BIG

PICTURE

STRATEGY

BIG

THE SIX CHOICES THAT WILL

PICTURE

TRANSFORM YOUR BUSINESS

STRATEGY

MARTA DAPENA BARÓN

WILEY

For general information on our other products and services or for technical support, please contact our Customer Care Department within the United States at (800) 762-2974, outside the United States at (317) 572-3993 or fax (317) 572-4002.

Wiley publishes in a variety of print and electronic formats and by print-on-demand. Some material included with standard print versions of this book may not be included in ebooks or in print-on-demand. If this book refers to media such as a CD or DVD that is not included in the version you purchased, you may download this material at http://booksupport.wiley.com. For more information about Wiley products, visit www.wiley.com.

Library of Congress Cataloging-in-Publication Data is Available:
ISBN 978-1-119-71206-0 (Hardback)
ISBN 978-1-119-71208-4 (ePDF)
ISBN 978-1-119-71207-7 (ePub)

Cover Design: Wiley

SKY10028116_071321

Contents

Introduction

Planning: You Are Using the Wrong Tools

Back in the early 2000s, I was a vice president of marketing at GE, a diversified global company then admired for its management discipline and track record of steady growth. I worked for the equipment leasing arm of GE Commercial Finance. We financed equipment such as copy machines, computers, earth movers, etc. A few years before I joined, the company had adopted the "balanced scorecard" methodology to develop a prioritized list of goals as well as metrics to track progress toward those goals.

The objective of using the scorecard method was to align all departments on the health and direction of the company. The scorecard was a one-page summary divided into financial, human resources, commercial, and operational measures, and it reported whether or not each department met the prescribed goals. The scorecard was calculated weekly.

But if the scorecard method was supposed to create a consensus on a forward-focused strategy, it failed. The only way the system brought us closer was physically: leaders from each team would meet in a room every Monday morning to review the latest scorecard. Yet because each team was motivated by different incentives, the metrics conflicted. Reaching some of the targets made achieving others impossible.

For example, the operations team had aggressive cost-cutting goals, while the sales and marketing teams had double-digit revenue growth goals. These turned out to be diametrically opposed objectives.

As a case in point, to achieve its expense-shrinking goals, the operations department outsourced customer service to a low-cost overseas call center. At the same time, it also established stricter standards for the condition of equipment coming off lease. Customers returning equipment that were missing manuals, or that had slight scratches, were charged additional fees.

Although this helped with operations' bottom-line goals, it generated lots of complaints and calls to the customer service number. Because the call center staff were poorly trained and weren't native English speakers, this worsened rather than improved our customers' service experience.

Needless to say, many customers were not willing to increase their business with GE, and our sales that year were nothing short of disappointing.

My time at GE taught me a memorable lesson: lack of organizational alignment can derail performance, even as everyone is working hard to achieve their own goals.

Popular models like the balanced scorecard are ill-suited to overcome problems that are embedded within the culture, values, and habitual ways that people in companies think and act.

I eventually left GE to become a management coach and consultant – to GE as well as other large companies – and have worked to remedy the learning gaps I see in the planning-to-execution process in organizations.

Big Picture Strategy represents an evolution of the *Big Picture Framework,* a method I describe in the textbook *Marketing Management: The Big Picture.* The methodology presented here has evolved over years of working with global organizations, and from teaching as well as learning from coaching thousands of executives. The Big Picture Strategy approach centers on six choices any company needs to make in developing a marketing strategy.

The idea behind the Big Picture Strategy model is a straightforward one. You have six choices to make when creating a go-to-market plan for your company. Yes, they are hard choices. But there are just six. These six choices are represented by the 6Bs, which stand for brand, business category, bodies, beliefs, behaviors, and benchmarks. Make them thoughtfully – use facts and logic rather than intuition. Include your cross-functional team. And you're on your way.

Note the word we used: *choices.* It's an important one, so keep it in mind as you read on.

Big Picture Strategy in 6Bs: Searching for Simplicity in Complex Markets

What led me to this choice-based method was my experience working with a variety of organizations both large and small. It taught me that organizations capable of creating incredible value could wallow in debilitating dysfunction.

As a consultant and as a marketer both, I was frustrated to see that teams facing difficult problems often resorted to simple solutions, often based on intuition, because they lacked adequate tools for a more thorough analysis. The tools and methodologies they were using did not take into account the complexities of the many interrelated variables involved in broad market-based issues.

The hope is that these tools will drive managers to use logic in place of intuition, and cross-functional problem-solving instead of siloed decision-making.

It all starts with creating a common purpose around the banner the company carries to market: its **brand** (the first B).

Companies may be organized in silos, but they go to market as a single or limited set of brands. Each of those brands competes against others that customers consider when looking for a solution that addresses some problem they have. Brands are arranged in categories as customers try to make sense of what is commercially available. In other words, companies are systems that operate in business categories, that are themselves systems. And the Big Picture Strategy methodology is itself a system-based methodology.

What is a system? A system is a set of interdependent agents, each vying to progress with, or at the expense of, other actors. When we conceive of a company as a system that is represented by a brand, we realize that planning needs to take into account all the cause-and-effect relationships within that company / system. What happens in customer service affects sales. What happens in operations affects finance. What happens in marketing affects operations and, of course, sales.

Within a system, to communicate everyone needs to speak the same language. And to know what decisions to make, everyone needs to know the right questions to ask. This is what Big Picture Strategy delivers.

What Big Picture Strategy Gives You

Developing go-to-market plans using the Big Picture Strategy systems-based method returns important benefits.

Getting Rid of the "In-the-Drawer Strategy"

The Big Picture helps companies avoid "in-the-drawer" strategies. Let me explain.

During my corporate career, I participated in many strategic planning cycles. Almost all of these strategy development projects were painful – and most were not worth the pain.

The traditional strategic planning season is a difficult time for marketing and strategy directors: our teams have to facilitate work sessions with cross-functional partners who'd rather be anywhere else. We spend many hours collecting data, running analyses, and preparing many versions of the strategic plan. Then, when the big day comes, presenting the plan to management feels like a college exam – replete with butterflies in the stomach.

But even when the plan is clever and the presentation goes well, everyone simply goes back to work. The plan is forgotten, and the status quo endures.

Most strategic plans I worked on during my corporate tenure ended up in a virtual or physical drawer, never to be looked at again.

The lesson? Great strategy without execution is a waste of time and resources. Alternatively, great execution without strategy yields erratic performance and missed learning opportunities. The model presented in this book solves both of these situations by linking strategic decisions with their executional implications.

Pulling Down the Organizational Tower of Babel

Over my years working with commercial organizations, I have noticed that marketing vocabulary is used loosely. Even basic terms like *customer* or *market* are defined differently, depending on who is speaking and in what context. More sophisticated terms like *segmentation* or *customer profitability* are even more broadly interpreted.

And the divide between teams can be about more than just words. Much of the gap between functions is due to organizational structure or incentives that drive an us-versus-them mindset. A salesforce compensated on short-term sales will pursue low-margin transactions and resent the marketing manager who resists discounting. These gaps can be made worse due to different philosophies that drive teams to undergo different training and orientation.

Unspoken assumptions and mental models can pit teams against each other. Ineffective cross-functional communications are difficult to change. What's required is a common methodology with a powerful common vocabulary. That's what Big Picture Strategy offers.

Moving from a Product to a Customer Orientation

Most companies still focus strategic planning around products rather than customers. They measure product profitability, which drives a short-term sales orientation. The alternative is to build a customer-focused company; one that is driven by *customer* profitability, which is attentive to customer retention rates, not just product margins.

Moreover, a customer orientation drives a brand orientation, as the brand – rather than the product – is the locus of customer loyalty. Products are still important, of course, as they are delivery vehicles for the brand promise, but as such, they are tools, as opposed to the primary hub of organizational activity.

By shifting strategic planning units of analysis from products to customers and brands, you can have a transformational impact on your entire organization. Key decisions your company makes, such as what business categories to participate in, which opportunities to pursue and prioritize, which customers to service and in what ways, how to develop value propositions, how to price. . . all these decisions shift when we build our strategy starting with the brand and we adopt a customer and long-term value approach rather than a product and short-term sales mindset.

Stryker Corporation, a global medical device company based in Kalamazoo, Michigan, used these principles to catalyze growth across its entire corporation. It shifted away from price-competition in orthopedic implants, as its competitors were doing, and instead focused on helping its hospital customers drive patient demand by co-promoting robotic-assisted knee and hip surgery.

Going from a product focus to a customer focus is a paradigm shift for everyone in the organization. This is in part why the marketing language needs to be shared across the organization, rather than being limited just to the marketing department.

The Big Picture Strategy method teaches you this. Marketing is no longer the name of a department that prepares sales aids and organizes trade shows. Marketing is the process and discipline that the entire organization shares to successfully develop and sell products and services. Importantly, the marketing-driven organization conceives of brands and customers as strategic financial assets and thinks of products and services as the tools used to build those assets. It uses 6Bs to steer the company in creating and expanding category-leading brands and customers who wish to partner with them.

From a Goods-Dominant Logic to Value-Dominant Logic

Moving from a product focus to a customer focus shifts the mindset of the organization toward providing customer value. This is a good thing. Because when companies move from product profitability to customer profitability, success metrics also move downstream, closer to customers.

The focus of the organization thus transforms from selling the next product to demonstrating the potential for value co-creation by cooperating with customers.

Organizations that make this transition successfully develop intimate knowledge of how customers can derive value from working with them. The focus of the company is thus no longer on sales transactions alone but on cooperating with customers to co-create value. The selling organization is no longer being paid just to deliver a product but is being compensated for providing proven expertise. The brand's value proposition becomes a value promise, and the execution of that value promise is carried out through a combination of services and products that are tightly integrated.

Futura Industries, an aluminum extrusion company based in Utah, built a tremendously successful business using these principles. It segmented customers not by purchase volume, as their competitors traditionally did, but rather by identifying companies whose business models would benefit from responsive and reliable service. It shifted its pricing method from the industry standard practice, which is based on weight, to value of the end application: aluminum shower enclosures are priced significantly higher than aluminum designed for carpeting applications.

Core to this shift is developing a value focus that is product-service agnostic. This is one of the key tenets of the Big Picture model.

From a More-Is-Better View to a Strategy-as-a-Constrained-Choice View

The view that more is better applies to some things in life but not to strategic choices. To use a metaphor, a key principle in modern warfare is that successful strategy involves concentrating firepower on the right battlefield, not scattershot over a large geographic area.

Likewise, a prime directive in marketing is to define business categories precisely, to identify specific customer opportunity in a chosen market category, and to develop single-minded promises to customers. In developing innovation, companies may be overwhelmed by the magnitude of the opportunities available. Successful brands follow a very precise path to developing strategy, however. As it turns out, a limited set of choices is available for each company and each brand. The Big Picture Strategy method uses 6Bs to force a sharp focus on what those choices are.

Not surprisingly, great marketers are disciplined in the methods they use to uncover the choices that exist for their brand(s). They are careful to select the one(s) that looks most promising, given the unique strengths of their teams. This principle of selection and focus is particularly important in marketing because our decision-making takes place under a great deal of uncertainty.

Moreover, the market is a very noisy place, and we cannot control many factors that affect us. We need to be purposeful in the selection of the battlefield – that is, the business category we compete in – and concentrate our firepower (our organizational resources), if we are to learn what works and what doesn't. This is why choices are so important in the Big Picture model. The right strategy is as much about what you choose *not* to do, as it is about what you choose to do.

In this book, you will learn about the Big Picture Strategy model, and how to use it to help your company's strategic planning process. Chapter 1 defines the 6Bs in the model and explains why they are important. Chapter 2 explains that there are four go-to-market strategies and explains how to use the 6Bs to select a strategy. Chapters 3 through 8 explore each of the 6Bs in depth.

My hope is that this book will change the way you approach, analyze, and solve customer-based and competitive strategy problems.

Organizations that implement the Big Picture framework in a disciplined manner experience transformative change in their marketing strategy and commercial practices. Integrating the Big Picture methodology into organizational processes involves the following practices:

- Define and continuously enhance the company's core competence.
- Define and prioritize shared goals over individual functional ones.
- Follow a long-term consistent approach to developing yourself, your organization, and your business category.
- Tightly integrate strategy development and tactical execution, using the right operational and evaluation benchmarks.
- Measure and disseminate critical customer and category information across the organization.

When adopted at a broad organizational level, the framework can generate the following outcomes:

- Substantially increase marketing investment efficiency and effectiveness.
- Improve the organization's ability to learn from its strategy-to-execution efforts.
- Drive customer retention and loyalty.
- Differentiate your brand.

1 Your Strategy, Your Choices

The traditional view of business strategy is that growth requires finding multiple wide-open market spaces, developing a portfolio of diverse breakthrough innovations, and achieving numerous "wins." But is this really true?

The problem with the "more-is-better" view of strategy is that it is complex and causes businesses to lose focus. Teams and resources are stretched. They are given too many so-called priorities. And, ultimately, they end up with little differentiation between their brand and others in their market.

Blame traditional strategic planning tools. Traditional strategy frameworks lack a systematic way to help businesses narrow down their options. And when it comes to planning and building successful brands, more is simply more, not better.

My work with some of the most successful companies in the world has convinced me that the best commercial plans emerge from constraints – from strategic *choices*. Some business leaders loathe choice because, in a sense, making a choice means accepting a loss in the hopes of scoring a greater gain. When companies develop customer-based strategy, choosing to focus on a specific group of customers requires that they not focus on others. The loss is clear, and painful to the company that sees each and every customer as a profit-generating opportunity. The gain still needs to be materialized. After all, there are no guarantees that we have chosen the right customer opportunity.

So, rather than developing a strategy that delineates a clear but finite path forward, many organizations develop vague plans that leave their options open. Their teams do not have a single goal but a long list of goals. Some organizations make this noncommittal approach work. After all, when not committed to any single metric, you can claim success when *any* metric improves.

During my time as VP of Marketing at GE's commercial equipment leasing business, we started the year with a double-digit sales growth goal. By October, as it became apparent the sales goal wasn't going to be met, management would shift to a bottom-line goal and start slashing spending, lowering pricing, and selling loan assets to be able to show a profit by year's end.

This way forward can work in the short term, but it will not deliver sustained growth. Absent a clear strategy that is supported throughout the organization, priorities will shift as personnel do.

Brands that lack a clear strategy can get by and become "familiar" to customers, but because they lack specific meaning, they fail to deliver high value to the organizations that own them. This is what happened to GE Appliances – known for making mid-market appliances but lacking a clear value proposition; Scion cars – focused on young drivers but lacking a youthful design – and Nokia smartphones, which focused on perfecting functionality but missed the importance of software and apps as the iPhone became popular.

Perhaps worst of all, this execution-without-strategy approach stands in the way of organizational learning. If a company doesn't make a choice, it might do well or it might do poorly, but either way, managers won't have a clear sense as to why things played out the way they did.

Giving Up Possibility to Realize Value

Go-to-market choices involve uncertainty because they are made within a system with many moving parts. And, as discussed, committing to a single strategy is hard because it requires giving up all the other possibilities.

But the good news about strategic choice is that just a few big decisions are required to develop with a successful strategic plan. As shown in Figure 1.1, a company needs to only make *six* choices to build its strategy: the **brand**, its **business** category, which **bodies** or customers to target, which customer **beliefs** and **behaviors** to drive, and which specific integrated **benchmarks** help operationalize the strategy and learn from its results.

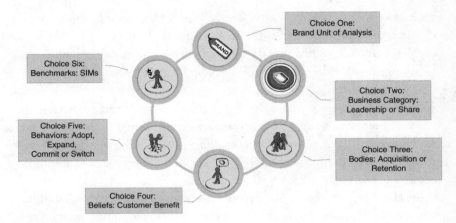

FIGURE 1.1 The 6Bs.

There are just six decisions a company must make in developing a go-to-market strategy.

Big Picture Strategy is a choice-based method that generates integrated strategy-through-execution plans. Each choice naturally constrains others that follow. This process forces discipline becaus it comes with strong internal logic that connects all elements.

Each choice bifurcates decision-making and leads to other logical choices, and then to others. Eventually, you build an integrated go-to-market plan – one that enables learning from each strategic cycle.

Teams that use this method end up with plans that actually get executed and measured, as opposed to simply being shelved and forgotten. Big Picture Strategy uses 6Bs to turn strategic planning into a learning tool.

While constraining your choices to drive competitive advantage might sound counterintuitive, the Big Picture Strategy method is very effective. Any business in any industry can use it. A variety of successful companies already use this framework to drive their most critical commercial decisions:

- **Johnson & Johnson** uses it to develops strategies for its medical device businesses.
- **Ecolab** deployed the framework to pinpoint growth opportunities in its institutional and food service businesses.
- **Copa**, the national airline of Panama, has used the framework to build its value proposition and identify relevant metrics, and to communicate strategy throughout the organization.

- **Stryker** aligns all its medical device business, enabling employees to share a common language to solve commercial problems.
- **W.L. Gore** develops strategy across its Gore-Tex fabrics business, alongside its industrial and medical device divisions.

Global companies that use the Big Picture method find that teams in disparate geographies learn from each other despite being in different business categories. Even when they use different technologies to solve customer problems, they finally have a *lingua franca* to communicate about customer-based strategy.

This book explains how to apply this decision-based framework of integrated choice to any business or goal-oriented organization. It is meant to be helpful to executives at any level and to function and in any size company.

This chapter addresses all 6Bs before diving deep into each one in subsequent chapters. But before we begin, I want to expand on the four different strategies that brands use to go to market. In our consulting practice at Big Picture Partners, we use a tool we call the "Go-to-Market Matrix" to compare these four approaches. Selecting one of the four is *the* foundational choice you need to make to align your organization on a single path forward. This go-to-market choice determines the trajectory of your options for the other six choices.

The Go-to-Market Matrix: Only Four Approaches to Going to Market

No two companies are the same, but when it comes to go-to-market strategy, there are just four approaches. And which of these go-to-market approaches is best depends on the **business category** orientation of the company, as well as its analysis of **customer opportunity**.

Throughout many years of working with a wide variety of companies, I have observed that having a strategy is much better than having no strategy at all. Just like that song says: "You gotta have a dream, if you don't have a dream, how you gonna have a dream come true?"

Choosing a strategic focus, a way to approach the market, is driven by how the company wants to grow.

There are only two ways to grow a brand when you take a customer-centric point of view: acquisition and retention.

And there are only two ways to grow a brand within a given market, or business category: growing by expanding the category (leading the way) or growing at the expense of a substitute within the category (through explicit competition).

The business category choice and customer choice are interdependent, and when combined, they yield four ways to go to market: the four strategic quadrants or the Go-to-Market Matrix, as shown in Figure 1.2.

There are two **leadership-focused strategies** and two **share-focused strategies**.

The two leadership-focused strategies, category development and brand expansion, represent go-to-market approaches that seek to lead customers and competition, by influencing how the former make choices and how the latter compete. These types of strategies are absolute in the sense that they present a way to go to market that avoids comparisons to competition.

Rather than spending to develop and lead a category, brands executing market-share-focused strategies grow at the expense of a competitor, presenting themselves as an acceptable alternative. The two share-focused

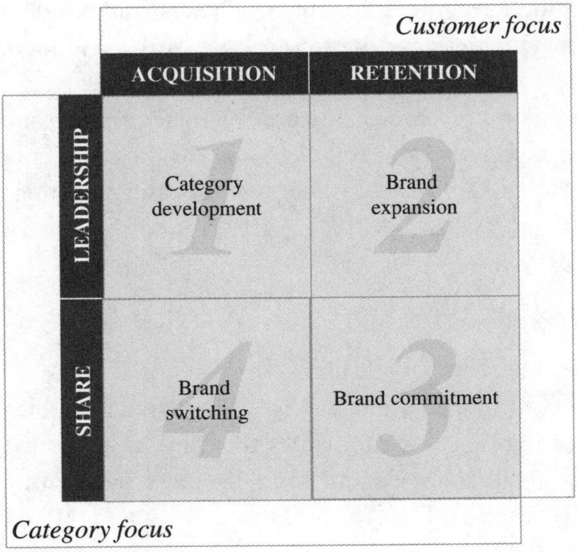

FIGURE 1.2 The strategic quadrants: just four go-to-market approaches.

The four strategic quadrants present four go-to-market approaches built around customer opportunity.

strategies, brand commitment and brand switching, are relative in that they invite comparisons. If successful, these strategies are short term, and they are chosen for efficiency reasons.

Strategy One: Category Development

Companies that possess significant innovations can reframe category boundaries. In this quadrant, the company creates a new category by increasing the importance of a benefit that it uniquely delivers. Growth comes from motivating noncustomers to try, and ultimately adopt, a new way of doing things.

In industries as diverse as snowboarding, high-performance electric cars, robotic surgery, and at-home boutique fitness, companies like Burton, Tesla, Intuitive Surgical, and Peloton have successfully executed *category development* strategies.

While diverse in their industry affiliation, these companies follow a common method to building their businesses: naming the new categories in a way that ignites market interest, creating customer awareness and excitement by identifying and engaging influential lead users, and building the regulatory and distribution infrastructure to turn that early excitement into sustained sales.

Importantly, they also communicate key features of their product and service offerings, enabling competitors to follow. A sign of the success of this strategy is the use of the category name by competitors and customers entering the category.

Strategy Two: Brand Expansion

Companies that have become category leaders, or that are hoping to establish leadership, may elect to execute *brand expansion* strategies. This is the most efficient path to growth for companies that have a large base of loyal customers. These companies expand their business by inviting "retained" customers to use the brand more consistently, or by upgrading to a higher-value version of their products or services. We call these *volume* and *value* strategies, respectively.

In this quadrant, companies develop incremental innovations to motivate retained customers to become more involved and loyal to the brand. Loyalty increases with product performance, especially if customers integrate the brand into their existing processes. This is a noncomparative strategy, and to maintain customer loyalty, brands shift from advertising product and service benefits to featuring customers in their advertising, reinforcing their brand choice and their affiliation to the brand. Pricing, distribution channels, and communications tools are also used to reward loyalty and encourage continued use of the brand.

Companies as diverse as Johnson & Johnson, Apple, and Volvo have successfully used this strategy to efficiently grow their businesses while cultivating ever-more intimate relationships with their customers.

Strategy Three: Brand Commitment

Companies executing a *brand commitment* strategy grow by focusing on multibrand customers, increasing their share of customers' wallets at the expense of a competitor.

Multibrand customers use the brand as part of a brand set but, unlike loyal customers, are not committed to a single brand. Companies that execute a successful *brand commitment* strategy are able to increase preference for their brands within a competitive set by creating a customer experience that is superior to that of the other brands within the set.

In executing a *brand commitment* strategy, companies present themselves as the best option within the specific competitive subset from which the customer purchases.

The success of *brand commitment* strategies is predicated on companies' ability to encourage consolidation of purchases. This can be achieved by integrating components of the product-service portfolio to increase pull-through to the brand, or by using contracts and financial incentives to gain a greater share of the customer's category usage. Airline loyalty programs and the streaming content wars waged by Netflix, Amazon, and Disney are examples of *brand commitment* strategies.[1]

Strategy Four: Brand Switching

Companies executing *brand switching* strategies grow by getting competitors' customers to switch to their brand. They research the target competitor's customers to understand the strength and type of relationships they hold with the competitive brand, and they mine those relationships for areas of relative dissatisfaction.

They then develop a similar solution portfolio, and also price it similarly to achieve a comparable offer. They select distribution channels that are similar to the competitor's and use implicit or explicit comparative communications.

A key to successfully executing this strategy is to enter competitive customers' consideration sets and become an acceptable alternative. They then execute to exploit their relative advantage and use comparisons to create the perception of substitutability.

Customer stories emphasize similarities between the brands and downplay the cost of switching. This strategy was used by Hyundai when it entered the US car market, Apple when it targeted IBM's corporate computer users, Samsung when competing against the iPhone, Sprint when it competed against Verizon, and countless others.

Selecting a Strategic Quadrant

Developing customer-based strategy requires assessing customer opportunity, delineating the major executional actions involved in each strategy, and comparing the entire strategy-through-execution implications of the quadrant choice.

The four quadrants offer a way to divide the universe of potential customers available to the brand: those inside the category and those outside; and those working with the brand already and those working with a competitive brand.

Go-to-market execution is relative to who the customers are and what they are doing today. The goal of a source-of-growth analysis is to construct a plan to reach those customers who are the most likely to benefit from working with your brand.

Once established, this method enables sustained growth in the face of changing customer and competitive dynamics. It's important to revisit the choices made with regular frequency as well as anytime there are any major changes in the competitive or customer landscape.

It's also crucial to use strategy-integrated customer metrics to pinpoint which strategic quadrant to choose and when to pivot from one quadrant to another as conditions change. This four-quadrant approach builds customer-based strategies that evolve as market conditions, customer behaviors, and company benchmarks change.

To select a strategic quadrant, first evaluate the four strategic approaches against each other – the 6Bs are hugely helpful as you conduct this *a priori* opportunity evaluation. And once you choose a strategic focus for your brand, make sure you use each of the 6Bs to ensure you approach commercial execution in a way that is consistent with the choice you have made.

The 6Bs: Choices That Drive Strategic Advantage

The choice as to which of the four strategic quadrants will deliver the most growth naturally involves considerable uncertainty. And some management teams opt to not choose, instead directing their sales and business development teams to secure "growth" wherever they see opportunity. The 6Bs should be used in conjunction with the four quadrants to frame and constrain choice, because these variables are interdependent.

An ideal strategy evaluation process entails analyzing each strategic quadrant one at a time, and then choosing the one the team is most excited about and feels most confident about executing. To "try on" a quadrant, the team considers each of the 6Bs decisions in that quadrant and then brings them all together to assemble a strategic narrative. Using the 6Bs to choose a strategy enables rapid iteration through go-to-market scenarios. Teams use the 6Bs and the four quadrants as a toolset to drive alignment and build a shared vision.

The Big Picture Strategy method gives teams a shared understanding of what they stand for, who is and who is not yet a customer, as well as who belongs to their competitive set. They use the four quadrants and the 6Bs to agree on a single goal that prioritizes all their activity. By the time they get to execution, teams that use the Big Picture Strategy approach are pulling in the same direction. Commitment to a single way forward and the curiosity to collect feedback along the way are the hallmarks of the learning organization. A learning organization is one that grows with each successive strategy cycle.

Choice 1: Brand

Many companies approach brand as a tactical rather than strategic question. I have worked with countless product development teams who treat branding as simply a naming exercise. They develop a product or service, determine its features and benefits, select a target audience, price it, and leave the "what should we call it" question to the tail end of the innovation process. This is incredibly shortsighted. More than ever before, in today's hyper-branded environment deciding what brand to assign your innovation should not be left to the last minute.

The choices you make about brand go well beyond its name and can make the difference between top-of-mind awareness for your product or service – and irrelevance. Whether contemplating a purchase within a grocery store or looking for consulting services, today's markets offer a dizzying array of options for both consumer and business buyers.

So when thinking about differentiating your products and services from your competitors', the role of brand as facilitating your customers' decision-making processes must be reframed. A brand is not simply identity. The brand is the promise the company makes to its target customers.

Your choices about brand should leap from an afterthought to the first question your development teams ask as they contemplate innovation. Also, when developing strategy, rather than starting work by asking about the market, competitors, and supply-and-demand forces, ask what you want your brand to achieve as it goes to market, what skills and resources are needed to support this ambition, and why customers might choose to ally themselves with your brand, given the multitude of functionally equivalent alternatives.

In short, think of the brand, rather than the product or service or even the company, as the strategic unit of analysis.

Here comes a choice – your first one.

If you intend to focus on a single value proposition and wish to concentrate on related business categories and customer groups, you should go to market as a single brand for all your products and services. This is called the *umbrella brand* approach.

You should use a *distinct brand* approach, with different brands for different product and service portfolios, if you intend to work with very different customer segments and categories and articulate divergent value propositions.

Alternatively, you can choose to combine these two approaches into a hybrid brand model. A *hybrid umbrella* is a brand structure with a dominant corporate brand – that is, one overall differentiated customer promise for all products and services – that uses sub-brands to help customers segment their needs more specifically.

And, finally, you can choose a *hybrid distinct* approach, which is a brand structure with relatively independent brands, each resourced with specialized skillsets to enable them to offer differentiated touchpoints across their customers' journeys. However, these independent sub-brands include a few common elements across the brand portfolio that remind customers of their membership in the corporate brand family.

The Brand as a Strategic Unit of Analysis

Adopting the *brand as strategic unit of analysis* is required in order for your brand to function as a customer unit of choice – that is, for the brand to deliver uniquely valuable customer experiences.

Branding is the discipline required to make your brand matter, and it involves much more than designing arresting logos and attention-grabbing visuals. The design of brand architecture needs to be done in concert with fundamental strategy decisions, such as what business or businesses you choose to be in, and what the brand should stand for in those businesses.

To orchestrate your brands, you must first look within your organization and contemplate what is uniquely valuable about it. Of course, value is relative, so you must consider very specifically what skills and resources you have relative to your competitors and relative to your own commercial ambitions. In other words, connect the brand to the core competence of the organization.

A core competence is a set of distinctive skills that are unique in the category, that are difficult for competitors to imitate, and that lead to differentiated brand promises. But here is where your choice of brand approach matters. If you're building an umbrella brand, you should utilize a single core competence across all your service and product portfolios. But if you are going to market with distinct brands, you must build additional core competences by customer segment.

Conversely, if your organization has different teams endowed with highly diverse skills, you may want to cultivate those resources separately and go to market with different brands; whereas if you have a single team with a single set of skills and resources, and limited ambition to expand beyond the existing scope of your business, you may choose to go to market with a single brand.

The point is, brand and core competence choices are inextricably linked. They must also be integrated with customer and category choices, which together drive downstream decisions about value proposition and execution.

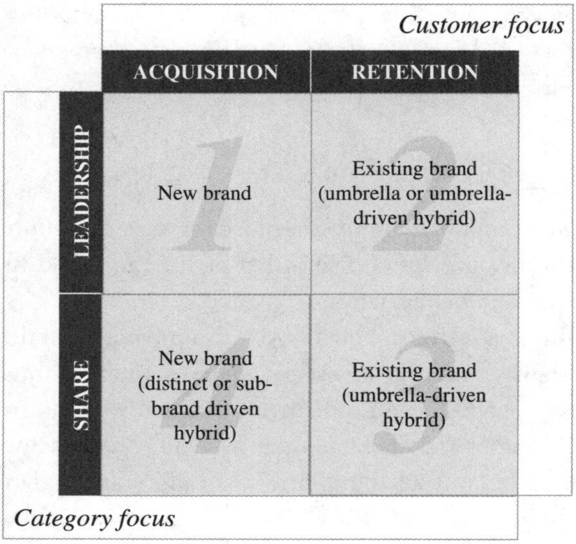

FIGURE 1.3   Brand focus and the four strategic quadrants.
Creating a new category often involves launching a new brand. Retention strategies are most efficient if they leverage existing awareness through an umbrella or umbrella-driven hybrid brand.

Although many companies choose a brand architecture and a strategic focus independently, customer acquisition strategies, especially those involving the creation of a new category, generally involve creating new brands. Retention strategies, conversely, are more efficient when the company utilizes an existing brand, either under an umbrella or umbrella-driven hybrid brand architecture. Umbrella brand architectures facilitate customer retention because they benefit from the brand awareness already created with existing customers. Figure 1.3 elucidates the relationship between brand architecture and strategic focus.

The brand decision is interdependent from the business category decision, which is the second B.

Choice 2: Business Category

Brands compete in categories. Managers can conceive of *business categories* as battlefields – spaces where their brands vie for attention from customers in competition with functionally similar offerings.

Think of the category, then, as a set of brands, all of which are acceptable to the customer. In other words, the category is the customer's consideration set. It is from this set that your customers will choose when attempting to satisfy their needs.

The definition of the business category is critically important for any brand. And yet many companies simply skip this important step when setting their business strategy. The category is what drives resource allocation in your organization: from how employees think about the business, to how they spend their time. Many managers take their business category as a given rather than a purposeful choice. The category definition directly influences strategy; therefore, the category must be defined prior to making other market strategy decisions.

Choosing your category is foundational to your business strategy. Knowing your category is critical for deciding how you go to market. Do you choose to act like a category leader, and try to expand the category and derive growth from that expansion? Or do you adopt a go-to-market approach where growth comes from taking market share from a competitor within the category? This choice is dependent on the parameters of the category.

Decades ago, management thought-leaders identified a bias that drives businesses to define categories narrowly, in either technical or product terms. What is produced is what defines the business category.

For example, the thinking was that if we operate trains, we must be in the railway business, or if we publish a newspaper, we must be in the newspaper business. Product-based category definitions are to blame for the disruption caused to railway and newspaper companies as customers found more convenient ways to travel, and more timely ways to get current event information than reading print newspapers.

A better way of defining the category is by the *benefit* the product or service offers the customer.

Only Two Category Strategies

Now, there are just two category strategies: a *leadership-focused* or a *share-focused* strategy.

Companies that choose a *leadership focus* create or become the default choice in their category. They must develop trailblazing strategies. They must launch breakthrough products and services, frame value propositions in new ways, and develop novel approaches to access customers and capture value.

Companies that choose a *share focus* within an existing category develop relative strategies. That is, they succeed by inviting comparisons to another brand and emphasizing a single point of differentiation.

For example, when the Korean car maker Hyundai entered the US market in the late 1980s, it chose a *share-focused* strategy to gain a foothold in the market at the expense of established Japanese automakers. This highly focused strategy consisted of launching inexpensive car models that imitated features available in higher-end vehicles to invite comparisons to Japanese companies.

Hyundai leveraged traditional mass media channels and promoted long warranty periods to build credibility. Conversely, when BMW launched the Mini Cooper brand in the United States in 2001, it chose a *leadership-focused* strategy, reinventing the category from driving to motoring, benchmarking against motorcycles rather than SUVs, launching multiple product models simultaneously for maximum impact, and deploying highly visible communications through Hollywood movies and colorful billboards.

Leadership-focused and *share-focused* strategies are starkly different, as are the activities and investments that underpin them. A clear choice must be made so as not to dilute the strategic impact of the firm, or as the old proverb goes, "*He who chases two rabbits catches neither.*"

Business categories are constructs devised by marketers to frame how customers make decisions. We address customers in the third B, the *bodies;* this is because whether you are marketing to consumers or businesses, successful go-to-market strategy requires you to engage specific people.

Choice 3: Bodies

Just as there are only two category strategies, there are only two ways to grow a brand: retain existing customers or acquire new ones. These two growth objectives require different activities and different investments.

The disciplined business strategist selects one of these two primary growth goals. A customer *acquisition* focus is critical when creating or entering a business category or when seeking geographic expansion. A customer *retention* focus is critical when seeking to consolidate the company's leadership position in the business category, when operating in a fragmented category with little customer loyalty, or when the brand is being assailed by competition.

Companies that focus on customer *acquisition* invest to create awareness and deliver information about their brands. They focus resources on the development of highly differentiated innovations, and as they are readying them to launch in the market, they emphasize customer education and ease-of-use features to maximize adoption. They price to encourage trials, creating pricing programs that effectively remove price as an objection. "Try-free-for-30-days" and freemium programs are examples of this.

Companies pursuing this strategy structure distribution channels to reach noncustomers and train their salesforces to assess the fit of potential buyers with the brand.

Copa Airlines designated half of its Latin American markets as *acquisition* and then budgeted accordingly, as *acquisition* activities are up to five times more resource-consuming than *retention* activities. The airline budgeted more for new markets than established ones even when it seemed counterintuitive to local employees. Copa Airlines then established market-level metrics to identify *acquisition-retention* tipping points, so that personnel managing regional budgets would be alerted when it was time to shift strategies from *acquisition* to *retention*.

Acquisition and *retention* also drive brand structure choices. Companies that focus primarily on *acquisition* follow a distinct branding approach.

Entertainment Arts grows by creating new brands for its gaming, each to appeal to a customer group seeking a different experience. The Madden franchise focuses on gamers who enjoy the thrills and "hard plays" of American Football, whereas the SIMs franchise focuses on gamers who enjoy stories about nurturing a family and building a community.

On the other hand, companies that primarily rely on customer *retention* for growth tend toward an umbrella brand approach. Starbucks built thousands of stores to deliver the benefit of convenience to its loyal following. It also let other retailers, airlines, hotels, and supermarkets sell its coffee, creating a sense of ubiquity for the brand and making it synonymous with premium coffee. Within its stores, Starbucks also expanded on the success of its coffee by adding teas, frozen drinks, and breakfast and lunch items to encourage repeat visits throughout the day. And by encouraging its customers to install its Starbucks-branded phone app, which they use to order and pay for products, it gains a high level of insight about what its customers like and what messaging and promotions are most effective in driving purchases.

In general, it's safe to say that a portfolio of brands supports customer acquisition, and a single brand is better to support customer retention efforts.

Of course, investing to acquire customers must be balanced with investing to retain customers. Successful brands balance acquisition and retention growth goals and resources. These integrated approaches are called *acquisition with retention in mind*, and *retention with acquisition in mind*.

Acquisition with retention in mind requires carefully managing front-end commercial operations to target customers who are likely to have high retention rates once converted to the brand. Retention with acquisition in mind requires building and then utilizing current customers to act as brand ambassadors to acquire new customers.

The choice of the customer focus must be aligned with both upstream and downstream decisions, from how to structure the company's brands to how to use commercial resources.

The *bodies* choice – that is, the decision to focus primarily on customer acquisition or retention, and the *business category* choice, that is, the decision to either go to market as a category leader or to take market share by comparing to another brand in an existing category yield four distinct pockets of customer opportunity, delineating four strategies, as is shown in Figure 1.4.

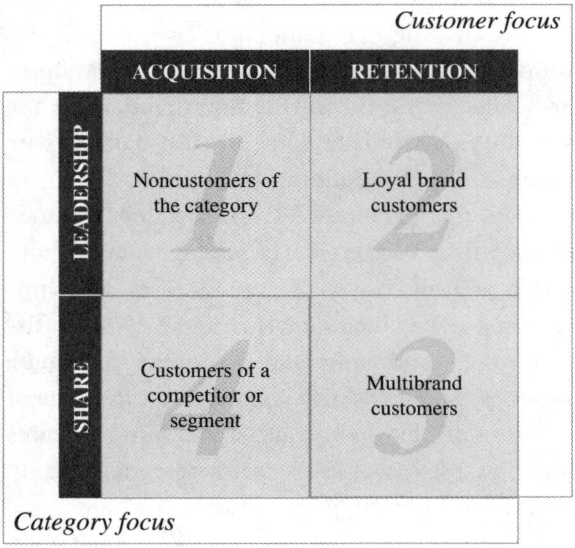

		Customer focus	
		ACQUISITION	**RETENTION**
LEADERSHIP		Noncustomers of the category	Loyal brand customers
SHARE		Customers of a competitor or segment	Multibrand customers

Category focus

FIGURE 1.4 Customer focus in the four strategic quadrants.

The strategic quadrants summarize the sources of volume available to a brand, clearly establishing **who** we are focused on to enable our brand growth goals.

Brand, business category, and bodies takes us halfway through the 6Bs. With those choices made, let's consider the next B, *beliefs*.

Choice 4: Beliefs

Marketers are in the business of changing customer *beliefs*. Traditionally, this job sits squarely with the communications team within the company or an external agency. While it seems ideal that specialized professionals take charge of design and messaging, in many organizations this separation of the creative activity has created a disconnect between what the company says and what it does. Grand marketing messages lift expectations to a level that inevitably leads to customer disappointment. The Big Picture Strategy method integrates communications into the company strategy.

Companies credit a variety of competitive factors with driving the success of brands. However, to develop a conceptual model for which brands will ultimately succeed you need to understand benefit dynamics in business categories. Brands that conform to a category are considered substitutable; that is why they are grouped together. Brands in categories offer a variety of common benefits, and yet two benefits establish differentiation enabling customers' choices: a *category* benefit and a *differentiating* benefit.

Given that multiple brands compete within a category, the category provides a bundle of benefits: the *category* benefit plus others that have the potential to become *differentiating* as brands attempt to take market share from the category leader through comparative strategies.

Category plots (see Figure 1.5) illustrate benefit *importance* and the customers' *perception* of the performance of each competitor on the category and *differentiating* benefits.

Teams can use relatively simple research tools to identify which key customer benefits delineate a category, and then develop a category plot and a competitive plot to identify the *category* and the *differentiating* benefits of each competitor. By plotting the competitors in a business category, teams can identify whether benefit *importance or perception* needs to change to drive brand differentiation.

Followed over time, benefit importance ratings and brand perception ratings form a powerful conceptual model to explain why some brands are able to sustain performance while others come and go.

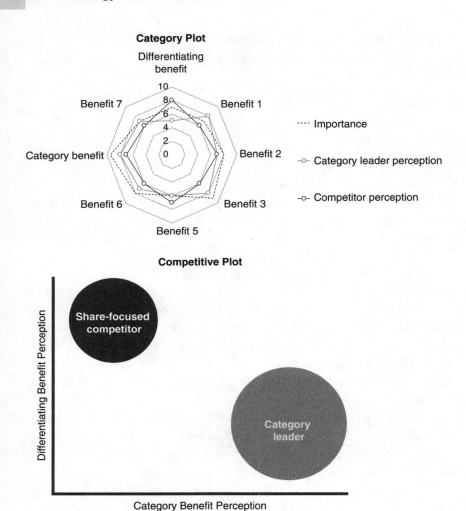

FIGURE 1.5 The category and the competitive plots.

The category and the competitive plots illustrate the benefit value of a business category and help leaders identify a differentiating benefit.

Identifying a single *category* or a *differentiating* benefit that a brand can own, and then investing to increase its *importance* and the *perception* of the brand's performance on it, is one of the most useful exercises that organizations can do to select customer segments.

Most importantly, the *category* and *differentiating* benefits constitute the essence of winning value propositions that are constructed to support the brand strategy, prioritize execution, and build brand differentiation.

Companies that are establishing new categories or leading in existing categories should make their brand names synonymous with the *category* benefit. Brands seeking a share focus within a category, and therefore differentiate against the category leader, will instead focus on a *differentiating* benefit.

Brands seeking to acquire new customers will need to magnify the importance of a benefit – adopting an *importance* focus – whereas brands seeking to retain customers may need to instead focus on improving the perceived value of their offer, adopting a *perception* focus. Figure 1.6 shows the relationship between the brand strategic focus and the customer belief focus.

Changing what is important to customers requires understanding how they make choices. You can then shift the relative weight of a benefit in their brand choice by helping them understand how that benefit affects them and what they care about.

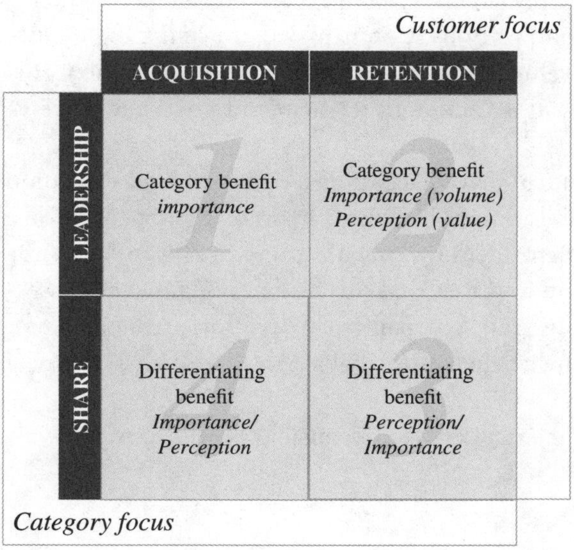

	Customer focus	
	ACQUISITION	**RETENTION**
LEADERSHIP	Category benefit *importance*	Category benefit *Importance (volume)* *Perception (value)*
SHARE	Differentiating benefit *Importance/* *Perception*	Differentiating benefit *Perception/* *Importance*

Category focus

FIGURE 1.6 Customer beliefs and the four strategic quadrants.

Brands adopting a leadership focus will invest to grow their brand with the category. They develop strong associations between their brand names and the *category* benefit. Brands seeking to earn share within the category will instead focus on a *differentiating* benefit. Brands seeking to acquire new customers will need to make their benefit more *important* – whereas brands seeking to retain will tend toward a *perception* focus.

Changing perception requires educating customers about the brand and the quality differences between its performance and that of its competitors.

When a company is seeking to create a new category or lead in an existing category, its ability to change customer behavior to adopt its products and services will be dependent on the perceived importance of the problem its products and services solve.

When a company seeks to differentiate its products and services from others in the category to earn market share, it will need to focus on its perceived performance relative to that of other brands in the category.

In other words (as is shown in Figure 1.6), leadership-focused strategies tend to have more of a benefit *importance* focus whereas share-focused strategies tend toward a brand *perception* focus.

Many companies attach catchy slogans to their brands that are helpful to gather attention. However, they are often not meaningfully connected to their core competence or their customers' needs.

Successful brands are represented by simple, yet profound statements connected to their value propositions. Companies that use the Big Picture Strategy method develop value propositions using insights about how customers make decisions: what is important to them and how they perceive brands' performance.

Value propositions, in turn, drive executional decisions, and execution is measured by whether it meaningfully affects importance and perceptions.

Sustainable growth is dependent on organizations' ability to target the right customers, understand how they make decisions, and how they assess brand performance. By doing this, companies can develop predictive models that connect people, their beliefs, their behaviors, and their support of particular brands.

With *beliefs* identified, the next choice to consider is *behaviors*.

Choice 5: Behaviors

Business leaders understand that growing their brands requires changing customer *behaviors*. Over the last two decades, companies have become particularly interested in predictive modeling and have collected inordinate amounts of customer transactional and touchpoint data, which they use to anticipate what customers might want based on past behaviors.

These powerful, predictive models are richest when they consider not just *what* is likely to happen but *why*. Indeed, *the most helpful predictive models connect customer behaviors to customer beliefs*. When a customer-based strategy is developed, we select customers we believe constitute the best opportunity for the brand, and that opportunity is contingent on our ability to change their behaviors in a way that benefits both them and us.

Linking brand strategy and execution requires connecting the organization's behavior toward customers to the brand strategy and value propositions. This is done with the objective of changing customers' behavior.

As Figure 1.7 shows, each strategic quadrant corresponds to specific customer behavioral goals. These are *adoption*, getting customers to accept and support a new category; *expansion*, growing retained customers' volume or the value they derive from the brand; *commitment,* getting multibrand customers to increase their support of the brand; or *switching*, motivating competitive customers to switch brands.

Execution is the discipline required to motivate diverse people in an organization to act consistently in articulating a common promise to customers. A key to successful execution is the ability of the commercial

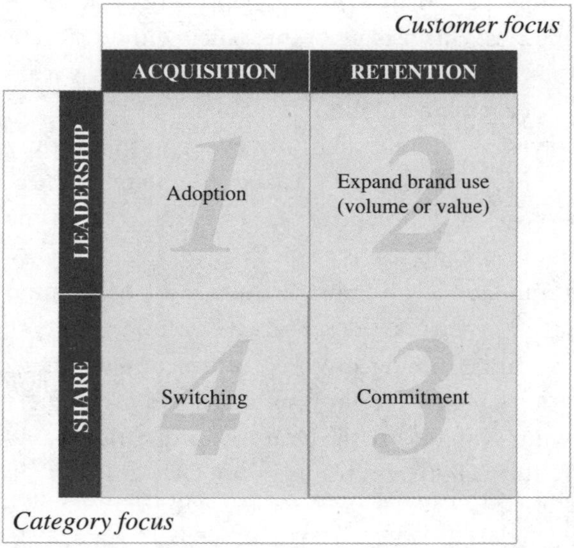

FIGURE 1.7 Customer behavior objectives and the four strategic quadrants.
Different brand strategies have different customer behavioral objectives.

leaders to create a narrative that excites and unites employees around a common purpose.

The strategy-aligned organization researches target customer beliefs and behaviors at each step in the customer journey and then builds an ideal customer experience prototype, noting the gap between the current customer journey and the ideal journey it is trying to create. It then enlists all functions and executional tools in the organization to close the gap between the current and the desired customer experience.

This is how Copa Airlines and Ecolab's Ecosure team executed their strategies. This is also how Peloton created celebrity brand ambassadors. Aligning strategy and execution requires specifically tying products and services, pricing programs, communications, and go-to-market channels to the brand strategy and value proposition.

This brings us to the last choice of the 6Bs: *benchmarks*.

Choice 6: Benchmarks

With the proliferation of analytics tools, commercial organizations have become awash with data. However, many struggle to prioritize and draw insights from commercial metrics. One reason for this is that without a well-defined question, metrics can add complexity to decision-making as team members debate the merits of each kind of metric calculated or measured.

All strategic choice involves uncertainty, and in the face of uncertainty many management teams simply use intuition. However, making subjective decisions intuitively exposes us to the many biases we hold about the world around us and about our organizations.

In running our training simulations with business teams, we have found that when faced with complex problems, the no-process solution – where the team skips the thinking and planning involved in designing strategy and simply moves to execution – yields inferior results. Even in cases where information is scarce, framing problems with the use of a question-based method, like Big Picture Strategy, motivates teams to use facts and logic in place of intuitive opinion.

The strategy-aligned organization shapes questions about their brand, business category, bodies, beliefs, and behaviors to conform to a strategic hypothesis, and sets metrics to test it.

The idea behind a process-driven strategic method is to set a long-term plan that gets refined through iteration. The Big Picture approach is an iterative process of inquiry. It reduces uncertainty and drives organizational learning by focusing on a few key metrics that articulate brand strategy and execution. With each successive planning cycle, the strategic questions become more nuanced and the metrics more detailed. As such, uncertainty is reduced progressively in the development of strategy and in the testing of strategy through execution.

Organizations using the Big Picture approach first choose a strategy, then set financial goals that are tied to it, as shown in Figure 1.8.

For these organizations, financial metrics are more than simply success criteria: they serve to drive decision-making across the organization.

The company that focuses on category development strategies is likely to set metrics to inform market development efforts. For example, it might measure initial interest during product demonstrations, the number of influential lead users that are trained, or their speed of adoption of the new technology.

The length of time to financial outcomes in this quadrant is protracted relative to brand expansion strategies, where the results can be realized more quickly. In the category development quadrant, financial metrics aim at tracking category growth or penetration relative to the total available opportunity, and at least initially, target top-line sales results rather than the bottom line.

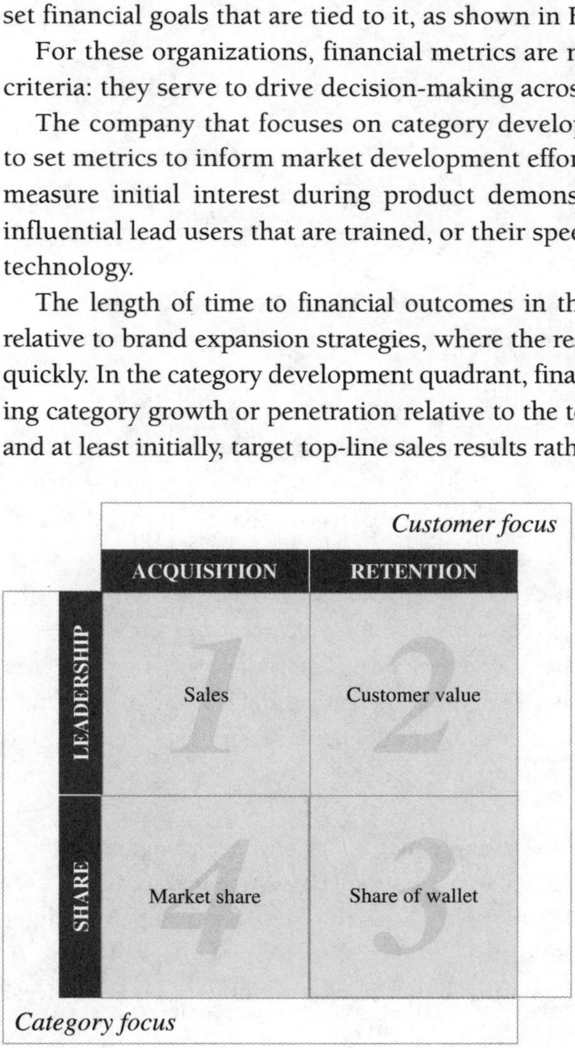

FIGURE 1.8 Financial benchmarks and the four strategic quadrants.
Companies should integrate their financial metrics to their specific strategy.

The company that executes a brand expansion strategy sets metrics to better understand the number of retained customers it has and how their touchpoints with the brand and other revealing behaviors correlate with their value and satisfaction. It then establishes a focused plan of action to lift customer value by encouraging lower-value relationships to trade up or use the brand more consistently.

The time to financial results of these strategies tends to be shorter, and the nature of the financial bets less risky. Key financial metrics include customer lifetime value and company profitability.

The company that adopts a brand commitment strategy is focused on improving its standing within a tightly defined competitive set by increasing the commitment of its multibrand customers. Its goal is not to expand the total business being conducted in the category, but rather, to displace an alternative by showing customers the experiential benefits of consolidating purchases and use.

Relative brand preference metrics, like top-of-mind awareness, can be used to gauge the extent to which the brand is able to obtain more attention than its competitors.

The financial metrics that accompany both *share-focused* strategies are relative and include market share and revenue share. The success of a *brand commitment* strategy is best assessed by computing share of wallet – that is, the percentage of customers' spend in the category that is allocated to our brand as proxy for their relative commitment.

Brand switching strategies also use relative metrics of performance, including relative benefit perceptions and the importance of their differentiating benefit relative to the category benefit. The goal of these strategies is to motivate customers of a targeted competitor to defect, and accordingly the organizations will set metrics to understand the rate of competitive customer acquisition and relative market share to track progress in competitive customer switching.

Big Picture organizations see their metrics as strategic diagnostic tools that enable learning and sustainable growth. The systematic approach presented in this book builds on the basis of the fact that companies must make choices under uncertainty. It then utilizes simple logical rules to reduce uncertainty by articulating hypotheses, framing strategic choices, and then choosing and measuring the result.

2

Four Go-to-Market Strategies

Developing your brand's go-to-market approach may seem like a complex task with many implications. Indeed, it is. The best way I know to do this for any brand is to use the Big Picture's system of integrated choices, the 6Bs, in a step-by-step and iterative manner.

The Big Picture method reduces complexity by focusing your team on the six foundational elements that all go-to-market strategies must address: brand, business category, bodies, beliefs, behaviors, and benchmarks.

That said, there is another piece to the brand strategy puzzle. There are just four strategy archetypes a brand can pursue in going to market: category development, brand expansion, brand commitment, and brand switching. And in making the choice of which go-to-market strategy to pursue, the 6Bs are helpful again. Use them to "try on" each of these strategies, so your team can visualize the opportunities available to your brand in each scenario and the major go-to-market implications of that choice.

1. **Category development.** This is the strategy a brand pursues when creating a category or expanding it by bringing in new customers. It involves investing in category infrastructure, and motivating adoption.
2. **Brand expansion.** This is the strategy of a category leader that wants to grow efficiently by increasing the value it offers to its loyal customer base. It involves increasing the financial and emotional commitment customers have to the brand.

3. **Brand commitment.** This strategy is for brands whose best source of growth lies with customers who use them only sometimes, that is, who buy from a set of brands in the category – we call them multibrand customers. It involves motivating those customers to increase brand commitment at the expense of another brand in the choice set.
4. **Brand switching.** This strategy is pursued by brands entering a category that has an established leader or segment. The entrants choose to compete according to the rules established by the category leader, rather than attempting to reframe the category. Entrants use all "executional elements" to motivate customers to switch brands.

Figure 2.1 summarizes each of the four go-to-market strategies using the Big Picture's 6Bs to illustrate each one. The rest of this chapter complements this summary through detailed explanations and examples of each of the go-to-market strategies.

Strategy One: Category Development

A company going to market with a breakthrough innovation, something that brings vast improvement over current standards, may invest to create a new category. This strategy has been used by companies as diverse as Tesla, Splenda, Peloton, Barclays Bank when launching iShares Exchange Traded Funds,[1] and Cordis in launching drug-eluding stents, or GE Healthcare in launching a hand-held ultrasound.[2]

Creating a new category can be very profitable, and that is why companies attempt it. However, it is a difficult route to pursue. Successfully creating a new category requires more than reimagining established business models. Creating a category requires changing minds and teaching potential customers how to look at a solution space differently, changing how they choose.

Use the 6Bs to contemplate what it takes to create a new category, and then "try on" that strategy to see if it might be worth pursuing.

Brand

Do you have the resources to create a new brand?

The usual impetus for creating a new category is an innovation that is significantly better than what already exists. For this reason, most companies

	Brand	Business Category	Bodies	Beliefs	Behaviors	Benchmarks
Category Development	New (distinct for existing brand).	New (narrow) category, leadership strategy.	Attract noncustomers of the category by looking for the "disenfranchised" in other categories.	Focus on raising importance of a new benefit to drive category adoption or expansion.	Promote trial and adoption of new category through breakthrough innovation and customer education.	Measure category growth (new customers, sales, category penetration . . .).
Brand Expansion	Existing brand (umbrella or umbrella-driven hybrid) strategy.	Leadership strategy in existing category.	Focus on growth from current loyal customers.	New use or enhanced existing brand benefit.	Expand existing brand by reinforcing customer choice; increase frequency of use (volume) and/or upgrade (value).	Measure value of current customer base (CLV, profitability, brand value).
Brand Commitment	May be sub-brand driven hybrid or distinct (flanker brand).	Existing category, share focus for brands used as part of brand set.	Focus on multibrand customers.	Improve importance or perception of your brand's relative experience.	Increase multibrand customer commitment by targeting competitive brand and offering compelling experiential point-of-difference.	Grow share of wallet.
Brand Switching	May be sub-brand driven hybrid or distinct (flanker brand).	Strategy for brands that are not category leaders (in categories with a leader).	Focus on a single competitor's customers	Compare a single point of difference to highlight competitive advantage.	Motivate competitor's customers to switch through comparative execution (solutions, pricing, communications).	Brand growth is relative to competitor (number of customers converted, market share).

FIGURE 2.1 Summary of the go-to-market strategies using the 6Bs.

that create new categories also create new brands. Sometimes the company is created around the innovation and the company name becomes the brand name, as in the case of Dyson's cyclone vacuum cleaners, Tesla's performance electric cars, Peloton's connected fitness workouts, and W.L. Gore's Gore-Tex high performance fabrics.

If the innovation is created by an existing company, however, the company will benefit from creating a brand that separates the new product from its corporate identity, such as McNeil Consumer's Splenda natural sweeteners, Procter & Gamble's Swiffer brand, or Barclay's Bank iShares Exchange Traded Funds (ETFs). Creating a new brand gives a company a "fresh start" – a chance at an identity with no preexisting associations.

Either way, if you are creating a new business category, you will want to create a new brand. You thus need to answer the question, "Do we have the expertise and budget to launch and maintain a brand that is capable of breaking through the cacophony of the market space to birth a new category?"

Business Category

What is the return on your marketing investment?

Category development requires that you create a new solution space by building the market infrastructure for your technology or business design. Most of the time, this entails paving the way for customers, regulators, distribution channels, and even competitors to participate in the category. Absent other market actors, your category may not prosper.

Successfully creating the drug-eluding stent category required very significant investment. J&J, the manufacturer of the Cypher stent, ran two double-blind trials enrolling 1,400 coronary disease patients, lobbied to obtain higher reimbursement, partnered with a number of clinicians to generate ample evidence of the stent's effectiveness for a variety of patients, and educated thousands of interventional cardiologists on the benefits and use of the stent. Cypher commanded three times higher pricing than traditional bare-metal stents, making the effort worthwhile until competition displaced J&J from its dominant leadership position in the category.

Having a fantastic innovation alone does not guarantee success if you underestimate the time, skill, and investment required to erect the infrastructure required for the category to succeed. Then, of course, there is the issue of changing hearts and minds. Creating a new category requires you to change how people make purchasing choices. A new category must bring a new benefit with it, and consumers need to be educated about that benefit.

Bodies

Which noncustomers will you target?

Creating or developing a new category requires attracting potential customers who, by definition, are from outside the category, and who are likely also new to your company. To profit from creating a new category, you need customers to adopt the category and to start using the brand. Who will lead the way?

The ideal target will be customers within an existing category who feel latent dissatisfaction – that is, they have some problem with their current product or service, a problem they may only recognize when you show them a great solution.

When Tesla launched in 2006, it targeted reluctant buyers of gas-guzzling fancy sports cars; for Splenda, it was people who were in the low-calorie sweetener category but worried about the impact of chemicals on their health.

Also, your first customers should provide exemplars for others contemplating whether to join the category. Selecting the right customers is always important, but particularly when you are creating a new category.

Peloton identified that there were 22 million people in the United States going to boutique gyms and 60 million who owned home-based exercise equipment. Some percentage of those people would likely be interested in getting the same amazing workout of a boutique gym while staying in the convenience of their homes. The opportunity seemed significant. And Peloton specifically targeted celebrities, who were already in great physical condition, among its first customers and also chose fitness instructors with the potential to become social media influencers.

When considering whether to create a new category, first estimate the number of people who may be interested in your offer; these are people who can come to value what you wish to sell and who exist at the fringes of related categories. Customers at the fringes of another category are fertile ground for belief and behavior change.

Beliefs

What is the likelihood you will be able to compel noncustomers to want what the new category offers?

Motivating potential customers to adopt an entirely new way of doing things requires convincing them that the benefit is worth the risk of trying something new.

Moreover, success here requires a two-step belief change: convincing potential customers that the category is worthwhile, and convincing them your brand is trustworthy. A category that lacks trustworthy brands is a category sure to have a short lifespan.

The hoverboard category gained notoriety due to celebrities and teen influencers, like Justin Bieber, whose hoverboard dance videos went viral. Hoverboards – battery-powered self-balancing scooters priced between $300 and $900 – were every teenager's dream during the 2015 Christmas season. Less than six months later, hoverboards had turned into parents' nightmares, when the Product Safety Commission recalled more than 500,000 because of severe risk of explosions. The category was almost wiped out when parents lost confidence in the manufacturers' practices. Ultimately, hoverboards did survive, but have been overshadowed by electric scooters that are not plagued by safety concerns.[3]

Brands that profit from creating categories are successful in capturing customers through a novel benefit – and are also able to elicit trust in the viability of a new brand.

Behaviors

How many people will actually purchase?

Creating a new category requires people to fundamentally change behavior. Yes, it is important to carefully curate lead users, but that is not enough. Motivating people to change behavior requires a groundswell of opinion and role modeling, not just from credible experts, but also from peers and social networks.

The Instant Pot brand was created in 2009 when two ex-Nortel software engineers invented an electric pressure cooker that combined the speed of stove-top pressure cookers and the hands-off benefit of electric cookers. Despite the obvious benefit of the invention, it was not until 2015 that it grew into a movement, a veritable category. How?

The inventors gave free Instant Pots to a few hundred food bloggers, and after positive reviews they focused on a single distribution channel, Amazon, to achieve their volume objectives. Amazon featured the Instant Pot in its 2015 Prime Day sale, and the brand sold tens of thousands of units. Despite its accessible looks, people needed support to feel success with the machine, so Instant Pot created a Facebook group seeded with food blogger reviews and recipes. New customers flocked to the group and, once successful, reciprocated by sharing their own recipes. The key to the explosive growth of the innovation was the creation of a community of use that engaged in self-reinforcing behaviors.[4]

Benchmarks

How do you measure whether you are executing on your strategy? And how do you learn from its outcomes?

Marketing metrics can drive your team's early successes to become self-sustaining, all while helping the team learn along the way.

When creating a new category, you can be blinded by the sheer size of the opportunity available to your innovation. You could point out that even with three million Instant Pots sold, fewer than 10 percent of American households would own one. This doesn't matter. The question is, how many people do you need to trial the innovation during the first few months to achieve financial sustainability, and how will you execute on that activity? How many need to buy it within the first year for your brand to survive? What channel of distribution will you use to reach the people most likely to be interested in your offer? And how will you know you have, in fact, been successful in creating a category, and with it, a self-reinforcing community of use? Using the first five Bs to define a specific strategic narrative and then establishing congruent benchmarks (the sixth B) will answer these questions.

The key to category creation is having a self-sustaining business model, one where the execution of your strategy with a few customers helps you acquire more just like them. In a sense, the goal of every category development strategy is to accumulate enough loyal customers to be able to efficiently shift into a brand expansion strategy.

Strategy Two: Brand Expansion

Whether having created a category or having entered a category and garnered a large base of customers, brands find sustainable growth by executing a strategy that focuses on loyal customers.

This is the strategy that BMW, Gillette, Arm & Hammer, Dyson, Panera Bread, Starbucks, Apple, and so many other brands pursued once they achieved a critical mass of loyal customers. Although these brands still invest in acquiring customers, the majority of their investments and profitability come from existing customers.

A brand expansion strategy is efficient because it builds on the success and value the brand has already demonstrated. Launching new products and services in the hopes customers will welcome them is always risky, but the risk is lowest for a brand that has amassed a large base of "friendly" customers. A brand expansion strategy is the type of strategy you want to experiment with when your organization is a category leader or is at the cusp of category leadership.

As before, the choice to employ this strategy is made on the basis of a 6Bs opportunity analysis.

Use the 6Bs both to calculate opportunity and to "try on" this strategy. Consider each B in sequence, collecting as much data about it as possible and contemplate how you might execute on it by strategy.

Brand

Does your brand have top-of-mind awareness status in the category?

Brand expansion strategies are for category leaders. In this context, category leadership does not necessarily mean having the highest market share; it does mean, however, that the brand establishes a reference for the category or has top-of-mind awareness: being the brand that customers think of first.

Top-of-mind awareness brands can leverage trust and positive associations to efficiently launch new solutions that further increase goodwill and customer value. The Volvo brand had been synonymous with driving safety for decades, but during the 1999–2010 period, changes in ownership affected its investment capacity.[5] Throughout that decade, sales declined as the safety features that had differentiated Volvos became standard for most brands, and yet Volvo was able to retain a base of loyal customers who still identified the brand with safety. As a result, years later, Volvo was able to reinvigorate its brand and its sales through product redesign and focused advertising. In 2014, Volvo used its safety positioning as a platform to launch the XC 90 and compete against BMW and Mercedes in the luxury SUV category.[6]

Business Category

How will the category grow?

Brand expansion strategies rely on a symbiotic relationship between the brand and the category as a whole. There are many potential ways for categories to develop over time. The hallmark of a category leader is that it delineates the specific path the category will follow over time. Tesla's new all-electric car models can drive farther and farther on a single charge; Gillette's razors achieve closer and closer shaves over facial contours; Apple's iPhones have increasingly better cameras. As category leaders, these brands can "force" others in the category to add similar features to their solution portfolios to maintain relevance in the category.

Bodies

How many loyal customers does your brand have?

A brand expansion strategy relies on the support of loyal customers to extend the solution range or solidify loyalty through more consistent use.

To execute on a brand expansion strategy, you need to be able to activate loyal customers.

Activating loyal customers is a separate effort from selling products designed for them. It requires reflecting their preferences and self-image, so as to make them feel part of the brand. It also requires sincerely soliciting their input and co-creating with them.

This is something the Instant Pot brand did well. It first executed a category development strategy: it promoted the product through Amazon and social media and contributed significant resources to helping new customers make the most out of it. It then amplified them by disseminating recipes and thus bringing them recognition, setting off a positive self-reinforcing loyalty cycle. Once it achieved a large critical mass of retained customers, the company successfully extended its product range, introducing four sizes and six types of Instant Pot cookers, but also taking the brand into other categories, such as milk-frothing machines, coffee, air fryers, and blenders.[7] Once activated, loyal customers followed the brand to other spaces in the kitchen where the Instant Pot could have immediate resonance and its benefit of speed could establish differentiation.

Loyal customers can become "brand ambassadors" who not only promote the brand but also become invested in its success and provide additional ideas for improvements.

Beliefs

What is the main reason your customers prefer your brand? How can you enhance that benefit to expand volume and reliance on the brand?

Companies executing a brand expansion strategy possess a clear value proposition. Their customers may be diverse in terms of demographic characteristics, but they share common values espoused by the brand. Apple customers value intuitive design; BMW owners value driving performance; Dyson customers value appliance power and design. These brands can expand efficiently, utilizing the credibility earned in one category to motivate customers to use it more often or to follow it to other product or service offerings where the brand benefit is relevant.

Brand expansion happens in one of two ways: horizontally or vertically. Horizontally, the brand can expand to adjacent benefit spaces, categories where the value proposition can travel credibly. Dyson, having earned a reputation in appealingly designed powerful air-related technology, expanded across vacuums (upright, corded, cordless, and for many specialized uses) and beyond them into fans, air filtration, hair and hand dryers, heaters, humidifiers . . . even air-circulating LED lights.

The brand can also expand vertically, that is, across price points within a category. The appliance brand Blendtec acquired customers with a powerful and premium-priced kitchen blender encased in plastic. Later, it sought to motivate existing customers to trade up by introducing a stainless-steel model with touch-sensitive controls. Stryker, the global medical-device company, offered manual stretchers for emergency medical services (EMS), but also stretchers that are electric-powered and fully featured to deliver a higher level of medical personnel and patient safety.

It is not enough to get current customers to double down in their *beliefs* about the brand. Brand expansion strategies succeed by changing current customer *behaviors*.

Behaviors

What percentage of current customers will increase their brand volume or value?

When executing brand expansion strategies, you can profit from customer loyalty by motivating current customers to increase the value they co-create with your brand (and the price they pay). Alternatively, you may leave prices unchanged and increase their usage occasions. We call these value and volume strategies, respectively.

In the United States, perhaps one of the most famous volume strategies is that of Arm & Hammer baking soda. The product was originally marketed in the 1800s as a baking additive, and later expanded from cooking to other home and personal care uses by educating customers about baking soda's odor reduction and cleaning properties. Customers complied, adding baking soda to other household cleaning products, placing baking soda in their refrigerators to eliminate bad odors, and even washing it down their sinks![8]

Value-based strategies consist of introducing a premium version of the product or service in the hope that the customer will trade up, as Blendtec did with its stainless-steel casing. Of course, brands do extend their offerings both up and down price points seeking to grow through customer retention and acquisition, respectively.

Premium and price-focused brand extensions must maintain value proposition consistency with the existing product portfolio to be successful. Whether you hope current customers will trade up through a premium offering, or noncustomers will try the brand through a less expensive offering, any product that carries the brand banner must deliver on the brand promise. Regardless of the price point, any product in the Mercedes portfolio must deliver on the luxury and comfort promise of a Mercedes Benz, and any Dyson-branded appliance must perform superbly.

Marketing metrics in brand expansion strategies track the behaviors of customers over time and across the solution portfolio to understand the best customer targets to pursue and the organizational behaviors that yield highest profitability.

Benchmarks

What are the best leading indicators of long-term brand and customer value?

In setting benchmarks, brands executing brand expansion strategies prioritize long-term category leadership over short-term profitably. Amazon is a good example of this. Since its first letter to shareholders in the company's 1997 Annual Report, Amazon leadership has publicly stated that it is willing to sacrifice short-term profitability and instead "relentlessly focus on customer experience."

Brand expansion leaders integrate metrics into the design of the customer experience. Members of Amazon's Prime program pay a flat annual membership fee to get expedited free shipping, special discounts, and free streaming content. The program offers the company's most committed customers a better experience than those who use the site casually. As of December 2019, Amazon had convinced 65 percent of Amazon shoppers – about 112 million people – to become Prime members.[9] The program is designed to collect a variety of customer metrics.

Amazon customizes the experience of every single visitor to its site. Even for new visitors, content is customized based on demographic data, such as location. Yet the customer experience is much more customized for repeat customers and even more so for Prime members. Previous product purchases, searches, and content preferences (accumulated through Prime video, Amazon music, Alexa, and Amazon Kindle purchases) are used to present highly customized suggestions. The point here is that customer benchmarks are not just useful to evaluate performance, but they are also an integral part of the customer experience design toolset in a brand expansion strategy.

Amazon's Prime members spend more than twice the average of non-Prime members, and their retention rates are 93 percent during the first year of membership and 98 percent after two years.[10]

Strategy Three: Brand Commitment ▬▬

A company undertaking this type of strategy is not a category leader and is not immediately seeking category leadership. This strategy is used by companies who estimate that their largest relative opportunity lies with customers who are *multibrand* users.

Multibrand usage often occurs when the differentiation among brands in a category is slight or because customers seek variety among a small set of brands. In these cases, many customers become either convenience- or product-feature shoppers rather than selecting brands as a result of a holistic feeling and strong preference toward a single brand.

Brands in categories where repeat purchases are made spontaneously naturally find themselves in this kind of situation. When making an impulse, variety-seeking, or unplanned purchase, the brand that has more mindshare at the time of a purchase or consumption also gets a larger share of the customer's wallet.

For categories subject to frequent repeat purchases or use, top-of-mind awareness and availability are critical as mental and physical ubiquity drive sales. However, we don't just find brand commitment strategies in product categories where people tend to make purchase decisions on the spot (beer, cereal, wine and spirits, and chocolates). We also find them in industrial markets where purchases are split among different brands either to manage risk or because the difference among vendors is too small to justify using a single brand. We also find such strategies used in other categories where customers naturally seek variety, such as clothing, video streaming, music and entertainment, food, and so on.

Brand

Can your existing brand inspire increased commitment?

Relative to a brand switching strategy, a company executing a commitment strategy has the advantage of working with current customers, people who like something about the brand or at least are used to it. Unfortunately, those customers have become accustomed to using the brand only sometimes. They are used to splitting purchases and have likely developed a resistance to being in a single committed relationship. In truth, this is okay, as the goal in a brand commitment relationship is to increase relative commitment rather than to obtain blind loyalty.

A brand commitment strategy is short term, relative to a brand expansion strategy. The goal here is to increase the customers' share of category spend or use to build sufficient credibility to eventually shift to a brand-expansion strategy, where you act like a market leader. Due to the proximity of the brands, a significant risk in the execution of a brand commitment strategy is igniting a price war or features war.

For decades, Energizer and Duracell battled over battery features and benefits. Energizer developed a drumming bunny mascot that epitomized its battery life, but Duracell was able to trademark a similar bunny for use in Europe and Canada. They engaged in lawsuits, starting in the 1980s and still continuing as of the time of the writing of this book.[11] At times, they have fought over "bunny rights" and most often about battery-life claims.[12]

Business Category

How to resize the category?

Both in brand commitment strategies and in brand switching strategies, your concern is not how to improve the health of the category but rather, how to become more relevant within it. Accordingly, your opportunity analysis should just focus on a portion of the business category. Here, you need to understand the opportunity represented by a set of brands within a broader solution space.

If you are a brand like Disney+ or Netflix, you are contemplating the opportunity to shift viewing time to your service within a limited set of options. If you operate a hotel, your functional category is not all hotels in a competitive franchise but rather other hotel brands with similar amenities in a local market. In a brand commitment strategy, resize your category to being just the set of brands among which your customers choose. You then need to understand their choice drivers.

Bodies

What is the split between loyal and multibrand customers?

Multibrand customers are not simply light users of the brand. Instead, they are people who are relatively committed to the category overall but who split their purchases among multiple brands. To be able to accurately estimate the number of multibrand customers, first start by designating the level of usage and belief that identifies loyal customers and then examine the rest of the customer base. Next, collect both brand sales and category spend by customer. Then understand the reason for their partial commitment.

Multibrand usage occurs due to shared decision-making, cost-management concerns, the need to mitigate supply risk, or simply because customers want variety. When purchase decisions are taken by groups, it is important that you understand each of the decision-making roles and their motivations.

Most medical supplies today are purchased under multiyear and multi-specialty contracts negotiated on price and availability. Powerful purchasing stakeholders, who are compensated based on their ability to decrease costs, may work with multiple device companies to drive competitive pricing. Clinicians may throw their support behind only a few product brands they consider critically important to their patient outcomes and may maintain relationships with several companies to stay abreast of innovations in their field.

A key to being able to split customers into loyal – people who use and prefer your brand – and multibrand – people who use your brand sometimes and lack a strong preference – is to understand the specific beliefs that drive customer behaviors.

Beliefs

Why do customers use multiple brands? What would make them more committed to yours?

The key to executing a brand commitment strategy is to understand *why* customers allocate purchases or use to multiple brands. Here, we seek to increase our brand's relative preference and will thus want to make a specific comparison.

The key to changing customer behaviors is understanding the beliefs that drive them. Customers may purchase multiple brands driven by a general lack of specific interest in the brand; driven by convenience, availability, or price; to manage risk or relationships by keeping multiple vendors engaged; or due to very specific brand-performance considerations. The execution of a brand-commitment strategy is different depending on the reason for multibrand usage.

In the credit-card category, where many customers are price sensitive, credit-card companies increase their customers' share of spend with their brands by launching co-promotions with retailers or vendors already popular with their customer base, also increasing convenience. Conversely, in categories where customers split purchases seeking specific benefits, brands may instead add variety to their offers to increase their shares of wallet.

Because a multibrand customer is familiar with multiple brands, you want to focus your belief-change efforts on an *experiential* benefit, achieve superiority in it, and then emphasize it so as to make it loom larger the next time the customer comes to purchase.

Brand commitment strategies do not always involve explicit comparisons. If customers are already evaluating brands prior to purchasing, companies are better off making implicit rather than explicit comparisons so as to avoid increasing their competitor's brand awareness, or further decreasing the perceived difference between already undifferentiated brands. Hotels in a local market compete fiercely against each other by monitoring their room rates and amenities such as free breakfast or upgraded rooms and making offers that are relatively better than their close competitors. Streaming services such as Netflix, Amazon Prime Video, Hulu, and Disney+ have been waging a closely contested war for viewership. The average American subscriber watches 3.4 services.[13] The top reason for choosing one rather than another service is "interesting content," and as a result the top services are constantly vying for exclusive rights over popular shows and movies (like *Friends*, *The Office*…) as well as investing to release their own original content.

Behaviors

To what extent will multibrand customers increase their commitment to your brand? And how do you need to execute to drive that commitment?

A key question in considering this type of strategy is: What percentage of your multibrand customers' purchases will you be able to capture? If customers are using multiple vendors to manage supply risk, there may be a ceiling to your brand's potential share of wallet.

If customers use your brand as part of a set because they perceive performance differences to be slight, then you will want to execute on a brand commitment strategy that builds separation between yourself and competition to gain an advantage. This is what Duracell did relative to Energizer. By refocusing on product innovation, it was able to reframe the debate between the two brands away from just battery life to other factors such as shelf life (Duracell claims its batteries last 10 years on a shelf).[14]

If customers are driven by convenience, then relative availability, lower price, or ease of ordering or disposal may be more critical.

Finally, if customers split purchases to get different experiences from different brands, then you may be able to add variety to your offer as a way to increase their brand commitment. Kellogg's Special K cereal brand added a variety of products over the years to increase its share of the breakfast category.

In considering a brand commitment strategy, you want to have specific customer-level metrics that help you assess your progress in increasing your customers' commitment to your brand relative to the level you targeted.

Benchmarks

Are you able to increase share of use or spend and relative brand commitment?

A key question to answer to validate whether to execute a brand commitment strategy is how many multibrand customers you have. You also want to measure "share of wallet" and then continue to look for changes in this share. Interestingly, if your execution is successful, over time your customers will become more committed to your brand, and you will eventually want to shift to a brand expansion strategy. Measure relative brand preference and correlate belief in your brand's differentiating benefit to the progress you are making in increasing multibrand commitment to your brand.

A brand commitment strategy is one of two competitive strategies – that is, those strategies that invite comparisons between your brand and that of a specific competitor. The other competitive strategy is brand switching.

Strategy Four: Brand Switching

Brand switching strategies are employed by companies wishing to establish a foothold in a category with a new product or service that, in some way, is better than the category leader's offer but is not sufficiently differentiated to reframe category boundaries.

This is the strategy employed by companies like Hyundai when it launched the Genesis model, a reliable sedan priced lower than the comparable Toyota or Honda model. This is also the strategy used by Outlook, the Microsoft email engine, with comparable features to Google's Gmail but claiming to be more respectful of customer privacy. It is the strategy used by Samsung Galaxy smartphones, priced similar to Apple iPhones, but featuring faster processors and more advanced performance features.

As with the other strategies, use the Big Picture's 6Bs to estimate opportunity and envision execution.

Brand

Is your brand an acceptable substitute for the brand you are targeting?

If you want to execute a brand switching strategy, first succeed at becoming part of the conversation when the category-leading brand is brought up. When Hyundai introduced the Genesis model into the United States in the 2008–2009 time period – its first model capable of competing in the luxury sedan category – the brand literally shot a commercial that took place in a German auto company's boardroom, and featured management struggling to pronounce *Hyundai* correctly. A few years later, the Hyundai Genesis became the car of choice for customers seeking luxury sedan looks at an affordable price. In fact, the company has a feature on its website where customers can compare Genesis models to Jaguar, Alfa Romeo, BMW, and Mercedes. In reality, the company is more likely to be successful in luring potential buyers away from Lexus and Acura than from European brands. And yet, by presenting itself as an alternative to established luxury brands, Hyundai has been able to increase its market share to just under 5 percent of all cars sold in the United States.[15]

Business Category

What is the role of your brand relative to the category?

When executing a brand switching strategy, you are not attempting to redefine the category. Your investment is much more targeted and, hopefully, much more efficient. A brand switching strategy is generally employed by a brand entering a new category and seeking to take share efficiently while establishing credibility. The hope is that by comparing itself to the category leader, the brand will be able to gain the attention, credibility, and eventually financial resources to pivot to another strategy, either brand commitment or brand expansion.

Bodies

What specific group of competitive customers could you compel to switch?

When executing a brand switching strategy you are not seeking to convert all customers of a competitive brand, just those who you can make feel disenfranchised enough to seek an alternative. To estimate opportunity, understand what percentage of a competitive segment or brand can fall into that group.

In 2016, Sprint launched a brand switching campaign against Verizon, targeting customers who could be made to care more about price than network reliability. Sprint hired Paul Marcarelli, an actor who for a decade had touted Verizon's superior network reliability in a series of commercials where he repeated, "Can you hear me now?" Paul, a face and voice everyone identified with the Verizon brand, was now urging customers to switch and give up 1 percent in network reliability and pay 50 percent less. The campaign was the most successful in the company's history, with more than 8 million YouTube views and more than 300 million impressions on social media. Upon news of the campaign's success, Sprint's shares gained almost 30 percent. Despite this, Sprint was unable to increase its market share. The company was acquired by T-Mobile in 2020.[16]

Beliefs

What relative weakness of your competitor could you amplify to motivate switching?

In executing a brand switching strategy, the brand is introducing itself to customers who have never experienced it. In this case, having novel technology or other easily comparable points of difference is helpful initially. It is common for a brand switching strategy to present a lower price for similar performance to that offered by the category leader. Like Sprint in its efforts to target Verizon customers, Shark vacuums earned share by offering a cheaper alternative to similarly featured Dyson vacuums.

When executing a brand switching strategy, you can either present your brand as a cheaper alternative to the category leader or as offering superior performance for a similar price. To motivate customers to switch brands, first mine and amplify their dissatisfaction with a brand they currently use. Be careful, however, and pretest your value proposition to make sure that it has the power of not only changing beliefs but also driving behaviors.

In 2013, Microsoft targeted Gmail with direct web ads telling customers that they were being Scroogled because Google was selling their personal data. Outlook asked Gmail users to sign a petition to be sent to Google, demanding that it change its business practices. Despite reaching millions of Gmail users (the ads appeared online and also on major cable networks) and persuading more than 100,000 people to sign its petition,

Microsoft was not successful in getting customers to switch away from Gmail to Outlook.[17]

Of course, a brand switching strategy – just like any other marketing campaign – must change both beliefs and behaviors to be successful.

Behaviors

What executional investment must you prioritize to motivate switching?

If you are executing a brand-switching strategy, direct all executional investment to encourage favorable comparisons to your brand. This entails presenting the product in the same way as your competitor, in the same points of distribution, for a similar price, and communicating similar performance claims to their customers. As the Sprint example aptly illustrates, successfully taking market share against a category leader requires more than changing beliefs.

Develop a realistic estimate of the number of people who will change their behavior and of the purchases each of them will make.

Benchmarks

How many customers of your target competitor will you persuade to switch?

The key metrics when executing a brand strategy are relative. They depend on the brand from which you seek to earn shares. These include the number of customers from the target brand who are aware of your competitive offer; their beliefs about the importance of the positioning benefit your brand offers as well as the perceived perception of your performance; and the number of competitive customers researching your offer, trialing, and eventually converting to your brand.

How to Select a Go-to-Market Strategy

There are four ways to take a brand to market. Which one should you choose?

Developing go-to-market strategy requires decision-making under uncertainty. The framework presented in this book is designed to reduce uncertainty by identifying the key variables and their relationships.

Brand		Business Category Bodies			Beliefs		Behaviors		Bucks				
Branded Unit of Analysis	CC	Category definition	Customer strategy	# Targets	Before	After	Before	After	% Converted	Converted bodies	Purchases per customer	Price	Revenue potential
Your brand name	Core competence	Business category name	Leader of category or earn share from competitor	# bodies in target audience	Current customer belief you want to change	Desired customer belief	Current customer behavior you want to change	Desired customer behavior	%	#	# purchases/ customer	$	$ sales opportunity

FIGURE 2.2   6Bs opportunity analyses.

Selecting a go-to-market strategy is an iterative process; it requires you to estimate customer opportunity in a given strategy and then consider what it would take to execute on that strategy. You want to choose the strategy with the best return, given your budget and time frame, and as compared to the other three approaches. So, how can you do this?

First, use the 6Bs system of integrated choices to conduct opportunity analysis. Identify the most likely choices for each of the 6Bs by the go-to-market approach. Develop assumptions for each B, estimating the number of potential customers available, the required belief and behavior changes, and the most likely financial outcomes.

For most organizations, sustainable growth comes not from having the best intuitive go-to-market plan but from developing a sound plan, with a single-minded goal, that your team can get behind because it is based on facts and logic. Figure 2.2 illustrates the elements of a simple 6Bs opportunity analysis.

Use the 6Bs to estimate the opportunity of each of the four go-to-market archetypes.

Once you have prepared an opportunity analysis, use the 6Bs to sketch the executional implications of each strategy. The team should then feel empowered to choose one of the go-to-market approaches, with the knowledge that it has three other strategic scenarios it can activate should they become more appealing than originally considered. For this purpose, set marketing metrics to indicate when to shift from one to another strategy.

Think of marketing metrics as learning tools that connect strategy with execution. Set metrics for each of the 6Bs to understand which strategy to choose; to keep your team's focus on the specific goals earmarked by each of the 6Bs; and to help them self-correct if you veer off course.

3 Brands

In today's hyper-branded environment, the brand decision is critically important; it makes the difference between ubiquity and irrelevance. The brand is the customer's perception of the company, and so the purpose of the brand must be clear.

And yet, many of the companies I've worked with simply let brands happen. Setting the brand strategy requires engaging in self-reflection about who you are. And, in turn, answering that question entails conducting organizational soul-searching to identify unique skills and resources.

Therefore, as you consider your brand, you must ask two important questions:

1. Who are we?
2. What are we good at?

The answers to these questions can neither be vague nor narrowly focused on the here and now. Your organization and its markets are complex systems in a constant state of change; defining the brand and the strategic capabilities of the organization that supports it must be forward-looking exercises. It's vital to consider not just what the organization and brand stand for today, but also what they will mean in the future.

This chapter helps you frame and answer these two questions. Together, they enable your brand choice.

Who Are We? Brand Architecture Enables Customer Choice

The traditional definition of a brand is that it is a symbol or logo that identifies the company's products and services, as distinct from competitors' offerings. But for decades, marketers have correctly argued that a brand is not simply identity. And yet, most business-to-business organizations still treat branding as simply a naming exercise, and many underperform even that basic function.

In fact, many organizations act like nervous parents who have planned all aspects of their procreation, but on the eve before bringing a new life to the world are still pondering the name. And some of them opt for waiting to see the baby to decide what name might suit their child best. They work through features and benefits, select a target audience, price the innovation, and leave the "what should we call it?" question to the tail end of the launch process.

It is also not unusual for mergers and acquisitions teams to get far down the acquisition process before addressing what will happen to the acquired company's brands; and in some cases, there is no plan for what to do with them until product portfolios are integrated.

Identity is a basic function of a brand. When brands are not recognized by customers and products are not correctly identified, even in the most basic way, the brand is not serving a useful function for the company.

One of my clients, a cataracts-lens company, has so many different and confusing brands that customers mis-order: the wrong lens is often brought to the surgical suite, delaying procedures. Another client recently discovered that only 25 percent of its professional customers correctly identified ownership of its largest brand, while approximately half of its customers thought it belonged to its competitor.

Indeed, brands can be a source of complexity and confusion. Yet when they work, they can be strategic assets, smoothing out business cycles, providing protection against disruptive competition, and adding value to the balance sheet. Brand value grows as customers use products and services and have positive experiences with the organization represented by the brand.

In short brand equity is the value of a brand above and beyond the *functional value provided by the company's product or service to the customer.*

At least in theory, brand equity can be measured by the magnitude of the price premium of the branded product over a functionally equivalent product that is not branded. For example, how much more does a diamond ring cost if sold by Tiffany & Co. than the identical ring sold by a no-name jeweler?

Brand: Defining Who We Are by Mapping the Customer and the Brand Journey

Brand equity is developed by the consistent communications and delivery of a promise, over time, as customers "journey" with the brand.[1] And companies that manage their brands proactively design a brand customer experience that runs in parallel to the customer journey, as shown in Figure 3.1.

Accordingly, maps of the customer journey are commonly divided into five steps: awareness, search and compare, purchase and initial use, habitual use, and post-purchase reflection. The brand plays a critically important

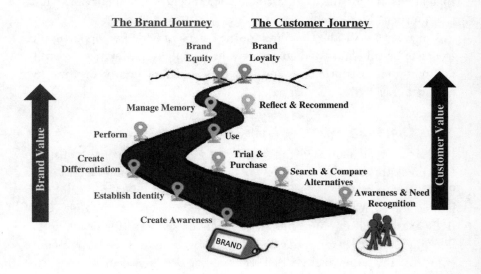

FIGURE 3.1 The customer journey and the brand journey.

To programmatically generate customer loyalty, brands should research and understand customers' journeys: the steps customers take in becoming aware, becoming interested, and finally buying and using, and deciding what to do afterward.

role in guiding customers along their journeys with the category, creating relationships along the way.

Throughout customers' journeys, the brand builds equity in stages as follows:

1. Attracting prospective customers' attention and interest.
2. Helping to connect with them while considering their needs.
3. Deepening that interest as it communicates a specific and valuable promise that motivates the customers to try and purchase the product or service.
4. Performing in a way that delivers on the promises made throughout the sales process.
5. Becoming a trusted or habitual companion that receives the good feelings co-created through the use of the brand.

We can examine the role of the brand in five stages, matching the steps in the customer journey. The 6Bs help you create a customer experience that aligns the brand to desired customer beliefs and behaviors along that journey.

If managed well, the customer journey steps provide five opportunities to create brand equity and company value as follows: awareness, identity, differentiation, performance, and loyalty. If managed poorly, they are five opportunities to destroy that value.

Stage 1: Brand Awareness

Attractive brand names, logos, and visuals, when used consistently, can help break through the cacophony of daily life and get potential customers to pay attention. The *awareness* function of a brand refers to its ability to garner attention for individual products and services (for example, Dove Body Wash), for an entire line of products or services (for example, the Dove line of skin care products), or for a corporate unit or for the entire company, including many different types of products and services (for example, Unilever Personal Care versus Unilever Food).

The awareness function is iterative. It provides the bookends of the customer experience. The brand causes us to pay attention to a company's product or service offer, and after we've had a good experience with the product or service, the brand reminds us of the good feelings that, over time, we come to associate with the brand, continuing to add to its value. As such, the brand serves as both an attention aid and a memory aid.

Stage 2: Brand Identity

The *identity* function of a brand is not simply about recognizing the name. Customers develop specific associations to brands, and place them in a category, that is, next to other brands they would consider simultaneously. This is called a *consideration set*.

BMW is associated with luxury high-performance cars and SUVs and is likely placed alongside Mercedes and Audi. IBM and Accenture are associated with IT consulting; Lindt is associated with chocolates and placed next to Nestlé. Michelin is associated with tires and placed next to Bridgestone and Goodyear.

Successful brands have clear and consistent identities. The associations customers attribute to the brand are homogenous and uniform, across all assets carrying the brand name. To achieve these associations, the brand name, logo, and colors must always be similar across every product and service within the portfolio of a single brand.

The importance of consistency in branding goes beyond appearance, as all service interactions with the brand must also be consistent and unique among the alternatives available to a customer.

The experience of walking into a McDonald's restaurant or a BMW dealership must be consistent regardless of location. It helps that McDonald's has a yellow distinctive logo, but beyond that, the experience in the stores, from the drive-through wait time, to the menu displays, to the bathroom cleanliness, to the food experience, must all deliver according to a brand standard shared across all franchisees anywhere in the world.

Similarly, walking into a BMW dealership feels like stepping into the lobby of a luxury hotel, although the details of the decor in Milan, Italy, may differ from those in Dayton, Ohio. The takeaway for the potential customer is that BMW is a purveyor of luxury high-performance personal transportation, regardless of the market.

Successful brands come immediately to mind when the customer has a specific need in a solution class that is served by the brand and where the brand is present. The unaided recall element in the brand equity model is also called *top-of-mind awareness*, indicating that the brand comes to mind as part of a consideration set without explicit prompting by the company.

Stage 3: Brand Differentiation

Valuable brands also carry a *differentiation* element. Beyond creating awareness for the brand and identifying the type of need a product or service satisfies, valuable brands are synonymous with specific promises. The brand
causes products and services to stand out from the competition by offering
propositions that are unique among the competitive set.

If I want to purchase a high-performance four-door entry-level luxury
sedan, should I buy a BMW 3-series, a Mercedes 300, an Audi A4, or a
Lexus ES350? They all have similar engine functionality, technology, and
high-end leather options. However, there are differences. The BMW brand
appeals to drivers who like to feel the road. Mercedes is about luxury and
comfort, Audi is associated with design, and Lexus with reliability.

The brand not only helps identify each of the car models but also
helps customers match their personality and preferences to the distinctive
strengths of each of the alternatives.

Stage 4: Brand Performance

Awareness, identity, and differentiation motivate customers to use or consume the product. During use, the brand enters a *performance* phase. That
is, the brand generates judgments and feelings based on the customer's specific experience of using or consuming the brand.

These judgments can be both rational and emotional. The BMW brand
performs from a functional perspective as it delivers acceleration and handling, but also from an emotional perspective if the driver feels their social
status is higher by being part of the BMW club. The clothing and lifestyle
brand, lululemon, delivers on its performance promise of helping customers
achieve a healthy lifestyle through clothing that enables physical movement.
It also performs at an emotional level by incorporating fashion into fitness
and emboldening its customers to wear yoga pants to social gatherings.

If post-use judgments are positive, the customer can be said to be satisfied. A common definition of *customer satisfaction* is the measurement of
the difference between a customer's expectations about a brand and his or
her evaluation of its actual performance. Customers are satisfied if they
complete a purchase cycle and find that the brand has matched or exceeded
their expectations. And, at the end of this process, if customers are satisfied, they are more likely to re-engage with the brand without conducting a
full comparative evaluation again.

Stage 5: Brand Loyalty

As customers associate positive experiences with a brand, it becomes more valuable to them, and eventually they develop *loyalty* to it. Brand loyalty describes a relationship in which a customer relies on the brand in a habitual manner, integrating it into their own processes while rejecting offers from other brands.

These brand-customer relationships can be based on ease of use, ease of access, or just convenience; they can be rational, based on the brand's recurring performance of a specific job the customer wants done; and they can be emotional, if the customer becomes personally invested in the brand, feels passion for what the brand stands for, and tells others about it.

Given the role of the brand as a guide to the customer along their journey, a brand is not how those inside the organization think about the company, it is what customers think and feel when they see or experience it. BMW is a luxury performance car company. 3M is an innovation-focused company that builds things we use at home and in the office. Facebook stands for keeping us in touch with our friends and communities. These are all external customer perceptions.

And yet, internal opinions do matter because for a brand to have a specific and valuable meaning, the company behind the brand must build that meaning. And the tools that are used to build a brand are the skills and resources of the internal people who support the brand.

In today's hyper-branded environment, you cannot be successful in creating valuable brands unless you also conceive of brands as *strategic units of analysis*. Marketing is not just communications and commercial operations; it is the entire process a company uses to *go to market*. In that context, brands are the assets that take a company to the market.

In other words, brands represent who the company is in the market from a customer experience perspective. Customers choose to purchase or not to purchase at a brand level.

What does it mean to say that brands must be treated as strategic units of analysis? It means that when developing a go-to-market strategy, brands establish *who* the organization is and *why* customers should buy from it.

There is inherent circularity in brand building and competitive advantage. The brand is the asset that represents what the company stands for in the market. Once a successful brand is built, one with clear, differentiated, and valuable meaning, the brand sustains the company and its products and services.

But the brand cannot stand for something that is not uniquely and genuinely owned by the company. Attempts to reposition a brand away from the true activity of the organization can fail and can even backfire unless the company purposefully integrates its activity in the market to its brand communications. In 2005, GE launched a rebranding effort, and, under the banner of *EcoImagination*, attempted to advertise diesel engines and coal-fired power plants. Internally, people at GE felt that *EcoImagination* was a big success. Externally, however, customers asked how it was possible for GE to position itself as environmentally conscious while investing in fracking, coal-fired energy, and diesel. That campaign did not stick, and GE's brand image as an industrial company remained.

Do Brands = Products?

What is the difference between a brand and a product or service? Brands are strategic intangible assets of the company. Products and services may also be company assets, but their role is tactical rather than strategic. Brands establish who the company is in the market. They establish the company's overall promise. It is then the role of the products and services to deliver on that promise. Brands are used to establish the strategy, and products and services are components of the execution of the strategy.

One big disadvantage of a product-based business is that products are subject to temporary lifecycles of investment, growth, maturity, and decline. A business must grow even as products are retired and replaced. This is where brands help. The brand lifecycle need not be subject to the peaks and valleys of the product lifecycle (see Figure 3.2). If managed well, brands can grow in value, theoretically forever, even as technology is upgraded, and existing products are replaced.

Brands offer customer benefits that are constantly updated and augmented with the successive introduction and retirement of products and services. Therefore, if you want to build a sustainable company, you should conceive of your organization as a collection of well-managed brands, rather than as a collection of products.

The Honda brand stands for engine superiority, and the company has successfully extended it into a variety of business categories where that meaning is valued, including automotive, boating, landscaping, generators, racing, aircraft, and recreational sports.

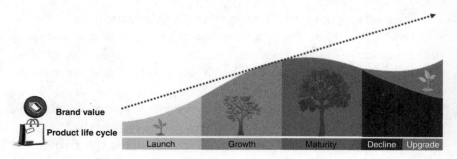

FIGURE 3.2 Product lifecycle and brand lifecycle.

Products are tactical tools of the company and are subject to lifecycles with phases of growth, maturity, and decline. When brands are treated as strategic tools, they can increase in value even as products are retired and replaced.

The distinction between products and services is no longer a very useful one in today's economy. With more than 75 percent of the US and EU economies deriving their gross domestic product from services,[2] few companies today purely sell products or services. Somewhat counterintuitively, most B2B companies I work with get paid when they deliver products, and yet they derive their competitive advantage from their services, which are often included with a product "for free."

Indeed, many well-managed organizations have become focused on value, and have shifted to being product-service agnostic. Years ago, IBM made servers and laptop equipment, and Marriott provided hotel services. Today, IBM derives most of its revenues from selling consulting services, and Marriott sells the robes and even mattresses used in its top-tier hotels. The simultaneous advent of digital-enabled automation and increased focus on selling experiences, have resulted in an economy-wide movement to "servitize" products and "productize" services.

Subscriptions no longer apply to just services; they span many product and service categories. Both product and service sellers prefer that customers pay a subscription rather than purchase a single unit outright. Automotive customers increasingly lease rather than buy their cars (the percentage of cars leased in 2020 was more than 30 percent, up from fewer than 20 percent in 2010).[3] Media companies used to sell newspapers and magazines. Today they sell information services. Subscription and service contracts benefit from brand inertia and therefore tend to be quite sticky.

Selling subscriptions rather than products helps create that relationship inertia. That's because when customers subscribe to a service plan or a subscription-based ownership plan, their relationship becomes less centered on the product itself and much more on their interactions with the brand.

A subscription-based relationship drives many touchpoints between the company and the customer, and therefore many opportunities for the brand to establish its value proposition and deliver value to the customer. So, in a sense, rather than inevitably driving a passive connection between brand and customer, brand inertia can be a source of value and loyalty.

For these reasons, the product-versus-service debate is a thing of the past. Success in both products and services centers on companies' ability to establish a service promise and deliver on that promise consistently over time.

Brands become valuable only if customers associate them with clear and differentiated promises. Those associations are built over time through repeated and consistent experiences. Products and services are responsible for delivering those experiences. In other words, products and services are *features* or attributes of the brand. They, in turn, have detailed physical, technological, or operational features.

Because the features of a product or service deliver benefits to the customer, as is shown in Figure 3.3, brand value builds if and only if the products sold under the brand name *deliver the specific valuable experiences* proposed in the brand value proposition.

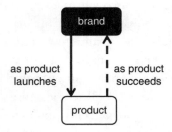

FIGURE 3.3 Brand and product value.

There is a symbiotic relationship between products and brands. At product launch, a well-established brand adds value by imbuing the product with awareness and meaning. As the product becomes accepted and is successful, value flows back, as specific positive associations are attached to the brand.

Every product in the portfolio has an obligation to support the equity of its master brand by delivering an experience that lives up to the brand promise. Products and services should be resourced relative to their role and centrality versus the brand promise. The product in the portfolio that delivers the brand promise with the greatest fidelity ought to also be the most salient and celebrated. The BMW M models epitomize the performance promise of the brand; they may not be the best-selling nor the most profitable for the company, and yet they are prominently featured in the company's communications and dealerships.

The creation of brand equity is a learning process for both the brand and the customer. In a congruent brand portfolio, each product and service communicates a consistent benefit. When the brand and its products are not aligned, however, no brand equity is created because no association exists back to the brand.

Motorola, the US-based electronics company, experienced wild success with its Razr clamshell phone, launched in 2004. But as the cell phone category gave way to the smartphone category in 2006 and 2007, Motorola was not able to capture much of the equity created by the Razr. The Motorola devices that followed the Razr looked different, carried different product brands, and functioned differently from the Razr. The lack of consistent design and functionality – with its smartphone products even having different names – is a reason the brand lost meaning and value in the marketplace.

With that in mind, let's take a look at the ways companies organize brands.

Brand Architecture and Customer Choice Units

Brand architecture is the organizing structure guiding a company's brands. Brand architecture guides how a company's brands are related to and are differentiated from one another.

Companies go to market with a variety of brand architectures. Some companies use a single brand to identify their entire product and service portfolio, while other companies create different brands for different divisions or portfolios.

Companies also create brands to identify specific product lines, or even ingredients or features of specific products.

Dyson goes to market with a single brand across multiple categories, from hair dryers to lighting, whereas Johnson & Johnson uses different brands for different business categories: Ethicon is its surgical products brand, and Janssen is its pharmaceutical brand.

The pharmaceutical company Pfizer uses different brands for different medications, such as Advil for pain relief, Viagra for erectile dysfunction or Robitussin for coughs. Well-known "ingredient" or "feature" brands, like Apple's Retina displays or Gore-Tex fabrics, identify specific components of products or services.

Some companies' brand architecture corresponds to careful design. However, many companies simply let brand architecture happen. Their brands are a result of acquisitions, product launches, management changes, and internal politics, rather than the result of purposeful design.

Brands that are organized logically, and have clear and valuable meanings, are successful because they demand little cognitive effort from customers. This is why, as you commence planning work, you should ask, "Who are we?" in the context of how customers view their options. Decisions about which brands to create and maintain, and how to resource and deploy them in the market, should match how customers want to buy.

Brand Architecture Options: An Overview

Companies that manage their brands purposefully choose a brand architecture that best enables their corporate strategy. As shown in Figure 3.4, there are four broad options for brand architecture: an umbrella structure, a distinct structure, and two hybrid-branding structures: umbrella-driven or sub-brand driven. Each type of brand architecture is described below.

Key Types:	Umbrella	Hybrid Umbrella-Driven	Hybrid Sub-brand Driven	Distinct
Customer Experience:	A common customer experience across all products and services	Customer experience dominated by the umbrella brand	Customer experience dominated by the sub-brand	Customer experience unique to each sub-brand
Example:	Dyson McKinsey & Co. BP (oil company)	Porsche Cayenne Intel Pentium	Residence Inn Marriott Courtyard Marriott Springhill Suites Marriott	Louis Vuitton Bvlgari Moet & Chandon Dewalt

FIGURE 3.4 Four types of brand architecture.

There are four main types of brand architecture, each with significant strategy and customer experience implications.

Umbrella branding is structuring the company around one brand for all products and services. A company should choose umbrella branding when it wants to deliver a single customer experience across all products and services.

In umbrella-branded companies, the corporate brand is a strategic unit of analysis dictating the value proposition, the category strategy, and major executional priorities. This does not mean that in developing their go-to-market strategies, umbrella-branded companies have a single strategic plan. Different portfolios may manage their own budgets and tactics, even if major strategic decisions are taken at the umbrella-brand level.

Companies that wish to appeal to very different types of customers simultaneously are best served by creating *distinct brands*. Companies should create distinct brands if they want to offer different customer experiences under each of their brand banners. Distinct branding affords companies flexibility to create value propositions that are different, and could even be conflicting, in the same or in multiple categories. Accordingly, they are managed independently as separate *strategic units of analysis*. Unilever sells personal care products under the Dove and Axe brands, and while they are in the same personal care category, Axe sells deodorants with a value proposition of *sex appeal,* while Dove stands for *real beauty* and *self-esteem.*

Few companies follow a pure umbrella or distinct brand architecture. Many live somewhere in the middle and create **hybrid** brand architectures. There are two types of hybrid architectures. They are distinguished by the different roles of the umbrella brand and the sub-brands owned by the company. They are called **umbrella-driven hybrids** and **sub-brand driven hybrids**.

Umbrella-driven hybrids go to market with powerful master brands but also utilize sub-brands with somewhat differentiated value propositions. These companies might have started as umbrella-branded companies, but over time evolved into a hybrid structure.

Sub-brand driven hybrids have relatively independent sub-brands although they are connected by membership to the umbrella brand. Companies may move into these types of hybrid architectures as their portfolios expand. As this happens, the sub-branded units require independence in their go-to-market strategies to create differentiation internally, as well as to grow, while maintaining a connection to the umbrella.

When it comes to making purchases, customers should not have to learn how a company is organized to find out if the brand is a good solution for them. Customers are interested in understanding, in the easiest way possible, why they should choose the brand instead of the other options available in the market. If brands are going to function as valuable strategic assets of an organization, they need to be structured in a way that fits with how customers make choices.

Now, with this understanding of the four types of brand architecture, let's take a closer look at umbrella branding.

Umbrella: Going to Market with One Brand

The biggest benefit of umbrella branding is efficiency. Once established, the corporate brand supports the product and service portfolio. The halo effect of positive associations with the corporate brand assists with every product and service launch.

Take, for example, the Dyson appliance portfolio. The company sells vacuum cleaners, fans, and hand and hair dryers. The Dyson *brand promise* is strikingly designed air performance. Each product leverages common technology and design features, and congruence is achieved by building to a common standard as much as possible. This includes not only identity elements like packaging, colors, materials, and components, but also more functional features like accessories, shapes, touchscreens, and other engineering elements.

Each product and service in the Dyson portfolio shares common features with all others, and those common features carry the brand identity and the brand promise. The products have similar switches, colors, and design. Each product delivers a specific functional benefit to fulfill the Dyson promise across a variety of applications or categories – from vacuums to hairdryers to air-cooled LED lights. Essentially anywhere in one's life where you can use air performance, Dyson has, or could credibly develop, a solution.

Well-designed air performance is equally carried through to service aspects of the brand. Dyson wraps services around its products, and the company maintains continuity through service standards, long warranties, immediate replacement in case of product failure, and highly effective training videos, which use special effects to augment the product performance features.

Finally, Dyson's communications reinforce the brand promise through content that showcases performance data, whether communicating the percentage of allergens their air purifiers eliminate, long battery life, or powerful suction. All aspects of the Dyson brand are synergistic and all strengthen the Dyson brand equity. Products, services, and communications are designed around a common customer experience so that as the target audience learns about and uses the brand, the value placed on well-designed air performance grows.

As the Dyson example shows, the benefit of umbrella branding is that equity elements (awareness, differentiation, loyalty) lower the cost of launching new products and services congruent with the brand. As additional products and services are successful, they further increase equity for the umbrella brand, providing synergistic relationships between the brand executional elements and the brand equity.

The disadvantage of umbrella branding stems from the truism that a brand can't both be perceived as differentiated and expand limitlessly. Over time, companies that go to market with a single brand and use it to enter different business categories or markets find this type of brand architecture constraining.

Companies that push on with a single brand across vastly different categories can thus end up sacrificing some of the differentiation value of their brands.

Yamaha, the Japanese conglomerate, leads in musical instrument sales for both professional and amateur musicians. It also sells motorcycles, but the value proposition (belief) that sets the brand apart in musical instruments does not carry over to motorized vehicles. As a result of being in both categories, as well as in additional categories, the Yamaha brand doesn't have a particularly clear meaning.

Relatedly, although the Dyson brand has helped the company move from vacuums to hand dryers, hair dryers, and fans, when Dyson announced it was creating a new electric car in 2017, company enthusiasts were intrigued but a bit puzzled.

James Dyson claimed his brand simply stands for *ingenuity*: "Having an idea for doing something better and making it happen – even though it appears impossible."[4] However, the Dyson brand does not carry equally easily into electric cars as it does, say, fans. And no one was terribly surprised when in late 2019, after significant investment and even a working prototype, the company announced that it was abandoning the project.

An additional downside of umbrella branding is that failure in one part of the brand system is likely to negatively impact all elements in the portfolio. British petroleum (BP), the oil company that was responsible for an environmental disaster in the Gulf of Mexico in 2010, suffered not just in the US market but globally, as customers temporarily boycotted its gasoline stations. The company's lack of environmental safeguards in the Gulf of Mexico didn't just affect its operations in the southern United States but its operations worldwide.

Given all this, when should companies go to market as a single brand for all their products and services? They should use an umbrella brand architecture if they intend to focus on a single value proposition and wish to concentrate on related categories and customer groups. However, they should keep in mind that although umbrella branding drives efficiency and helps focus resources, it does have constraints and risks.

When those risks become too great, it can be beneficial to develop distinct brands.

Distinct Branding: Going to Market with Multiple Brands

Companies should use a distinct brand architecture if they intend to work with very different customer segments and, therefore, need to articulate divergent value propositions.

Unilever developed two distinct personal care brands for people who might be demographically similar but who hold fundamentally different motivations. Unilever brands Axe and Dove both sell deodorants and personal care products and are similarly priced. Yet Axe targets people who are motivated to increase their sex appeal while Dove targets people who want to increase their self-esteem.

Distinct branding can separate segments and categories. BMW, a company that uses an umbrella brand for most of its products and services, developed a distinct brand when it launched Mini Cooper – an entry-level luxury compact performance car designed to deliver fun rather than serious driving performance. Although some overlap exists, most of BMW's portfolio competes in the luxury sedan and sports utility categories, while Mini Cooper competes in the compact car category.

Distinct branding can also help separate customer groups within a category. In 1992, the US company Black & Decker created the DeWalt brand to establish itself as a credible power tool supplier to the professional trades after it realized that the Black & Decker brand carried a stigma as just a home, DIY brand.

Distinct branding enables a company to extend its business horizontally, that is, across multiple categories and benefit spaces – as Unilever, BMW, and Black & Decker illustrate. It also enables expansion from a pricing perspective. In 1989 Toyota created Lexus to go beyond its customer base and appeal to a luxury-seeking segment of customers.

While umbrella branding can be risky in cases of a product failure or a market entry misstep, distinct branding can protect the core business in these instances. However, the obvious benefits of flexibility and insulation from risk associated with distinct branding do come with two disadvantages. First, creating and maintaining multiple brands is expensive, and companies tend to underestimate the resources required to successfully launch and operate a new brand.

When companies find either branding approach – umbrella or distinct – too constraining, they can turn to hybrid branding, which combines the two.

Hybrid Branding: The Best of Both Worlds?

Hybrid branding attempts to combine the efficiency advantages of powerful umbrella brands with the flexibility offered by distinctive sub-brands. Well-designed hybrid brand architectures can lower the cost of product launches while providing flexibility to spin off or retire the sub-brand in case course correction is needed.

Companies can utilize a well-known brand to attract immediate attention, while using a new brand to seed curiosity, energize the corporate portfolio, and provide protection against me-too competitors. In an umbrella-driven hybrid brand, a valuable corporate brand is associated to a new, and therefore unknown, sub-brand, granting the latter immediate credibility. When Porsche first launched its first sports utility vehicle (SUV) in the US market in 2003,[5] it created a sub-brand, the Cayenne.

Well-managed brands are strategic assets of the company; however, brand equity can turn negative if the products in the brand portfolio disappoint or their value propositions are not aligned to the umbrella. This was a concern for Porsche when the Cayenne first launched. The first model year received negative reviews from Porsche traditionalists, who at the time were mostly male and highly involved in the engine and mechanics of their vehicles. In a sharp departure from this tradition, Cayenne was a car for safety-conscious parents. Whether intentionally or not, the eventual success of the Cayenne caused the entire Porsche brand to be repositioned from a brand that appealed to performance purists to a brand that is better known for luxury finishes and comfort. Interestingly, since the Cayenne was introduced, the Porsche brand has more than tripled in value, propelled by other luxury sub-brands, such as the four-seater Panamera and the Macan line of compact SUVs.[6]

A hybrid brand can help a company reposition its offerings and create flexibility to retire brands if they do not perform as expected, or to spin them off and make them independent in case of a run-away success.

In the early 2000s, Hyundai, was perceived as a low-quality brand in the United States because its reputation was largely staked on the Excel, a model brought to the US market in the 1980s that had been plagued by quality problems.

But in 2008, Hyundai sought to change its brand perception by debuting the Genesis, a premium model that assured reliability through the longest warranty policy in the industry, 100,000 miles and 10 years – more than three times as long as the standard three-year warranties offered by most car brands.

Also, in response to the financial crisis of 2008 and in a rare gesture of empathy, Hyundai offered buyers the ability to return the car if they were unable to make car payments because they had lost their jobs.

Partially as a result of these two tactics as well as its quality improvements, the Genesis had record sales and was also named 2009 car of the year by JD Power and Associates. In 2017, Hyundai spun off the Genesis as a separate brand,[7] capitalizing on its earlier successes and providing a viable path for the company to enter the premium segment and compete with brands like Acura, Infinity, and even Lexus.

The Hyundai Genesis is an example of how hybrid branding can provide the flexibility to pivot between a corporate-driven strategy and one that is more independent and driven from the sub-brand.

While hybrid branding can confer the company flexibility, hybrid branding can get complex and confusing. As internal resources are stretched, the company may not be able to deliver distinctive value propositions with clear common elements driven by the umbrella brand, along with clearly differentiated elements driven by the distinctive portfolio elements.

Marriott hotels groups brands into various customer segments (Luxury, Premium, Select, Longer Stays), and within each group there are "standard" and "distinctive" properties, making up eight sub-categories of hotel properties, each with multiple brands.

In the standard grouping, brands such as Residence Inn, Springhill Suites, and Courtyard operate independently and have differentiated value propositions, but to the average business traveler who only stays at these properties occasionally, the differences between these brands are not terribly clear. As a result, many business travelers are confused, not just about how the Residence Inn is different from the SpringHill Suites hotel but also what to expect from a Marriott hotel experience.

Successfully operating a brand requires sound strategy and execution. For a sub-brand to add equity to the company's products and services, it should have a distinctive promise that is different from the umbrella brand, yet not so distant as to seem incongruent with the rest of the portfolio, as this would potentially damage the umbrella.

Brand Architecture: How to Choose

Treating the brand as the strategic unit of analysis helps to develop strategic congruence; that is, alignment of the brand promise and the skills and assets required to support the brand. Alternatively, if simply branding as naming, the brands may succumb to anonymity.

Who are we? This question ultimately means, at what level in the brand architecture does the organization develop strategy? The answer to this question has resource implications.

The company that goes to market with distinct brands will organize in small teams with specialized skills and resources to support independent and differentiated customer experiences. Rovio Entertainment, the company that developed the mobile electronics game Angry Birds, develops other games (Battle Bay, Fruit Nibblers, Sugar Blast), each with a different theme. To the extent that Rovio wants its games to deliver different benefits to customers – such as education rather than simply entertainment – it requires not just different cover stories and graphics but also different software development skillsets for each brand.

Alternatively, the company that goes to market with a single brand will tend toward centralized management to deliver a single customer experience across products and services. BMW and Dyson deliver a single brand promise through shared resources, from advertising and communications, to product development and commercialization, to service and customer relationship management.

Conversely, for companies with hybrid-branding models, aspects of the customer experience controlled by an umbrella brand may be resourced at a more centralized level than aspects corresponding to the sub brand. Marriott hotel brands deliver specific experiences, but are all tied together through common reservation systems, a loyalty program, and corporate cleanliness and customer safety standards – common elements that remind guests of the Marriott affiliation. This is very important for maintaining strategic congruence.

As I show in Figure 3.5, the brand architecture choice must be made in the context of other commercial strategy decisions, including value proposition, resources and cost, time frame, and need for risk mitigation.

When making judgments as to whether to launch a new brand when an innovation is brought to market, consider the associations that exist to your current brand, as three concentric circles corresponding to business category, bodies (or customers), and value proposition. To the extent that you wish to articulate a value proposition that is vastly different from those expressed by your current brand portfolio, you may be best served by creating a new brand.

Perhaps the most important requirement for success in launching a brand is investment in specific resources necessary to deliver on its goal and value proposition. In other words, brand architecture and core competence are interdependent choices.

With the answers to who we are identified, let's consider the second important question that enables your brand choice: *What are we good at?*

Umbrella	Hybrid Umbrella-Driven	Hybrid Sub-brand Driven	Distinct
one overall	Value proposition		one per brand
lower (long term)	Relative cost		higher
centralized	Resource allocation		decentralized
focused	Strategic options		flexible
high impact	Product failure / risk mitigation		low impact

FIGURE 3.5 Brand decision matrix.

The brand architecture choice is a strategic decision; one that both drives and is influenced by other decisions in the 6Bs framework.

What Are We Good At? Competences Enable the Brand Promise

While there are divergent views of what drives companies to achieve sustainable competitive advantage, an inside-out view made popular by C. K. Prahalad and Gary Hamel states that the key to sustaining advantage lies within the walls of the company.[8] This view states that the key to sustainable competitive advantage comes from the core competence of the company, its unique and differentiating skills.

The inside-out perspective directly connects to the Big Picture Strategy method, a brand-based and customer-centric view of marketing strategy. That's because, for a brand to be successful, it needs to be *authentic* in projecting what is special and different about the company that supports it. That can only come from within.

If a brand is the promise of a specific valuable customer experience that is differentiated from competitors' promises, core competences and strategic assets are the skills and resources that enable the organization to deliver on that brand promise.

Of course, companies need many skills and resources to be successful in their businesses. But a few of those skills and resources are core – or strategic – because they directly enable the brand promise.

A core competence is a set of skills that:

- Are *unique* to the company within its business category.
- Are *difficult or impossible for competitors to imitate,* in part, because they are deeply embedded throughout each of the functions of the company.
- Are *pervasive* in the company: they permeate the values and culture of the company and are embedded in the managerial processes of the organization.
- Fuel the company's *competitive advantage* through the creation of strategic assets: resources that the company uses to deliver differentiated customer benefits.
- Require *continued investment*, both through investment in technology and through hiring and training of people who can augment the company's competences.

Core Competence and Strategic Assets

As Figure 3.6 shows, the *core competence* drives the brand promise through *strategic assets*.

A competence is know-how or skills that are unique to the company and its employees – they are valuable, but they travel with people and cannot be easily traded in the marketplace.

Competences generate assets – resources that have intrinsic market value. In other words, *core* competences are inputs that yield strategic assets as outputs. Core competences can manifest themselves in four primary ways: through employees' knowledge and skills; through technical systems; through managerial systems and processes; and through the culture of the organization.

The strategic assets that come from core competences can be tangible or intangible. Their function in a go-to-market model is to deliver differentiated and valuable benefits to customers. Store locations, manufacturing facilities, and even products are often included in listings of *tangible* strategic assets. Patents, brand reputation, and customer relationships are *intangible* strategic assets.

Core competences and strategic assets are intimately connected in self-reinforcing processes. When employees in an organization possess skills for innovation, over time the organization can create valuable related assets, such as strategic R&D centers, intellectual property and patents, or creativity templates. In turn, having those innovative assets makes the company more attractive to prospective employees who seek to work at a company that values creativity – improving its core competences. And because the

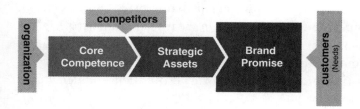

FIGURE 3.6   Core competence, strategic assets, and customer benefits.

The core competence of an organization is the skillset used to create strategic assets, which are the differentiated resources the company uses to deliver its brand promise.

company has a creative workforce, it further improves its strategic innovation assets and its reputation for innovation.

A company that has a core competence at software or hardware technology skills can, over time, generate differentiated software and hardware assets which, in turn, make it more attractive to technically savvy managers, who add to the firm's core competence. It's a never-ending circle – just think of Amazon, Google, or Apple.

A company led by inclusive leaders who have a core competence at being customer-centric and providing amazing service, will over time, develop related strategic assets such as strong customer relationships, customer service courses and processes, and service programs that have great reputation in the market. In turn, the company's reputation for being a great place to work that values employees and customers will attract customers who crave that kind of environment and improve on it as they join the company, expanding its list of core competences.

The core-competence concept comes down to this: just as people succeed when they focus on their innate skills and develop the self-discipline to exploit those skills, the key for organizations to sustain competitive advantage is to focus on a single discipline, and then build a value proposition and culture to support it. Dyson built core competences around industrial design and air-flow engineering and developed a culture that encourages innovation and research and attracts independent thinkers.

Surprisingly, there are only three distinct value-driving disciplines that differentiate a company:

1. **Product leadership.** Through technical innovation and high-performing products.
2. **Customer intimacy.** Through a service-oriented and flexible operating model that results in valuable customer relationships.
3. **Operational excellence.** Based on price or convenience due to having an efficient operating model.[9]

Each of these value-driving disciplines requires unique core competences (skills) and assets (see Figure 3.7).

Why focus on only one of these disciplines? Because core competences and strategic assets are very resource intensive. A company cannot simultaneously develop all three types of disciplines. Aspiring market leaders must choose one of them to excel.

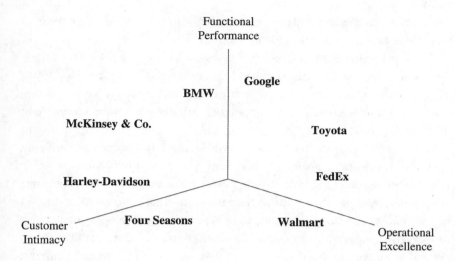

FIGURE 3.7 Value disciplines (core competence types).
There are three broad types of core competences. Companies will want to focus on one while keeping up with their competitors in the other two categories.

Although competences are internal to the company, they must be defined in the context of customers. Customers who select a brand do so based on the outcome of its organizational core competence. People who select a Dyson vacuum cleaner expect uncompromising product performance; people who select a Toyota demand reliability.

The company building an umbrella brand leverages a single core competence across all its service and product portfolios, whereas the company going to market with distinct brands may need to build additional core competences, one per brand.

Given that there is no successful brand without a corresponding core competence, and no reason to build a core competence if it is not going to be monetized through a brand, the brand and core competence choices are inextricably linked.

Auditing Core Competences, Strategic Assets, and Benefits

Auditing your core competence is critical to understanding the source of your brand's differentiation. The core competence audit starts by collecting customer feedback about the differentiating benefits of the products or services.

Customers should be asked: *"What are the main reasons you buy from us over alternatives?"* Look for specific benefits: fast delivery, fair pricing policies, or ability to resolve issues with a single contact rather than general statements like *trust* or *quality*.

We conduct focus groups where internal cross-functional teams are shown the customer-benefit research and together they build a diagram, like Figure 3.6. To develop the diagram, start with one or two top customer benefits and develop hypotheses regarding the strategic assets and core competences that generate those benefits.

Once the internal teams have developed their core competence/strategic asset/benefit diagrams, it's time to measure the competitive advantage of the company. You do this by breaking down each of the assets and competences into specific operational steps that can be benchmarked against other organizations.

For example, service benefits may be linked to relationship assets and to relationship development skills. If you believe that your company is differentiated by its ability to develop customer relationships, ask yourself: what specific processes and technology do we employ? How do these compare to what other companies do?

To measure the core competence, conduct cross-industry benchmarking. Don't just compare to companies in your category, as you are trying to be better than them. Look across industries and markets globally and find organizations known to be good at your core competence. Once you have located appropriate analogs, understand the specific operational ways in which those companies develop skills.

In designing brand architecture, do not ask how many trademarked names to manage, but rather, how many groups of distinctive skills and resources the organization has or can build to achieve its strategic ambitions (customer assets, category presence, financial leadership). The brand architecture choice is a commercial strategy choice and needs to be made in the context of questions about resource concentration and specialization, risk tolerance, time frame, and strategic focus.

The Brand Choice and the Go-to-Market Matrix

The answers to the brand questions *Who are we? What are we good at?* should motivate you to examine your brand portfolio with a goal of maximizing the relevance and value of your brand assets. Doing this requires that you connect your organization's distinctive skills and assets (including the brand) to the value the brand promises customers. Answering these questions is an iterative process and requires self-reflection.

Brands are strategic assets upon which your company's strategic planning is built. The goals of brands are to create equity by building awareness, performance, association, and loyalty.

Strong brands are actively managed over time through consistent execution, and in turn, deliver value to the organization. This can only happen when the marketing function works constructively with the rest of the functions in the company. They all need a common purpose to deliver the specific experience promised to customers.

The brand is a promise of a valuable benefit that becomes the reason you and your colleagues come to work every day. A brand promise that is tied to the skills and resources of the organization is within the reach of its employees and gives purpose to their work. It is not surprising that some of the world's most valuable brands are owned by the best-managed companies, as shown in Figure 3.8.[10]

A brand can be an incredibly valuable asset, but only if resourced and managed through consistent and integrated execution.

Brand architecture arises from the commercial strategy of the company and, in turn, enables decisional efficiency when it is time to execute on the strategy. A brand portfolio that is lacking in architecture will create unnecessary complexity and confusion for both your employees and customers.

A company's brand architecture and the meaning of its brands must be developed in the context of other critical decisions about business category, bodies, beliefs, behaviors, and benchmarks. And as the brand decision is influenced and influences these other choices, they must be considered both one at a time as well as jointly. Importantly, consider what is your go-to-market approach and how brand impacts that decision (see Figure 3.9).

A company that seeks to grow through a diversification strategy, that is, by developing innovations that compete in diverse categories or by engaging customers with different benefits, may consider honing skills at launching, growing, and retiring or selling brands. Utilizing a distinct-brand strategy or a hybrid sub-brand driven strategy may lower the cost

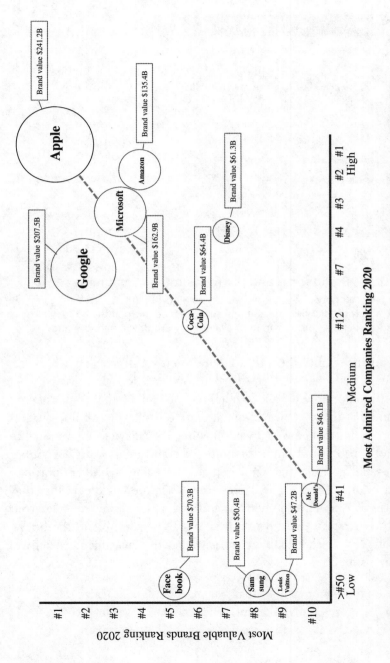

FIGURE 3.8 The worlds' most valuable brands and the worlds' most admired companies.

Many of the worlds' most valuable brands belong to the worlds' most admired companies, indicating a relationship between company core competence and brand value.

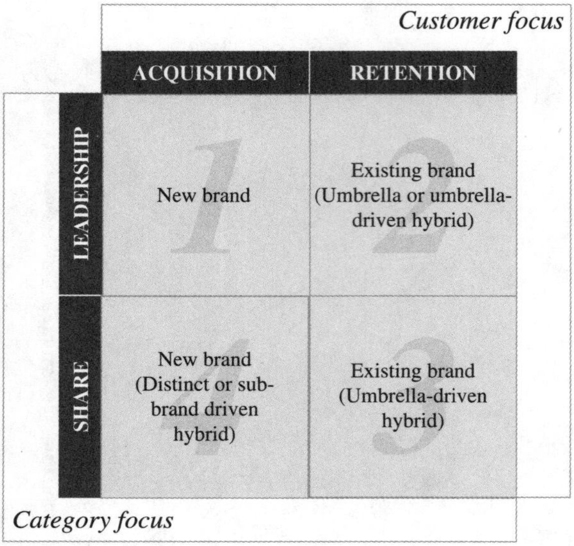

		Customer focus	
		ACQUISITION	RETENTION
LEADERSHIP		New brand	Existing brand (Umbrella or umbrella-driven hybrid)
SHARE		New brand (Distinct or sub-brand driven hybrid)	Existing brand (Umbrella-driven hybrid)

Category focus

FIGURE 3.9 Brand focus and the four strategic quadrants.

Creating a new category often involves launching a new brand – an existing company may create a new distinct brand. Retention strategies are most efficient if they leverage existing awareness, through an umbrella or umbrella-driven hybrid brand.

to the company should there be a failure in either strategy (where to go, who to focus on, what skills are needed to succeed) or execution (what products to build, how to talk to potential customers, how and where to sell and at what price). Once companies are established and find success with a few brands that enjoy a loyal following, they may elect to rationalize their brand portfolio and shift to an umbrella brand architecture. Of course, companies may go to market with a single brand and a coherent portfolio of related products and services they use to acquire customers that they then successfully retain. In choosing a brand architecture, consider your go-to-market strategy, and how your strategy might evolve in the future; and of course, your core competence as well as the investment capacity of your organization.

4

The Business Category

Traditionally, organizations take a top-down approach to strategic business planning. Executives consider industries, markets, and supply-and-demand patterns in that order. However, the Big Picture Strategy uses 6Bs to reframe strategic planning. You start at the bottom and work your way up. This is an important and fundamental difference.

You begin by considering the brand. Next comes the business category: the space where brands compete for customers. Business category membership is an important part of your brand identity. Once executives realize the importance of managing their brands as strategic assets, they must also begin to pay attention to managing their business categories.

Categorization is the mental process by which humans group elements they consider to be similar, simultaneously separating them from other elements they consider dissimilar. From birth onward, humans categorize things to help us relate new objects or concepts to those that are already familiar. Rather than examining each new object or concept we encounter as entirely new, we simply scan it to see how it fits into a group of similar items.

Categorization is key to early childhood development. Without it, children would have to respond to each stimulus as if it were entirely new. Categorization in business is quite similar to categorization in early childhood. It is a learning process to conserve and make our mental resources more efficient. Throughout all industries, companies have developed a dizzying array of choices, too many for customers to consider one by one. Like children, customers naturally arrange brands into categories.

In retailing, where customers are faced with brand choices lining aisles (or virtual shelves), category management was formally developed as a discipline to structure decisions regarding the presentation of products in a store. This encompasses everything from which brands to include, to how and where to display them, to all other tactical decisions, including pricing and communications.

A central tenet of category management is that categories should be treated as strategic business sets because brands within a category are interrelated and considered as a group by consumers. As shown in Figure 4.1, categories are grouped around distinctive customer benefits that all brands within them must deliver. Categories function as consideration sets, while brands function as customer choice units. Brands are allowed to be members of a certain category because they are *substitutable* with the other members. That is, customers consider that all members of a category provide similar benefits.

A category is also a competitive field. Within it, a group of brands vie for customers' business. Brands within categories deliver additional benefits to differentiate themselves, enabling customers to make choices.

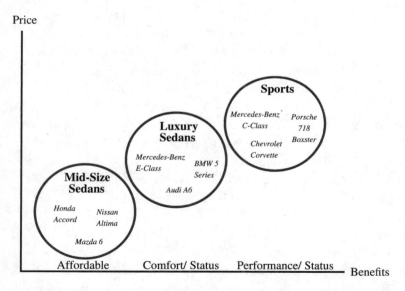

FIGURE 4.1 Categories are consideration sets. Brands are customer choice units.

Categories are groups of brands that offer somewhat similar benefits for a similar price. Brands within a category offer common benefits, and yet must also offer differentiated benefits to enable customers to make choices.

Choosing the right category is critical because doing so clarifies aspects of strategy: specifically, where to compete and how. Sadly, many strategy-development exercises gloss over the delineation of the business category.

Why Category Matters

Why is the category concept fundamental to business strategy? Although companies go to a specific market within a particular industry to sell their products and services, markets and industries are broad classifications. Industries are subdivided into markets, and markets are subdivided into categories. Long-term competitive advantage is decided not at the market but the category level.

So, to plan effectively, businesses should define where their product or service can best compete. Accordingly, choosing the right business category has important practical value for an organization. That value can be summarized as follows:

- **Establishes dominant logic.** Dominant logic is the shared understanding or conventional wisdom that prevails inside the organization. The category functions as the dominant logic for employees as they come to work each morning. How employees think about the business they are in affects the culture and norms of the organization. Are they developing an *at-home boutique fitness* experience, or are they in the treadmill business? The culture inside a company that makes hardware is different from that of a company that sees itself as a design-driven business.
- **Guides innovation.** What are the boundaries that define the company's innovation activity? A company that develops knee implants invests in materials engineering, joint mechanics, and development of instruments for knee-replacement surgery. A company that conceives of its business as joint pain management is more likely to invest in minimally invasive therapies, like injections of gels and stem cell-derived therapies to increase knee mobility and support bone strength and even regrow cartilage. One requires engineering skills and the other skills in biology and pharmaceuticals.
- **Establishes opportunity.** How large is the potential for the business? Is it in the millions or billions? The category definition drives these estimates. A company that is in the knee-implants business can

measure its opportunity by estimating the sales of implants by its competitors. For example, the total market sales of knee implants in the United States is estimated to reach $12 billion with about three million procedures by 2026. If the company instead defines its business as "alleviating knee pain," it will be able to seize a much broader opportunity, as approximately 15 million people in the United States suffer from severe joint pain related to arthritis.[1]

- **Determines competition.** Who are your direct and indirect competitors? In defining the business category, identify direct competitors: companies that build what we build, employ similar skills and technologies, and conceive of problems in a similar way. Also watch for companies that make substitutes for what you deliver to customers, but who approach problems from a different vantage point. Knee replacements and knee gel injections both may relieve knee pain and increase mobility, but they do so in very different ways. The companies making knee replacements compete directly in selling implants to surgeons but all of them ultimately compete as potential solutions to a patient's knee problems. Defining the category helps your team to exactly delineate who is a direct competitor or an indirect competitor, and whom you may ignore.

- **Sets customer expectations.** Think of the category as a set of benefits for customers. Category delineation, once established, sets expectations and thus enables choice efficiency. The name of a category conjures an image of the value customers receive from the brands within that category.

  A customer who needs a personal communications device could use a conventional mobile phone, a computer, a tablet, or a smartphone. Today, a customer looking for a portable communications device is most likely to consider a smartphone as they come at a significant discount to tablets and computers (although at a steep price premium relative to regular cellular phones). Although they are not as robust as tablets, they are more portable, and most come with powerful cameras and apps to enable users to participate in social media networks.

- **Establishes competencies.** Category membership determines the uniqueness of a company's skills, expertise, and assets. A company competing in luxury sedans requires different skills than one that makes economy sedans. This explains why when Hyundai spun off its luxury brand Genesis, it hired new staff and developed new dealerships.

Define the Business Category ━━━━━

So: what is your business? A natural tendency is to identify your business by labeling what you produce. If you make money by selling books, you are in the book business, if you make money by manufacturing mattresses, you are in the mattress business. However, simply letting category membership be determined by the environment around you or by your first response to the question of "what business are you in?' leaves to intuition a critical question that can affect the entire course of your go-to-market strategy.

Decades ago, marketers coined the term *marketing myopia*, referring to the managerial bias that drives business leaders to define business category in terms of the product or technology the company makes. The essential argument is that if we identify our business by what we make, we become focused on *how* we go to market rather than *why* we go to market. The problem is that category affiliation drives how customers view you, and customers don't care about the *how;* they care about the *why.*

Fundamentally, customers are interested in the degree to which your offer satisfies their needs better or worse than an alternative. People used to ride trains because it was the most efficient means available to traverse long distances. When cars became available, many quickly switched because cars offered much more flexibility in scheduling and routing. People used to ride taxis until the ride-sharing category, pioneered by companies like Uber and Lyft, offered a cheaper and more convenient way of traveling in urban centers.

There are three basic ways of defining a business category: *how* you make what you make; *what* you make; and *why* you make it.

You can use a simple *category definition tool* to "try on" these three different ways of defining your category and then choose the one that best fits. For each way of defining the category – *how, what,* and *why* – do the following:

- **Write down the category name.** Consider all possible ways of defining your business category, one at a time. For the *how,* what is the most distinctive feature of your product or service. For *what* you make, write down the generic name of your product or service. For the *why,* select a job or set of needs your product or service solves; and give that set a name.

- **List all the benefits.** Now, looking at the category name, write down all the benefits customers would expect upon hearing that name.
- **List your competitors.** Consider how those customers are currently fulfilling the need that you also solve. That is, list all the alternatives in their consideration set. These might be other brands or substitutes you had not considered before but that customers view as similar. If a customer wants to relieve *knee pain*, they may consider pain medication, steroid injections, physical therapy, or knee surgery. If a customer wants to get a knee implant, they may only consider Stryker, Depuy Synthes, and Zimmer Biomet.
- **Assess the fit between your brand and the category.** Is your current brand known and relevant in the category? Do customers associate you favorably with the benefits you believe they need?
- **List required competencies.** What skills and strategic assets do you need in order to supply all the benefits you have just listed?
- **Estimate the available opportunity.** What is the business opportunity you could achieve in the category? Is it worth it, given the investment required?

Based on the above, adjust your category definition – that is, narrow or broaden it to fit your goals and investment appetite.

Let's now look at some examples.

How: Using Features to Define the Category

Defining the business category by how you do what you do yields the narrowest category definition, one that focuses attention on your unique competences and resources. If you are running the Botox brand, you may describe the business category as *Onabotulinum A neurotoxins:* drugs that act by paralyzing muscles. This is the *how* approach. The advantage of this very narrow category definition is that it calls attention to the technical standards of the product. While narrow, this category confers clear differentiation to the brand: the FDA has stated that Botox is "noninterchangeable – which means that its safety and effectiveness cannot be claimed by any other product."[2]

Of course, going to market in a category that emphasizes a feature rarely makes sense long term because it focuses attention on a company's business model rather than the customer needs that business model satisfies. However, many companies use this feature-focused category definition approach when first creating a category, and it works for them. Creating a category by highlighting a unique feature of the brand can help erect temporary barriers to competition. This feature-focus helped Splenda, the sugar substitute, when it was first brought to market.

McNeil Nutritionals launched Splenda in 1992 with the tagline "Made from sugar so it tastes like sugar" to set it apart from artificial sweeteners, which at the time were marketed under the brands Sweet 'N Low, Equal, and Nutrasweet. Highlighting a feature – "made from sugar" – was a key ingredient in Splenda's early success.

For years, Splenda acted as the leader in a new category: *natural low-calorie sweeteners,* an in-between sugar and artificial sweeteners. However, in 2007, Merisant Co., the makers of Equal, successfully sued McNeil Nutritionals for misleading advertising, alleging that Splenda's slogan led consumers to think that it was healthier and more natural than other artificial sweeteners. Splenda ended up changing its slogan, which now reads, "It starts with sugar. It tastes like sugar. But it's not sugar."

The battle between Equal and Splenda is an interesting one. It is in essence a battle over category definition and membership. The marketing team at McNeil Nutritionals correctly identified that customers would be interested in a zero-calorie sweetener free of the negative health effects associated with aspartame and saccharine. After McNeil Nutritionals had to admit that Splenda is not natural, it lost its position as leader in the natural low-calorie sweetener category it had established. Interestingly, that banner has been taken up by other products with natural claims. Products with brands like Stevia and Truvia, extracted from the stevia rebaudiana plant, are marketed as natural sweeteners, and in recent years, the rate of growth of the natural sweeteners category has far outpaced that of artificial sweeteners.[3]

What: The Product as Category

The easiest way of defining the category for a product manager is to equate the category to the product type. When someone asks what business you are in, it seems natural to describe what you make or sell. It seemed natural for Dell, the American multinational electronics company that started its business in the 1980s, to define its business as computer manufacturing. And in 2003, when it expanded its business beyond computers to other electronics, to change its name from Dell Computer to simply Dell.[4]

A company that sees itself as a computer manufacturer is likely to improve the elements of a computer as a way to differentiate its product from others. A better computer is one that is ever-easier to use, faster, has a larger and higher-resolution screen, has more storage space, and has longer battery life. However, over time not thinking more broadly and considering all the reasons people use computers could mean that the company is investing resources in features that customers no longer desire. People use computers to create, consume, distribute, and store content. And as cloud-based computing emerged, we now do not need computers with lots of storage space. Relative to content consumption and creation, the availability of powerful smartphones and tablets has decreased our reliance on computers for many tasks. Conceiving of each these products independently, each with a specific category label that corresponds to a different product class, is likely to direct resources to improving technology and service features at the risk of becoming misaligned to the reasons customers use the products – overlooking shifting trends in consumer preferences.

A product-based category definition focuses attention on *what* we do. In a product-focused organization, this is the most natural way of looking at the world. However, it begins and ends with us, rather than the customer. In the end, the customer is product-agnostic and value-focused. For this reason, we should focus our attention not on what we make but on what customers need.

Why: The Category as Customer Purpose

An alternative to defining the category by what we make or how we make it, is to consider why customers buy from us. Allergan knows that people would prefer not to inject neurotoxins into their faces; they do it because they want to reduce facial wrinkles and are convinced that neurotoxins are the best available way to do so. By defining Botox's category as facial wrinkle reduction, the Allergan organization is thinking about its business the way customers do. As people age and start worrying about facial wrinkles, they may also consider skin peels, micro-abrasive treatments, Retinol, and Vitamin C creams and serums. The best way to get more customers to try the Botox brand is to understand the benefits that this broader competitive set brings to customers, and to demonstrate the advantage of Botox relative to that broad set.

This category definition should drive research into where people search for information about wrinkle reduction treatments and what causes them to move from over-the-counter cosmetics to more effective treatments. What causes women and men to seek professional help? What communications outlets do they use? What role does social media play, and what sources are trusted and which ones not? Ultimately, could the company shift its role from a manufacturer of neurotoxins sold to physicians to a trusted guide in the science of skin health as we age?

There are even broader ways to think of the business category, if we ask *why* yet again. For example, why do people who have wrinkles feel a need to reduce or eliminate them? Many women and men in their late 30s and early 40s report that the appearance of wrinkles makes them look older than they feel, and that reducing wrinkles is a way to regain congruence between their internal and external sense of self. Facial wrinkles is one concern, but there are others, such as sagging skin, thinning hair, teeth discoloration, and loss of muscle mass. Perhaps the marketers in charge of Botox should think of their business category in terms of high-performing beauty. And perhaps as they do, they may consider whether Botox is the right brand for that category.

If Allergan had a mission of becoming the premier aesthetics company in the world, it would care less about cosmetics, and more about the journey people endure in the pursuit of beauty. And, of course, beauty is defined by each person, and that definition changes as they age. Allergan could collaborate with its professional customers to develop an aesthetics protocol that could be transferred to end-customers through education on how to develop an aesthetics regimen that works to build self-confidence. The company could then sell software, content, and specific topical and injectable and capital products in combination. The pricing model would be based on a subscription to each individual's beauty regimen rather than selling injectable vials or creams.

Think of your business category in terms of *how* you make what you produce, in terms of *what* you produce, and in terms of *why* it matters. There is never just one way of defining the business you are in. Follow a structured approach to considering the alternatives and weighing them in terms of their implications (competences, competitors, customers, channel members, context – opportunity and regulatory issues). Figure 4.2 illustrates this process for the Botox example.

Iterating through all appropriate category definitions is a necessary exercise in making the business category choice.

Category definition / Type	Key customer stakeholder	Benefits delivered by category	Key competitors and substitutes (specific product / service)	Company competences	Brand relevance	Size of the opportunity
Broader why (customer purpose) **High performance facial aesthetics**	Final consumers	• Self-congruence • Self-confidence • Less invasive	• Injectables (fillers, neurotoxins) • Less-invasive facial treatments (RF ablation, laser, peels, micro needling . . .) • Double chin reducer (injectable) • Lash extensions • Teeth whitening • Hair regrowth	• End-user marketing (especially insight generation) • DTC consultative sales	Allergan may be more relevant	> $15 billion, Botox is approximately 9%
Why (customer job) **Medical wrinkle reduction**	Final consumers	• Wrinkle reduction • Facial contouring • Facial rejuvenation	• Neurotoxin brands • Fillers • Less-invasive facial treatments (RF ablation, laser, peels, micro needling . . .)	• End-user communications • Medi-spa sales and marketing	Botox	~ $10 billion, Botox is approximately 14%
What (product) **Neurotoxins for aesthetic use**	Medical professionals	• Wrinkle reduction • Flexible dilution ratios • Formulation and patient tolerance options • Varying time to onset • Storage options	• Xeomin (Merz) • Dysport (Galderma) • Juveau (Evolus)	• Medical professional marketing and education • Medical professional distribution	Botox	~ $2 billion. Botox Cosmetic is approximately 70% of the market
How (technology) **Botulinum A neurotoxins for aesthetic use**	Plastic surgeons and dermatologists	• Wrinkle reduction • 3-day onset (time to action) • 3-month duration of effect • Simple dilution ratio	• Xeomin (Merz) • Dysport (Galderma)	• Pharmaceutical R&D • Drug manufacturing • Medical professional education and distribution	Botox	$1.5 billion. Botox is approximately 90% of the market

FIGURE 4.2 Iterating through category definitions for the botox brand.

Category Names

When someone comes to market with something that is really new, they may find that it does not fit well in any existing category. Business category names originate from the need to describe an innovation and then finding that no existing label quite fits. The best category names call attention to an innovation by describing it in a clever yet distinctive way.

The category name and the standards or boundaries that regulate membership to the category get established simultaneously. This happens as the business model that originated the category gains credibility as well-known consumers accept it and as competitors adopt it. Category names tend to evolve over time, as consumer trends and business standards change.

Research on category names shows that the ones that are eventually adopted – which is not all of them by any means – strike a good balance between originality and familiarity. They must be familiar enough to be easily understood and yet original enough to excite and inspire potential customers to want to know more. And it is common for the companies who introduce winning category names to emerge as category leaders. The snow clothing and equipment company Burton coined the category name *snowboard*, which prevailed over the contender, *snurfer,* and established Burton as the category leader. When the multifunctional phone category was emerging in the 1990s, category names included PDA phone and camera-phone, but Ericsson's "smartphone" label prevailed.

Eventually, as a category name becomes widely accepted, it becomes infused with meaning. When we hear the word *smartphone,* we imagine a device with a large screen that, in addition to being capable of making and receiving phone calls, has email and texting capabilities, has a powerful camera and the capacity to operate third-party productivity and entertainment applications. The meaning of the category is derived from the features of the products and services in the category. And this means that as the category name is established so are technology standards for the companies participating in the category.

Defining the category membership of a brand is an important step in setting its strategy. In going to market, we face the choice of participating in an existing category or creating a new category. Companies create new categories as a way to draw attention to an innovation and in an attempt to define differentiated value. Alternatively, companies can elect to participate in existing categories, and conforming to existing standards, if they decide that the most efficient way to go to market is by competing under existing category rules, rather than rewriting them. The next sections examine these choices in detail.

Leadership-Focused Strategies: Expanding the Category

In going to market, companies can use a share-focused or a leadership-focused strategy. A brand that goes to market with a leadership-focused strategy will observe six rules of leadership strategies.

1. Sell the Benefit

Category leaders gain and retain leadership by establishing the importance of what the category, and they themselves, bring to the world. The impetus for a category is an innovation that is different enough from what exists already as to defy existing category lines. But for the innovation to warrant a separate grouping in customers' minds, the benefit proposed by the new category must be important enough to capture their imaginations and desires.

Companies can increase importance by highlighting the virtues of the category benefit or by augmenting a problem, and then presenting their brand as the unique alternative to solving it.

The drug-avoiding stent category was created to solve a problem in a medical procedure called angioplasty where metal stents placed in a coronary artery to resolve a narrowing or blockage tend to become plugged with plaque or cholesterol after some time. In 2003, Johnson & Johnson launched Cypher, a new kind of stent that offered a polyester covering mixed with a drug that prevented plaque buildup in the stent. The company created a new category.

In 2012, Procter & Gamble launched Tide Pods, laundry detergent pods to address a common problem: when doing laundry, measuring how much detergent to use is challenging, and using the wrong amount can result in clothes that are not clean, or can damage clothes and laundry machines. The laundry pods category now accounts for almost 10 percent of the $50 billion laundry detergent market.[5]

2. Make Your Brand Synonymous with the Category

Category leadership refers not only to market share or financial metrics, but also to the space the brand occupies in the minds of customers within the category. Market share and mind share often go hand in hand. Amazon is the undisputed market-share leader in online retail in the United States, and it is also the mind-share leader. The Amazon brand has become synonymous with online shopping.

Other times, a company might not be the market share leader and still hold a mind-share leadership status. The Apple iPhone may not be the largest market-share brand in terms of number of phones sold, but it is seen as a category leader in smartphones. Similarly, when consumers thought of the hybrid car category, the Toyota Prius brand traditionally held top-of-mind status.

Achieving top-of-mind status is beneficial because it means that most customers in the category will not make a purchase without first checking that brand. Most people interested in a hybrid car will look at the Toyota Prius. And as they do, they will notice its features, most notably those which establish the core benefit of the category – like energy efficiency for hybrid cars. They will then use that standard to assess other brands in the category. Even when customers purchase something else, the top-of-mind brand influences their perceptions about the category.

3. Avoid Comparisons

Imagine that you have just purchased a house and need to buy a new furnace. Your neighbor has recommended you purchase a Trane-branded furnace; he tells you that Trane is the category leader in residential furnaces. Since you have not purchased a furnace before, you do additional research. You first go to the Trane website and get a sense of the models offered and how Trane presents the features and benefits of each.

But as you look closer within the Trane website, you find a table comparing Trane to other leading brands. You had heard of Trane prior to your neighbor's suggestion; however, you had never heard of the other brands in the table. Now you are considering other brands. How do you decide? Trane comes highly recommended, but when you look at energy ratings, heating power, and wireless features, you realize that the brand that was recommended is not the only choice.

Here's the point: To gain or retain leadership in a category, the brand must not compare itself to competitors in its communications. It should also go a step further and make those comparisons difficult. Brands that establish a top-of-mind association with a category gain advantage over potential competitors by becoming the reference that consumers use in evaluating their options.

Trane may advertise that it is the category leader, and as such, its products have technical or service advantages that are simply not available elsewhere. Making the features of its products and services hard to compare reinforces the perception that the category leader's offerings are unique. Of course, they are; it is the category leader, right?

Category-leading brands can create or heighten the perception of uniqueness by presenting products and features in ways that are different from those of the competition. One way they may do this is by naming them differently, even creating "ingredient brands" for components that are especially unique.

Apple does this by branding particular features. For example, its computers and phones do not just have screens, they have Liquid Retina™ displays. Files are not transferred via file drop; that functionality has its own brand, AirDrop™. And users do not simply press on their phone screens to access features, they use 3D Touch™, another trademarked name. While emphasizing their uniqueness, companies hoping to become category leaders should share what is special about their components as well.

4. Set Category Standards

A leadership-focused strategy ties the growth of the brand to that of the category. Accordingly, the company assuming this competitive strategy will want to establish, influence and, as much as is possible, *control* category standards. This can range from setting the category name to establishing specific features, technology, or ways of interacting with customers that tie the category to the brand.

At-home boutique fitness, established by Peloton, centers on sophisticated hardware. It includes a spinning bike outfitted with a WiFi-enabled large touchscreen that streams live and on-demand classes and allows the rider to compete with other participants in highly motivational instructor-led and music-pumped classes. It would be difficult to imagine a competitor coming into this category and being successful in taking market share away from Peloton if it didn't offer a spinning experience with most, if not all, of these same features.

5. Develop the Category Infrastructure

Establishing a category and maintaining leadership involves investing in critical infrastructure that enables customers to access the category and derive the value it offers. This may entail clearing regulatory hurdles, publishing evidence or other data that establishes the performance of the category, establishing distribution channels and supply chains to ensure sufficient inventory is available to meet potential demand, and – importantly – educating customers on the benefits of the category. While it is expensive to develop and maintain the infrastructure of a category, the benefit of doing this work is that it increases the visibility of the brand and credibly establishes its position as the category leader. Also, developing infrastructure does go hand in hand with developing category standards.

When Tesla went to market with a high-performance all-electric car, it lobbied the US Congress to obtain and later maintain tax credits for electric vehicles. It also installed many electric vehicle (EV) fast-charging stations to provide a convenient energy supply to its customers. The company has also invested many millions of dollars in developing battery technology to extend range and to lower costs, including funding academic research and making a series of early-venture acquisitions. As its intellectual property is developed and published, Tesla's investment benefit not just the company but also its competitors. And yet, it is Tesla that is in the driver's seat. Its advanced battery technology establishes acceleration and range standards for any company seeking to compete in the high-performance, all-electric car category.

6. Develop an Ardent Following

People discount brands' marketing messages if they seem inauthentic. However, they place high currency on the opinions of people they know and like, people who are similar to them, trusted experts, celebrities, and even online reviews from people they don't know.[6]

Three powerful principles of persuasion – social proof, liking, and authority – can be additive in succeeding at stimulating demand for a category. A category leader should develop close relationships with key customers, not just based on those customers' direct revenue-generating capacity but also on their status within the communities the brand is trying to target. The early success of the Gatorade brand was due to its association with professional celebrity basketball players like Michael Jordan. When first establishing the all-electric performance car market, Tesla invited celebrities to a VIP-only event to pick up their new cars. The brand's status was aided by posts and sightings of celebrity customers like Brad Pitt, Kanye West, or Cameron Diaz.

Share-Focused Strategies: Growing Within the Category

Share-focused strategies are the opposite of leadership-focused strategies. A company that executes a leadership-focused strategy makes the brand appear unique, setting standards and making it an obvious choice. In contrast, companies executing share-focused strategies present the brand as a preferable alternative. A brand that goes to market with a share-focus strategy will observe these rules of successful share-focused strategies:

1. Invite Comparisons

Understanding how customers think of categories and make choices within them is critical to executing share-focused strategies. When faced with a new item, customers examine it for membership in categories they know. The mental process by which they do this involves identifying similarities and differences. If they consider a brand to be similar to others they have encountered before, they assign it to a category. And yet once they have decided they are interested in the benefits the category offers, they still need to differentiate the choices within it to make a purchase. Category membership and brand choice come down to points of parity and points of difference – that is, the elements of an offer that establish what other brands it should be compared to, and the elements of an offering that establish how it's different.

The first step in taking share is becoming part of the target customers' consideration set – that is, inviting comparisons. The category leader is responsible for setting standards in the category. Accordingly, share-focused strategies entail executing well enough on those standards – those points of parity – to be brought into the category conversation. At the same time, you need to carefully delineate a single-minded point of difference to give customers a clear "why" they should choose the brand instead of the category leader.

This is the strategy that T-Mobile used after John Legere became CEO in 2012. At the time, T-Mobile had just 10 percent market share of the US wireless service category, while AT&T and Verizon each held 40 percent market share. Mr. Legere outlined a strategy focused on taking share from AT&T by presenting itself as the more customer-centric and service-oriented option. To execute this strategy successfully, T-Mobile had to address points of parity: performing at an acceptable level of reliability and service. To this end, T-Mobile invested more than $8 billion to improve its network reliability. The strategy worked, and by 2016, T-Mobile's market share rose from 10 percent to 16 percent, making it the third-largest carrier in the United States.[7]

2. Build Relative Advantage

The value proposition offered by a category leader establishes the primary benefit of a category that no other category meets. Conversely, the value proposition of a company looking to gain share within an existing category is relative to a brand within the category, generally the category leader's.

A company seeking to take share is trying to appeal to customers who are already in the business category and using a category-leading brand. They can therefore be assumed to understand and, for the most part, like the value proposition of the category leader. The company seeking to take share should acknowledge and build around the offering of the brand it is targeting. T-Mobile did not present itself as the only option in wireless service, but rather offered a value proposition that was relative to that of Verizon and AT&T, emphasizing comparable reliability and service at a lower price.

There are two basic ways to develop a share-focused value proposition: to get target customers to believe they are overpaying for the value they are currently receiving or to get them to believe they could get something even better for the same amount or just a bit more money.

3. Create and Amplify Dissatisfaction

To successfully get customers to switch brands, you must convince customers who are using your targeted competitor to believe their current choice is no longer their best option. In other words, you need to take seemingly happy customers and sow unhappiness.

All successful share-focused campaigns establish comparisons between two options, and some go as far as vilifying the category leader. This approach is risky, as brands that present themselves as heroic in the fight against some evil corporate giant can generate counterargument and reflect a negative image back on the attacker. This is why, when used, comparative communications must be either tactful or ridiculous. Tactful share-focused communications are fact-based and may use implicit comparisons, not calling out the target company by name, but implying it. Other companies use humor or exaggeration to lighten the mood of the target audience and poke fun at their brand choice in a "light" manner to try to avoid counterargument.

In the first decade of the 2000s, when Apple was trying to take share from Microsoft, it used comedy and two actors, John Hodgman as PCs and Justin Long as Apple, in a series of commercials that essentially made fun of Microsoft for being old-fashioned and hard to use. Similarly, in 2012, T-Mobile called itself the "un-carrier" and created advertising that featured actors impersonating AT&T and Verizon as identical and boring corporate guys unable to respond to the demands for high-speed service from an iPhone and a high-speed Android phone.

But successfully taking share does not require poking fun at the competition or running attack ads. A share focus is primarily about becoming part of the consideration set, and that should be done through pricing, product features, and the distribution channel, in addition to communications. Vizio entered the LCD television category in the early 2000s with a simple strategy: manufacture TVs that look very similar to high-end models, are of reasonable quality, but are cheaper than traditional brand-name TVs. Then, Vizio encouraged comparisons by placing the TVs in the same stores – Costco and Sam's Club – and right next to Sonys and Samsungs with similar features. The company went from being number 15 in 2005 to becoming the third-largest brand in terms of units sold in the United States in 2020. And it did so with little to no advertising.[8]

4. Build Relative Core Competence

Because share-focused strategies are relative, they require a reference to execute against. Successful share-focused strategies come from companies embracing a *number two* brand role and growing at the expense of a competitor or a specific segment within the category. The number two brand role is one that is a slightly "better" or "cheaper" choice than alternatives.

In a share-focused strategy, you must select the target carefully because that brand sets your strategy. You will want to be seen as a better alternative for a specific reason. Specifically, when executing this type of strategy your team needs to agree on the answers to two questions:

1. **From whom?** How will you execute your go-to-market strategy so that you are considered to be similar to your target?
2. **On what benefit will you dominate?** That is, what relative strength do you believe will attract your competitor's customers? This refers to the value proposition you wish to create, of course. But importantly, it also refers to the core competence and strategic assets you will require to be successful.

For example, within the fast-food category, Subway took share from McDonald's by delivering the message that "Subway is a healthier choice." This strategy worked because McDonald's conjured a very clear image in customers' minds. It was unhealthy, but it was fast, convenient, and priced low; many of these attributes were also assumed about Subway because it compared itself to McDonald's.

Of course, to work long term, a share-focused strategy must be supported by facts: that is, by a core competence and strategic assets that back up your superiority claims. Subway was successful against McDonald's because it developed a core competence through healthy menu design and food sourcing. It was able to bake bread within its stores, and consistently sourced natural and fresh ingredients for its sandwiches.

Samsung successfully took share from Apple iPhone, thanks to its relentless focus on a performance-engineering core competence while building related strategic assets – superior hardware, storage, larger screens – and delivering a benefit of faster performance than the iPhone.[9]

The Category Choice: Leadership or Share?

What Is Good about Leadership-Focus Strategies?

When successful, a leadership-focused strategy affords the brand top-of-mind awareness advantages. The category leader is a default choice. Salesforce.com is the default choice in the CRM cloud-computing category, McDonald's is the default choice in fast food, and Gillette is the default choice in men's razors. The category leader is the brand that gets the highest number of customer inquiries and generally has to spend the least to acquire customers.

Category leaders have higher profitability than brands with low market share. The relationship between category share and profitability increases as market share goes up. Reasons for this include economies of scale. It's cheaper to manufacture in large quantities because fixed costs get spread over larger volumes. Market power – buying raw materials, hiring agencies and consultants, and so on – is cheaper for the market leader because it wields scale and reputational power. And, of course, and possibly most importantly, it is easier to attract top talent in the industry as a category leader because professionals would prefer to associate themselves with the company that is in the leadership position.[10]

Importantly, the category leader benefits from competition because category standards – points of parity – are based on its core competence. Peloton created the *at-home boutique fitness* category to include live fitness classes, a recorded content library, and exercise equipment that incorporated high-definition screens and speakers. When companies such as NordicTrack and Flywheel, entered the category, they had to catch up to Peloton by offering similar features. This was good because it validated Peloton's business model, further affirming its category-leader status to customers.

The Downsides of Leadership-Focused Strategies

Still, leadership-focused strategies come with high costs and risk. The category leader is expected to launch new products and services with some regular cadence. Because many new products fail for a variety of reasons, being at the forefront of the category is expensive and risky, both financially and in terms of brand reputation. The category leader's failures are especially visible. Even though many thousands of new products fail every day, it is those launched by category leaders that fail most loudly. We've all heard of New Coke, for example.

Leadership-focused strategies are also expensive because expanding the category grows the business of direct competitors. Expanding a business category entails attracting new customers and investing in the category infrastructure. However, competitors benefit from the work of the category leader at a lower rate of investment; some of the investment by the category leader spills over to its competitors.

Soon after Peloton created the at-home boutique fitness category, Nordic Track followed. Nordic Track had a long track record in home-fitness equipment, including cross-country skiing machines, bikes, ellipticals, and treadmills. The company added a screen and software connectivity to its spinning bike under the iFit brand, hired instructors, and copied the Peloton model feature by feature. It then launched commercials so similar to Peloton's that it took viewers several seconds to notice they were not watching a Peloton commercial. This strategy worked; Nordic Track iFit reported 3.3 million subscribers by July 2020, fueled in part by Peloton's efforts, as well as the COVID-19 pandemic of 2020.[11]

What Is Good about Share-Focused Strategies?

Going after share is cheaper than investing to lead, at least initially. By establishing a comparison to the category leader, a new entrant gains efficiency in its communications and other executional decisions.

Being a second mover or a third mover – that is, following in the footsteps of a category leader – is less risky. There is no need to develop breakthrough innovations and educate reluctant customers. The work of the second mover consists in gathering intelligence regarding the missteps of the category leader and improving on at least one aspect of its offer.

A brand that is focused on share presents itself as a substitute for the brand it is targeting. It develops similar products and services, is present in the same distribution channels and at the same prices as the category leader, and then makes direct comparisons in its communications. As if it were drafting in a bicycle race, the company focused on share benefits from the momentum created by the category leader. Simply by following, a company that executes this type of strategy can grow its brand.

Share-focused strategies are efficient in the short term; they are less costly than leadership-focused strategies because they take advantage of the investments another company has already made in developing and growing the category.

The Downsides of Share-Focused Strategies

Share-focused strategies increase your risk of competitive warfare. If your share-focused strategy is successful, your brand will increase its business at the expense of a competitor. These strategies work best at the beginning of a company's life, especially for companies that are much smaller than the company they are targeting.

In these cases, the category leader, at least for a while, is likely to ignore the attack, and the company trying to grow share can do so unfettered. When Apple launched the first-generation iPod in 2001, it also designed earbuds that were shipped with the device. The earbuds were white, and over time Apple improved their design and acoustics. Then, in 2016, Apple launched the AirPods, wireless earbuds with microphones and many advanced technological and design features.

Since the launch of the first earbuds to the AirPods, a number of companies have profited from developing copycat products that look like and claim to function like the real thing. The reason these imitators have survived for so long without visible retaliation from Apple is that there are too many of them, and individually they are too small. Apple does pursue copycat products if they infringe its intellectual property rights – that is, when they are counterfeit products. But it is less likely to retaliate against small competitors who simply imitate the Apple design without misrepresentation.[12]

Large competitors that attempt to earn share face much higher retaliation risk, even early on. When Google launched its Google Plus service to compete with Facebook, Facebook immediately retaliated and began a corporate war that kept Facebook employees under *lockdown* – a term used at the company that literally means employees are required to work evenings and weekends. In a matter of just weeks, Facebook improved on all the features Google had imitated, forestalling a successful launch for Google Plus.[13]

Successful share-focused strategies are, by definition, limited. While in the short term, share-focused strategies may seem like a good way to preserve resources and lower risk, they do not work as well over extended periods of time. If you persevere and become the market leader, eventually a share strategy will no longer be a good option. Then, as market leader, you will have to start thinking about ways of expanding the category and distancing your brand from others. While some companies make that transition seamlessly, others struggle.

The Category Choice: The Competitive Frame

There are just two ways to go to market: acting like the category leader, focusing on expanding the category and avoiding competitive comparisons; or by inviting competitive comparisons, focusing on taking share within a category.

The choice of leading or competing is framed by the category definition. The category serves as a mental model for customers, a frame through which they examine the options available to them. Just as important, the category definition affects how employees conceive of their work, how they establish goals, how they develop value propositions, and then how they build products and services to deliver on them.

In a customer-focused framework, the category definition also delineates who specifically occupies each of the four strategic quadrants of opportunity: customers outside of the category and therefore not committed to any brand; customers in the category and loyal to our brand; customers of our brand but who also use other brands; and customers of a competitive brand. Defining customers and understanding their value is required for all companies wishing to implement customer-focused strategies. This is what I discuss in the next chapter.

5

Bodies:
The Customer Focus

What Is a Customer?

The word customer is derived from the Medieval Latin word *custumarius*, which means "pertaining to a custom or habit." And companies do think of their relationships with customers as habitual: customers buy and pay for a brand, use it, and come back for more.

The importance of customers to the health of a business is hard to overstate. I have never spoken to anyone who disagrees: whether nonprofit or for-profit; whether we call them customers, clients, or consumers. If people are not demanding the goods and services that we offer, our enterprise will not survive or prosper.

Brands are only as successful as their customer relationships. And yet, most of the companies I have worked with, use a managerial approach that *de facto* places products ahead of customers.

The product-dominant philosophy traces its origins to the Industrial Revolution conceptualization of a business: the company uses ingenuity, labor, and capital to build products. Those products are embedded with value, and that value is transferred to the customer when money changes hands and the customer takes possession of the product.

In product-dominant organizations, value is associated with the product, so the business is built around product lines. Prices are determined on the basis of product costs and margins. And competitors are judged on their ability to generate comparable or superior products. The goals of the business are to drive product sales volume and market share. The marketing function becomes a process-based department that supports sales and product managers, and is only responsible for the tactical aspects of product launches, promotions, and maintenance.

The product-dominant model myopically focuses on the short term: products are generated to be sold and must maximize their margins as individual units of value. This sometimes means that cross-product integration opportunities are missed; worse, it can lead to misallocation of resources and, ultimately, failure. The unfortunate fact is that you can have a fantastic product but still fail to capture customers. Better products alone do not correlate with competitive advantage.

Remember the Pepsi challenge? In 1975, Pepsi launched a blind-test competition, whereby people were asked to sip Pepsi and Coke in unlabeled cups. Most preferred the sweeter taste of Pepsi, at least in the first sip. Why was Coke then, for decades, able to capture more customers and market share than Pepsi? People preferred Coca-Cola, in part because they felt emotionally connected with the brand, in a way that they simply did not with Pepsi. The intangible aspects of a brand have always mattered a great deal.

Today, the marketing literature widely recognizes that the key to attracting, engaging, acquiring, and retaining customers centers around the customer experience offered and delivered by the brand. And even for industrial companies, the product itself is only a part of that experience. It is the company's complete offer and the customer's perception of that offer that matters, rather than product features alone.

Customer-dominant logic, in a sense, is also service-dominant logic. It recognizes that customers and brands are matched when the needs of the former are well-suited to the skills and strategic assets of the latter. Consequently, value is not only created in the production of a product but also in the interactions between people. As marketers in service businesses recognized decades ago, value is co-created between a brand and its customers rather than simply manufactured by a company.

While many companies have shifted to a service-customer focus from a product focus, a significant percentage have not. This is a paradigm shift that transforms the focus of the organization from short-term sales and market share goals to long-term customer retention and loyalty. A company must transform its vision from seeing customers as tools to achieve product volume objectives, to relationships they invest in – assets to be nurtured.

The W.L. Gore organization understands this. Its medical device sales representatives compete against other salesforces that are compensated on volume. The Gore salesforce is instead compensated through salary alone and maximize customer lifetime value by helping new vascular surgeons and interventional cardiologists develop their skills. As doctors' skills improve through the training and support they get from the Gore service organization, they come to identify with the brand and develop devotion to the vascular grafts and other devices that Gore makes. These surgeons come to associate their successful clinical outcomes and their even-more successful careers with the Gore brand. Conversely the company understands that its brand image depends on the ability of surgeons to deliver good outcomes and invests in ensuring its products are used optimally in complex surgical procedures.

The success of this customer-centric model hinges on the organization's ability to identify customers who are willing to actively collaborate with the company to create value. They must be prepared to invest time and other resources to learn how to use the company's products and services to fully enjoy that value.

Companies that have made the transformation from a product to a service model still make products, but they understand that the product is a tool used to engage customers and help them efficiently derive value from working with the brand.

Working with our team, Futura Industries, an aluminum extrusion company based in Utah, made this transformation in a category long considered commoditized. Their CEO refocused the company to differentiate on a service promise of reliability and responsiveness to customers. Futura segmented its opportunity by looking for companies who needed fast response times and flexible processes to accommodate change orders. It also priced its aluminum by the piece, rather than by the pound – uncommon in this market – to reflect the value of the product in its final application. For example, because shower door enclosures and truck grills represent high-value uses, they were priced higher than carpet metals or aluminum for applications with a lower value. Prices were also based on customer profitability rather than individual product margins. This effectively aligned the sales and the marketing teams to prioritize customer value.

How to Measure the Value of a Customer

If you think of the customer as a financial asset and the marketing organization as steward of the customer relationship, then marketing earns the respect of the other functions in the company by measuring and managing the financial value of that asset. How much investment does acquiring a customer require? How much investment is required to retain that customer? And how does the brand monetize that investment by generating cash flow from customer acquisition and retention?

Of course, not all customers who purchase and use your brand have equal value. The value of a customer depends on the profitability of what they purchase or cause to be purchased over their lifetime with the brand, minus the investment the company has made to acquire and retain that customer. This is what marketers call **customer lifetime value.**

The formula for customer lifetime value has two essential components: the customer margin and the retention rate. The customer margin, different from the product margin, is the net annual profit from doing business with a customer, and it holds an interesting and sometimes counterintuitive relationship to product margin, especially for companies selling multiple products and services to the same customer. This is because sometimes losing money on one product can be the key to maximizing customer profitability via the total portfolio.

In 2011, Amazon launched the Kindle Fire, a tablet carrying the brand of its successful eReader, the Kindle. The tablet launched at $199, which analysts estimated to be close to the fully loaded manufacturing cost of the device. But then, to accelerate sales, Amazon dropped the price to $100 in time for the Christmas season. Due to the price drop, and even though Amazon had forecasted to sell more than five million units, equity analysts punished the stock which dropped by more than 20 percent on concerns that the Kindle Fire would hurt Amazon's bottom line.[1] Instead, the Kindle is a profit driver for Amazon, as customers who purchase it are more likely to buy books and streaming content from Amazon – and more likely to order other products and eventually sign up for Amazon Prime. Of course, Amazon Prime customers spend much more with the company than the average. At the time, Amazon shares were trading at less than $170. Today, they are trading at over 20 times that number, in part because the company devised programs that, like the Kindle Fire and Amazon Prime, and sacrificed short-term product margin to capture customer lifetime value. The success of the Amazon brand is a testament to the superior value of customers over products. It's also a lesson in how to create customer relationships.

Categorizing Customer Relationships

It may surprise you to discover that most of the customers in your customer database have low or negative customer lifetime values. The Pareto principle, which states that for many phenomena, 80 percent of the effects come from 20 percent of the causes, applies to many things in life, including customers. When we work with organizations to help them understand which customers are most critical to their sustainability, we find that fewer than 20 percent of their customers account for the majority of their profitability. The rest of the customers may keep the organization busy and the salesforce transacting but are likely unprofitable. For this reason, the key to sustaining growth in an organization does lie in understanding what makes for a successful customer relationship.

Customer relationships, in many ways, are like other relationships. To work and to last, both sides have to engage to create value, and both sides must derive value. When this happens, there is an equilibrium. Just like in interpersonal relationships, in brand customer relationships it is unrealistic to expect continual bliss. There are good days and bad days, great service experiences and mediocre ones. But an ideal brand customer relationship is one that delivers financial return to the brand while satisfying the expectations set when the two agreed to transact. Ideal customer relationships are win–win relationships. They return high value to both the organization – net of the investment it has made in acquiring the customer – as well as to the customer.

Figure 5.1 shows a categorization of customers by their value to the company and the company's value to them. The companies I've worked with refer to all the people they do business with as "customers." And yet only some of those relationships can be placed in the *ideal* quadrant (high customer lifetime value to the firm and high customer satisfaction) – fewer than 25 percent, in my experience. The rest are either low-value or low-satisfaction customers: that is, *free riders* or *hostages*.

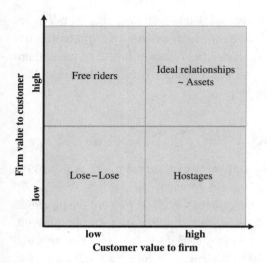

FIGURE 5.1 Customers as relationship assets.

A well-managed commercial organization categorizes customers by value and develops win–win relationships.

Hostages cannot be considered true customers because they are "locked-in" to a relationship with the brand due to the high cost of switching out of that relationship. Switching costs are due to structural, financial, legal, and emotional barriers.

Some switching costs are structural due to characteristics of the business category. For example, individuals and businesses making a large purchase of machinery can't easily switch until the end of the useful life of the equipment. Purchasing internet or cable services or tickets for air travel is also subject to structural switching costs, as only a few suppliers may offer options in a particular market.

Financial costs include contract breakage fees, the cost of disposing of existing capital equipment, the cost of changing internal processes to adapt to the new organization's sales or inventory management processes, and any other time or money required to switch brands.

Legal or contractual switching costs are also significant. Customers may be prevented from switching because they signed a long-term contract, as may be the case for wireless phone services or cable, or home security services. Medical device companies, consulting companies, and many other categories of businesses sell their products and services under contracts, which include penalties for early cancellation.

Switching costs can also be emotional. Especially in services, customers may stay with mediocre providers due to their concern that it is difficult – sometimes impossible – to evaluate a new service provider without actually switching. For example, you cannot know what it would be like to switch dentists unless you do.

In a "hostage" relationship – illustrated by the lower right-hand quadrant – the company gets a disproportionate amount of value from the customer. This may seem desirable for the company but is not sustainable. When the iPhone was first released into the US market in 2007, Apple gave AT&T exclusive rights to sell its wireless service contracts.[2] The company took advantage of this and made customers sign non-cancellable contracts, effectively locking them into a relationship with the company for two years. This worked in the short term, but within a year, AT&T competitors reacted by targeting those customers and offering to pay contract breakage fees.[3]

Not only are hostage situations not competitively sustainable, they tend also lead to negative word of mouth. Hostage customers who cannot get out of unhealthy relationships tend to share detailed negative reviews, which can dissuade other, potentially valuable, customers from working with the company.

In free-rider relationships (top left-hand quadrant), conversely, perhaps because the company lacks sophisticated customer metrics, the company misallocates resources to customers who do not bring sufficient cash flow to justify investment. For example, in short-term, sales-driven organizations, customers who do not spend much with the firm may get large discounts or a big allocation of high-cost customer service. For one of our clients, an intraocular lens company, we estimated that 85 percent of customers were responsible for just 15 percent of sales, while the remaining 85 percent of sales was by only 15 percent of the customers. In this organization, small customers getting the same service levels and discounts as large ones are effectively being given a "free ride."

Customer-centric organizations understand what percentage of their customer base falls under each of the quadrants in Figure 5.1. More important, they know why some customers are happy to partner with their organization in a productive manner. And they can manage others out of bad relationships with their organization. In other words, customer-centric organizations share operational definitions of who is an ideal customer.

Who Is the Customer?
Defining Customers

Whether you work in a business-to-consumer (B2C) or a business-to-business (B2B) company, you should think of customers as people. Yes, of course, your products and services may benefit an entire client organization, but the organizations do not make the decision as to whether to choose your brand. Specific people within them do.

It is useful to think of customers in terms of decision-making roles. In most categories and for most brands, there isn't a single customer: several people must come together and align on the brand choice.

You ought to ask: Who is signing the contract? Who is using the product? Who has budget responsibility for the purchase? Who interacts with the product or service internally? And who receives the final benefit, if the product or service is used in an assembly or process that ultimately ends up with someone else? Finally, are there people who are not directly involved with the product but whose influence could derail or advance the account-brand relationship?

Sales and marketing should track the specific people who carry out each of the decision-making roles required to choose, purchase, use, and benefit from the brand. In B2B organizations, where there isn't just a single customer, we call each of the people carrying out each of those decision-making roles "customer stakeholders." You can use a tool like that shown in Figure 5.2 to track customer stakeholder motivations, their decision-making power relative to your business category, and your salesforce's degree of influence / affinity toward each of them.

Track customer stakeholder power and your ability to influence them over time so you can plan how to engage and sell to organizations with different customer stakeholder dynamics. This type of analysis is a requirement to understand not just the more obvious behaviors that define a customer (what they are doing with us), but the beliefs (why they value us) that drive those behaviors across the client organization.

To be an effective manager, you need a nuanced understanding of who is and who is not a customer.

At the beginning of my tenure as an independent consultant, I worked with the airline of the country of Panama, Copa Airlines. I went to Panama to meet with Copa executives as part of my consulting engagement. During

Decision-making role	Stakeholder / org title	Key benefit sought	Rank stakeholder decision-making power (A rank 5 to 1)	Rank our ability to influence (B rank 5 to 1)	Prioritize: Select primary and secondary (A+B)	Commercial Implications
Decision maker Formal decision-making power						
Payer Controls budget						
Direct user Uses the brand						
Indirect user Most directly impacted by brand outcome; may weigh in on product choice						
Influencer Provides input that affects brand choice						

FIGURE 5.2 Aim and align customer stakeholders.

A key to resourcing the commercial team and to direct them to the right customers is to understand and track customer stakeholder dynamics over time.

our first meeting, we reviewed the tenets of the Big Picture framework and – as I generally do with senior managers – we tried to work through each of the 6Bs.

Copa was an umbrella brand, and its executives felt their core competence was flight operations – that "B" was relatively clear. We had a hypothesis but needed some validation. We then got to this "B," the bodies. I asked, "Who is your customer?" and the group chuckled. This question was too simple and its answer obvious. After we stared in silence for a few seconds, someone said: "A customer is someone who flies with our airline, of course." It was my turn to chuckle.

I then explained that I flew Copa to Panama, but I had not purchased the ticket – Copa had. I had never heard of Copa before our engagement. My flight experience had been acceptable but unremarkable (I omitted this detail). I did share that they were part of an airline alliance where I did not accumulate points, and, as a result, I would be unlikely to fly them ever again beyond our engagement. This left them pensive. Was I a customer of the airline?

When it comes to developing a truly useful definition of a customer, you need to understand not just who generates the most revenues for the organization and is most profitable for you, but for whom you create the greatest value. You need to understand both *behaviors* and *beliefs* from the people who are in a habitual relationship with your brand.

GE Aviation Retained Customer	Blendtec Retained Customer
Behavior • CFO of regional carrier with 75% of fleet under GE service contract	**Behavior** • Owns a Blendtec • Uses it 3x+ times/week • Gifts or recommends Blendtec
Belief • GE lowers fleet operational cost	**Belief** • Powerful • Key to healthy lifestyle

FIGURE 5.3   Retained customer definitions.

Customer definitions should include customer behaviors and beliefs and should enable you to count customers.

Define a customer then as someone who behaves like a customer and prefers your brand to a functionally equivalent alternative. Figure 5.3 provides two examples of customer definitions. If you are a manager, you should know how many customers you have, you should know why they prefer your brand, what makes them a valuable asset to your organization, and how they are different from unprofitable or unhappy customers.

If you sell capital equipment, whether it is blenders used at home to make breakfast smoothies, as is the case with Blendtec, or aircraft engines, as GE Aviation does, success requires more than simply selling products and receiving money for them. You must create measurable value for your customers; otherwise you run the risk of creating hostage customers, that is, people who may be purchasing today while spreading negative word of mouth about your brand and planning to leave.

The point here: don't take the bodies "B" for granted! A customer-focused organization tracks each of the people who have a decision-making role impacting its brand and maintains a clear delineation between those who are and those who are not likely to be win–win relationships.

Customer Loyalty

A customer relationship that is win–win is, by definition, a loyal relationship. Customer loyalty is generally described as commitment toward a brand that a customer develops over time after multiple positive experiences, and that manifests both in their behaviors and in their feelings toward the brand. Despite being perhaps the single most popular topic in marketing, with more than one million papers and books, customer loyalty is widely misunderstood.

Loyalty is a complex concept requiring a particular type of consistency on behalf of the brand to generate specific feelings in the customer. Loyalty depends on the business category. Loyalty depends on the person. And thankfully for managers everywhere, loyalty also depends on the company.

Categories that entail a big financial or emotional investment for the customer – and where consequently there is a high financial or emotional cost in case of failure – tend toward higher levels of loyalty.

It is no surprise, then, that brands that possess vocally loyal customers tend to sell premium products with lots of features, especially those that are consumed in public and those with a service element that give the company a chance to establish a direct emotional connection. It is easier for car and motorcycle companies to generate loyalty than for companies that manufacture paper napkins, laundry detergent, or medical supplies. And yet, Charmin toilet paper, Tide detergent, and Ethicon medical sutures are all relatively inexpensive products and all have fervently loyal customers.

Loyalty depends on company competences. Despite making a utilitarian and relatively inexpensive product, Charmin is the brand of toilet paper US consumers prefer by far with over 76 million people choosing it. Charmin's long-standing value proposition of squeezable softness, and its mascot – a bear – are both memorable and compelling to many US consumers.[4] During a conversation with a professional who travels internationally for work, when I asked, "Are there any brands you are passionately loyal to?" she responded, "Charmin toilet paper. I always pack Charmin in my suitcase, just in case."

Clearly, some people feel more strongly about a category than others, and that is why, even when a company behaves consistently toward its customers, it will not win a single type of loyalty but rather different types. This is not to say that companies shouldn't strive to develop specific loyalty profiles among their customers; however, even when they do, they are likely to end up with more than one type.

In fact, my research proves that there are three types of loyalty: heart, head, and hand. That is, emotional, rational, and habitual loyalty.[5] And these three types of loyalty are related to the three types of core competence I discussed in the Brand chapter: customer intimacy, functional performance, and operational excellence.

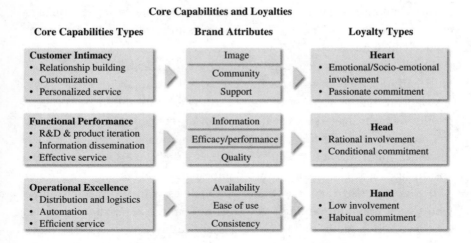

FIGURE 5.4 Relationship between core competence, brand attributes, and customer loyalty.

Although loyalty is dependent on individual customer and category characteristics, it is also influenced by the core competences of the organization, which create specific associations toward a brand.

Figure 5.4 shows the relationship between the core competence that supports a brand, the benefits the brand provides customers, and the types of customer loyalty the brand can aspire to maintain.

Heart Loyalty

A heart-loyalty relationship describes a customer who is passionate about a brand – this is the type of customer-brand relationship people traditionally identify with loyalty. **Heart loyalty** is based on an emotional connection to the brand. It is what drives some Apple customers to wait in line for hours for new iPhone releases or that motivates Mini Cooper drivers to get together on Sundays to drive and share car stories. Their emotional connection to the brand establishes an automatic bond with others who own it. Heart-loyal customers feel an ego-centered connection to their preferred brands. They are interested in learning about the category, but only through the perspective of the brand.

Peloton, the connected fitness company discussed in the Chapter 4 on business categories, benefits from its heart-loyal customers as they amplify the brand's messaging by, for example, retweeting the company's announcements regarding its fitness programming. Heart-loyal customers are likely to share stories about their positive brand experiences. These are the customers who are most likely to generate positive word of mouth, to tell friends to join the brand community, and to post reviews on social media.

Heart loyalty is more emotional than it is rational. While doing research on customer loyalty, I met many customers who professed such strong feelings toward brands as to seem irrational. A professional woman employed by a large medical device company told me that she adored her Jeep Wrangler. She told me that she had loved her car since first stepping into it; and, yes, it had poor gas mileage, was so unreliable that it had left her stranded twice, and was missing many automation features standard in similarly priced cars. Yet owning and maintaining her Jeep was "a labor of *love*."

Heart-loyal customers tend to be forgiving when their preferred brands have service or product mishaps. As a consequence, retention rates among heart-loyal customers are very high. Heart loyals are likely to delay purchase or use if the product is out of stock, and they are also likely to let the brand know when they encounter a product or service problem, to give the brand a chance to fix it. It makes sense, then, that loyalty actually increases after service recoveries.[6] This is because, like spouses, heart-loyal customers are invested in the relationship.

Heart-loyal customers tend toward repurchase and are uninterested in competitive offers. In fact, direct sales efforts by competing brands can backfire, as these customers may take attacks on their preferred brand as personal affronts. Sophisticated salespeople know that it is difficult to compel heart loyals of a competitor to switch brands. Instead of attacking the competitor, the salesperson does best by developing a long-term relationship with the target customer and patiently waiting in case that customer-brand relationship deteriorates due to a backorder, service problem, or as a result of repeated and unresolved quality issues.

Heart loyalty requires a level of commitment that most people cannot maintain with more than a handful of brands. Accordingly, there are few companies that engender that type of loyalty broadly within their customer base. And yet we do find heart loyals in aluminum extrusions and toilet paper. So, if you wish to cultivate this type of customer loyalty, you should develop a customer intimacy core competence: offering customized support and excellent service and fostering a sense of community within your customer base.

At Sephora, a cosmetics retailer owned by LVMH, there is actually a vice president of customer loyalty – someone whose role is to create unique experiences for its customers. In discussing her customers' relationships to the brand, the Sephora's vice president of loyalty states: "it's not about what their loyalty demonstrates to us, but what we can deliver to our clients that creates the most meaningful and connected experience with our brands."[7]

While heart loyalty can be somewhat irrational, **head loyalty** – conversely – describes a customer's rationally derived brand preference that is due to the brand's ability to satisfy a functional need.

Head Loyalty

Head-loyal customers support brands that offer the best performance for the price, based on their requirements. Head loyals are rational; they use the brand because it does something for them.

Head loyals are generally interested in product and service information. This interest in information and focus on product features and benefits makes head-loyal customers a better target for competitors seeking to acquire customers than heart loyals are. Head loyals are committed and involved with their preferred brand. And yet, because their commitment is rational, they can be persuaded to switch brands with strong rational arguments.

Companies interested in developing a rational – that is, head-loyal – customer base should invest in performance features that create measurable value for customers. They should carefully measure value and set price accordingly, knowing that competitive comparisons are inevitable. And from time to time, at least, customers will engage in rational evaluations of their offers relative to their similar brands in the category. To contrast with the many heart-loyal users of Apple iPhone, Android phone users have relatively little emotional connection to their devices. Instead, commercials for Android phones focus on features where iPhone is weak, such as water resistance.

The CEO of Futura Industries, the aluminum extrusion company based in Utah, described her head-loyal customers as the most demanding from a service perspective. She discussed how one of them, a manufacturer of treadmills and ellipticals, required a model redesign every two years, and expected Futura to lend engineering resources to them "free of charge." Despite expecting this free service, the customer would invite Futura's competitors to bid for the supply of the aluminum extrusions once the design was finalized. Futura had had the contract for over 20 years, and yet the bid process was in place to ensure that pricing was competitive. Head-loyal customers are the most likely to weight costs and benefits to avoid overpaying.

Finally, there is a third type of loyalty that has only recently been recognized. It is not highly committed, like head or heart loyalty, and yet may generate behaviors that are indistinguishable from high-involvement loyalty. It is loyalty simply based on *habit* or convenience. This we call **hand loyalty**.

Hand Loyalty

Hand loyalty is the type of loyalty that occurs because people don't want to rethink every decision they make every day. Hand loyalty purchasing happens as part of a routine and due to familiarity with a brand. For example, once consumers have decided to use a particular grocery store that is conveniently located and meets their shopping needs, they are likely to use it recurrently without considering other options. Ease of access is key to hand loyalty.

Within the store also, and especially for certain categories, shoppers are very likely to stick with a particular brand without considering alternatives. This can happen even though they don't have strong feelings about its performance and lack an emotional connection to it. For example, in categories that do not represent a high financial or emotional cost of failure, investing in gathering information about competitive offerings or searching for deals may not be worthwhile. Brands like Morton table salt have customers with this loyalty profile.

We might assume that hand loyalty is only really related to utilitarian products, those with few features and low price. But we actually find that hand loyalty occurs almost anytime that customers face a cost to switch out of a brand. People stay with some financial institutions and many service providers not because they provide something really special, but rather because the perceived differentiation among the brands in the category is not worth the hassle, time, effort, money, or learning cost required to change. This focus on convenience and consistency is a major distinguishing characteristic of hand loyalty.

Hand loyalty is prevalent in digital channels, where multiple brands are readily accessible and brands are preferred due to small access advantages, top-of-mind status with consumers, or due to automation of certain routines. Many people use a particular search engine such as Google or Safari because it is slightly more integrated with their computer manufacturer (PC versus Mac), or because it is what they have become accustomed to. In 2009 when the then-popular Firefox web browser switched its default search engine from Google to Yahoo, the former lost almost four percentage market share points. This happened because consumers did not bother changing their default settings on their web browsers and instead switched search brands.

In contrast to the vocal feedback a company can expect from heart loyals when there is a service or product issue, hand-loyal customers tend to leave quietly. Think of what you might do if your slightly preferred brand of salt or crackers is unavailable in a grocery store. You probably won't look for a store clerk and ask for help; you will simply examine the shelf and look for other brands you recognize, perhaps engaging in a little research by comparing their features and prices. You will then select a new brand and be on your way.

Effective customer management requires understanding loyalty types and measuring the loyalty profile of your brand.

Measuring Loyalty

Of course, loyalty is only useful if you can recognize and manage it. We might want to change the loyalty profile of our brand, and to do that we must first be able to find out what type of loyalty we actually have. How can you recognize these different types of customers? The three different types of loyalties are revealed when customers are asked about their preferred brands.

If you ask a customer about your brand and they give you big smile, they are probably heart loyal. If they shrug, they are probably hand loyal; and if they give you a list of reasons why they like the brand, then they are probably head loyal. **Ethnography** – research based on observing non-verbal cues as customers interact with brands – is very helpful in assessing loyalty types but hard to operationalize in an organization with many customers.

Thankfully, you can also use a survey instrument, which in just a few questions can help you tease out the type of loyalty customers hold with your brand. Those questions are included in Figure 5.5.

Just 16 questions establish the loyalty profile of your customer base. The survey uses a seven-point scale with scale anchors 1 (strongly disagree) to 7 (strongly agree).

Heart items

I feel passionate about <brand>.

If someone says something negative about <brand>, I will feel like they are attacking me personally.

I feel good when I think about <brand>.

I feel a connection to other people who also use / purchase <brand>.

The fact that I use / purchase <brand> says something about me.

I love sharing stories about <brand> with other people who also purchase / use it.

Head items

I expect <brand> to deliver on its promise every time.

An important reason I like <brand> is its quality.

If <brand> does not deliver as expected, I will be very upset.

I value <brand> for its superior performance.

One key reason to repurchase <brand> is that it works as expected.

Hand items

I buy / will repurchase <brand> out of habit.

I buy / will repurchase <brand> just because I am used to it.

I buy / will repurchase <brand> just because it is familiar.

I buy / will repurchase <brand> as long as it is easy to find.

I will keep buying <brand> just because it is convenient.

FIGURE 5.5 Establishing your brand's loyalty profile.

Understanding the loyalty profile of your brand is empowering. Going beyond that, to treating each customer in a way that matches how they relate to your brand, can extend their lifetime with your organization, thus enhancing brand value and profitability. The key to this transformative practice is to understand the connection between customer loyalty and company core competence.

Managing Loyalty

Once you have a sense for the loyalty breakdown of your customer base, you can relate customer loyalty back to core competence.

It probably makes sense to you that if you have a core competence for customer intimacy – the type of competence that Harley Davidson, the Four Seasons hotel, and the Ritz Carlton hotels have – you will tend to have heart-loyal customers.

Now, companies that are really good at operational excellence are generally really good at making their products and services convenient, available, easy-to-use, and consistently distributed. Those companies tend to find more hand loyalty amongst their customer base.

And, finally, companies that are really good at developing products, delivering information, and innovating, tend to develop head loyalty.

There is a relationship between the three categories of core competence: functional performance, customer intimacy, and operational excellence, and the triad that we find here: head, heart, and hand loyalty.

How can you use this in practice? First, assess the type of core competence your organization has, as I described in Chapter 3 on brands. Then, define a customer specifically and set the type of loyalty profile you would like for your organization. Now you can design a customer experience that utilizes the skills and resources your organization possesses to develop the type(s) of brand customer relationship that executes on your vision.

The Customer Journey Map as a Planning Roadmap

In Chapter 3, I introduced the customer journey and the functions of a brand that guide customers along their journeys to create specific experiences. Customer *acquisition* and customer *retention* are two broad areas of investment for the organization; brand and customer journeys delineate more detailed steps within those two broad areas. Accordingly, the customer journey map can be used as a customer investment roadmap.

While you need to guide and support customers throughout their journeys, the focus of your effort will be different when you are trying to acquire rather than retain customers. Brands hoping to grow by getting new customers and executing a *brand-switching* or a *category development strategy* will focus investment on the front end of the customer journey. Brands that have a lot of customers will find it more efficient to grow through retained customers by executing a *brand commitment* or *brand expansion strategy*. They will focus investment on the back end of the customer journey. Figure 5.6 shows a customer journey map annotated with acquisition and retention marketing investments.

There are only two ways to grow a brand's business: acquire or retain customers. These two growth objectives require different activities and investments. The disciplined strategist selects one of these two primary growth

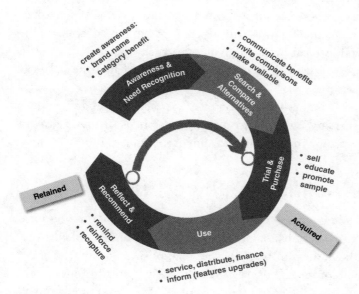

FIGURE 5.6 Using the customer journey for customer acquisition and investment planning.

You can use the customer journey as a roadmap detailing the investments your brand will need to make to acquire and retain customers.

	Acquisition	Retention
Solutions (products & services)	Breakthrough design and ease of adoption	Design to motivate upgrade or increase usage
Pricing	Trial programs	Continuity / loyalty programs
Distribution	Benefit expertise / more available	Support expertise / more selective
Communications	Awareness and information	Reminder and reinforcement (image and behavior)

FIGURE 5.7 Execution when focusing on customer acquisition and retention.

Customer acquisition requires not just more but also different investment from customer retention.

goals, budgets accordingly, and then develops feedback loops to capture some of the other goal. A customer *acquisition* focus is critical when creating or entering a business category and when seeking geographic expansion. A customer *retention* focus is critical when seeking to consolidate the company's leadership position in a business category, when operating in a fragmented category with little customer loyalty, or when the brand is assailed by competition.

The choice as to whether to focus on customer acquisition or customer retention is a necessary one because these two sources of brand growth require different specific investments, as shown in Figure 5.7.

Customer Acquisition Investment

If you are executing a strategy reliant on customer acquisition, you need product and service solutions that awaken a sense of wonder and curiosity in customers with whom your brand has no relationship. Ideally, the brand goes to market with products or services that represent breakthrough innovations relative to what the customer is using. And yet, customer acquisition requires that customers be able to adopt the new product or service easily. Your organization must be able to educate customers and ensure their first-use experience is positive and consistent with the benefits promised by the brand.

A customer is not acquired until they have experienced the benefit promised by the brand; it is not enough to have received their money. The work of the organization is not complete until the customer has also used the product and felt the experience. This is a really important distinction between the traditional sales focus and the more customer-centric focus in an organization. If your product is complex or expensive from a learning, process change, or financial perspective, the acquisition resources in the organization should also include training, equipment trade-in, process redesign services, and even financing. Acquiring customers requires helping them easily adopt the brand's technology, business, and service processes.

Acquiring customers requires thoughtfully using your resources to guide them along their journeys within the category. You need to make specific investments to execute on this strategic choice. Let's take a look at those.

Executing on a Customer Acquisition Strategy

When focusing on customer acquisition, you should develop products that ignite interest and trial. Either the product itself should be intuitive or the service experience around it should make it intuitive. If you sell capital equipment or for some other reason purchasing your brand requires a large financial, learning, or emotional commitment, you need to first understand each of these hurdles and devise a plan for how customers will overcome it. If you are switching customers away from a competitor, you might have a program specifically dedicated to transferring data, trading in capital, or learning the specific differences between the use experience of the two brands. Other times, especially if you are introducing a new category that requires significant financial, time, or emotional commitment to adopt and which offers a great experience, you may develop "light" versions of the product to enable customers to "get a taste" for what larger commitment might bring.

The organization behind Peloton understood this. As buying an expensive spinning bike and committing to a monthly subscription was a large objection to new customers coming onboard, the company designed an entry-level product: easy-to-use digital content to enable potential customers to experience the benefits of the brand.

Especially if you are executing a *category development strategy*, price is likely to be taken as an indicator of quality because customers are not familiar with the category or brand. You should price to highlight the value of your products and services.

Also, for experience-dominant products and services, which those customers need to experience to appreciate, implement pricing programs that remove price as an objection to trial. You can use introductory discounts; however, discounting can negatively impact the perceived value of the product. Therefore, finding a way to offer a free trial is a preferred way to entice potential customers to try your brand.

When it launched its first generation of all-electric performance vehicles, Tesla offered them at prices comparable to luxury sedans and offered generous test-driving opportunities, allowing would-be customers to keep the cars overnight.

The function and structure of your distribution channels should also reflect a customer acquisition focus. If you are executing a brand-switching strategy, you will want to structure your salesforce or distribution outlets so that your product can effectively reach competitive customers before they repurchase their current brand. If you are executing a category development strategy, the distribution channel should also reach your target customers and be able to create interest and deliver education.

Tesla placed stores in luxury malls or downtown locations with high pedestrian traffic. This is different from the traditional car sales model: dealerships are located in the outskirts of urban centers where real estate is cheaper and storing large numbers of vehicle inventory is inexpensive. Because it makes and sells its cars "to order," Tesla does not require locations with lots of room for inventory. Also, its store staff are not in charge of pricing and can't extend discounts, and are instead solely dedicated to explaining the benefits of the brand.

Finally, acquiring customers requires investment in awareness and informational communications. The goal of your content strategy is to let people know the brand exists, create interest, and establish positive associations between the brand and the customer benefits it provides.

The communications channels you use to transmit that content will also reflect an acquisition focus. While specificity in designating customer targets is always desirable because it drives efficiencies in distribution and communications, you will likely not be as targeted in your customer profiling when focusing on customer acquisition relative to retention. As a result, you will use communications channels that can reach a broad target audience (relative to communicating to your own customers). Depending on your category, you may use social media influencers, banner ads, magazine or journal ads, image-appropriate streaming ads, or other channels that enable you to expose the brand to your target audience and broadcast a message likely to be heard.

In summary, when growing through new customers, you should invest in activities designed to attract attention, garner interest, communicate broad benefits, and enable easy trial of products and services.

Retaining customers is complementary to acquiring customers and requires dedicated investment. This is why you must choose whether to primarily grow through customer acquisition or retention. We have looked at acquisition; let's now look at retention.

Customer Retention Investment

To grow with existing customers, support them in the choices they have already made. You should invest to help them achieve the experience your brand has promised, while partnering with them to measure the value they derive from the relationship. All executional elements are materially different when investing in retaining customers versus acquiring them.

Products and services are tools to deliver the brand to customers. In brand commitment and brand expansion strategies, your customers are familiar with your products and services. To reengage your customers, you will want to build on the technology or features they already like, augmenting them to motivate upgrades or increased commitment.

This is the design philosophy utilized by car companies such as BMW. The products in the BMW portfolio are numbered to indicate the order in which a customer might use them as their life progresses and they need more space and also have more disposable income.

Brands also grow through a retention volume strategy by getting customers to use the brand more often, perhaps by applying its benefits to different aspects of their business or their lives. By introducing new menu items, Starbucks gets customers to rely on its stores for breakfast or snacks, not just morning coffee.

Iconic brands that have grown through customer retention efforts have mastered the art and science of listening to their customers and translating use experiences into product and service enhancements and accessories.

Gillette has established a cadence of global product launches: each increasing the brand's performance on a consistent value proposition of providing a close shave with no irritation. Every three to five years over the last few decades, the company has launched a product that either delivered on the promise of a closer shave – by adding blades or by improving contouring by adding mobility to the razor head – or decreased irritation – adding lubrication to the razors and battery-powered vibration designed to decrease friction between the blades and the skin.

Successful product and service iterations maintain key components of the customer experience that attracted users to the brand initially. And yet, as the sophistication of the product increases it may become more complex. The BMW 3 series car launched today has many more features than the model launched in 1970, and a new driver needs to expend considerable time and effort to learn how to master them.

Investing in customer retention requires dedicated execution.

Executing on a Customer Retention Strategy

A well-arranged portfolio will have products and services specifically designated as "customer acquisition" and "customer retention" tools. For the Apple brand, products that are useful in acquiring customers are cheaper, have fewer features, and are easier to use; these include standard model iPhones, and less-featured iPads and computers. Products that motivate customers to remain with the brand and increase their commitment are more complex and generally also more expensive; they include the "pro" iPhone and computer models, the Apple Watch, and streaming services optimized to work on Apple devices, like Apple Music, Fitness+ or TV+.

In retention strategies the communications effort is focused on reminding and reinforcing customers, and tactically motivating them to upgrade or use more. Retention pricing programs may use bundling promotions or include loyalty incentives, or large volume, or step discounts.

The most effective loyalty programs are designed with an understanding of which products in the brand portfolio are most effective in getting customers to increase their commitment to the brand. Highlighting those products through temporary discounts may help increase sales from existing customers. Even better, you should think of ways of integrating them with the rest of the portfolio to enable them to pull the other products through. For example, if the accessories and spare parts work across all the products in the portfolio, then customers will be motivated to add more of your products, rather than going to another brand when they need a complement. Apple is more likely to motivate upgrades across iPhones, smart watches, and computers if customers can reuse peripherals and because their data is seamlessly available across devices thanks to the company's iCloud service.

Amazon Prime is a fee-based program for current customers that offers free shipping for an annual flat membership fee. The average Amazon Prime member spends around $1,400 per year, while nonmembers spend $600 on average. In 2020 the annual Amazon Prime fee was $119.[8]

As I have discussed already, if the function of the sales and distribution channels when you are investing in acquiring customers is to explain the brand benefits and motivate trials, their role in retention is to support and service the customer. In some cases, companies use different salespeople for customer acquisition and retention activities.

You might have not thought about your marketing execution in this way before. Conceiving of acquisition and retention as investments with different priorities drives great efficiency across all executional disciplines: products and services, pricing, distribution, and communications.

The Customer Choice: Acquisition Versus Retention

All companies across all their brands have to master customer acquisition skills. At critical inflection points in a brand's life cycle – when it first launches, when entering a new market, when facing a sudden sales slump – customer acquisition may be particularly important.

You might have thought that the best way get new customers is to target competition. A lot of my clients seem to gravitate toward *brand-switching* strategies when needing to acquire customers.

However, acquisition rates tend to be lowest, and costs are highest, from competitive conversions. Competitive customers have existing relationships with other brands, some involving loyalty, which you must disrupt in order to acquire them.

A common maxim in marketing states that "it costs five times more to acquire a customer than to retain a customer." Whether this number is accurate – diverse authors have quoted a variety of other numbers from 3 to 20 – it does make sense that customer acquisition is expensive relative to retention. Why? Because for acquisition you have to take people through many steps in the customer journey. They have to become aware and engaged in learning more, they have to recognize the information you provide as useful, and then they have to be motivated to try the brand. And customers can drop off at any of those transitions. That makes acquisition relatively expensive. However, once engaged, most people tend to be overtaken by inertia, making retention cheaper than acquisition.

Thus, if there is one metric that is indicative of the long-term viability of the brand, it is likely the *retention rate*. Companies with very high retention rates, in excess of 90 percent, have customers who stay with them more than 10 years. Generally speaking, these companies are sustainable. They have a business model that works.

An important part of the brand strategy choice is to focus on either acquisition or retention. Of course, both are necessary for your business to prosper, but they are two distinct growth levers with materially different executional ramifications.

Acquisition and *retention* also drive brand structure choices. Companies that focus primarily on *acquisition* follow a distinct branding approach. Genentech, the pharmaceutical giant, develops new branding for each drug it introduces as part of the effort to attract interest in its new therapies. Companies that primarily rely on customer *retention* for growth, like Caterpillar, tend toward an umbrella brand approach. Of course, this is not a hard-and-fast rule, and companies may shift their customer focus from acquisition to retention too frequently to justify altering their brand architecture. And yet, in general, a portfolio of brands supports customer segmentation and acquisition: a single brand is a better support for customer retention efforts.

Of course, investing to acquire customers must be balanced with investing to retain customers; successful brands balance acquisition and retention growth goals and resources. These integrated approaches are called *acquisition with retention in mind*, and *retention with acquisition in mind*. Acquisition with retention in mind requires carefully managing front-end commercial operations to target customers who are likely to have high retention rates once converted to the brand. Retention with acquisition in mind requires executing to build and utilize brand ambassadors to acquire new customers. The customer focus choice must be aligned to upstream and downstream decisions, from how to structure the company's brands to how to use commercial resources.

6 Customer Beliefs

Working through each of the Big Picture Strategy 6Bs progressively focuses your go-to-market choices by considering each of the questions posed by the framework. By the time you get to this B, beliefs, you have chosen a particular group of customers to pursue based on their business category and brand behaviors. You now further refine your target customer opportunity analysis by considering which specific customers to prioritize based on their beliefs.

The processes described in this chapter will make your marketing more efficient and effective. Understanding customer beliefs and targeting customers whose attitudes match your capabilities allows you to prioritize potential customers who represent a good fit, thus using your marketing budget efficiently. A detailed understanding of your target audience is also key to constructing a value proposition that compellingly (and honestly) represents your brand. The more compelling your brand's value proposition, the more effective it will be.

This chapter has two goals: to give you tools to identify a positioning benefit for your brand, and to help you to develop and articulate a value proposition built around that benefit. A value proposition centers on a single-minded, targeted benefit. The value proposition process should drive resource allocation toward people most likely to welcome your offer. You choose a single-minded benefit to prioritize customers, you execute on that benefit, and later you focus on customers who most need it.

Delta Air Lines' value proposition is to consistently deliver a superior travel experience (powered by happy employees).[1] Delta tends to be the most expensive US airline but attracts the most frequent travelers of any US carrier, people looking for convenience and a better onboard experience than what is available elsewhere.

Here, in the beliefs stage of the framework, you must make a choice. You must select a single-minded belief to represent your brand, a belief that meets two criteria: it is built on a customer insight that drives behavioral change in your target audience; and it represents a benefit your brand can deliver better than anyone else.

To be able to select that belief, you must first build a deep understanding of your target customers. Then you can develop a value proposition that utilizes that understanding and therefore speaks directly to them, using language they find both familiar and compelling. Let's start by presenting tools designed to discover and target customers' beliefs.

Step One: Discover Beliefs that Drive Brand Choice

Our beliefs influence which brands we pay attention to, and which ones we end up selecting, using, and trusting over time. Whether we use a standard cognitive process, where we first think then act and then feel; or act first, and then think and feel, brands acquire meaning over time and that meaning controls our attitudes toward them. Think of a brand, any brand. Now come up with words that describe it. What does this brand mean for you? For me, Icebreaker, a merino wool clothing brand based in New Zealand, conjures feelings of comfort and environmental responsibility associated with wearing humanely harvested wool.

As marketers our job is to embed our brand with specific meaning. We hope that the thoughts and feelings evoked by our brand match the needs of as many potential customers as possible, and work to develop positive and immediate needs-based associations. But meaning is personal and intimate. Customers do not (and cannot) generally volunteer deeply held attitudes. Asking a customer directly about their attitude toward a brand is unlikely to reveal the true nature of their beliefs. Most insightful beliefs lie beneath the surface of everyday conversation. To overcome this limitation, in our consulting work we use two qualitative research tools together: customer journey-mapping interviews and feature-benefit-value laddering.

Whose Beliefs Matter?

At this stage of your analysis, you can use the four go-to-market strategies, discussed in Chapter 2, to focus your research, as each of them corresponds to a distinct customer group. Should you focus on customers who are new to the brand or those who are already working with your organization? Customers within the category or those currently in a different business category? Those loyal to your brand, loyal to a different brand, or multibrand?

In selecting customers for your research, be mindful to preferentially speak to customers whose behaviors and demographic profiles resemble those in the group you hypothesize will be most attractive for your brand, based on a 6Bs opportunity analysis like the one I discuss in Chapter 2, the four go-to-market strategies chapter.

Customer Journey Mapping

I explained customer journey mapping in the bodies chapter. Customer journey mapping is an invaluable tool to understand the steps a customer takes to form a relationship with his or her preferred brands. Conducting customer journey in-depth interviews is also fundamental to mapping customer beliefs. A customer journey-map interview combines the mapping of routine behaviors with descriptions of specific service experiences that customers remember as being particularly impactful.

Experiences combine behaviors, thoughts, and emotions. And in customer journey interviews, we ask customers to recount incidents they view as critical to understand those experiences. A critical incident[2] is a specific event that has a significant contribution, whether positive or negative, to a customer's experience within a category and with a brand. During these interviews, we get customers to talk about experiences they consider important, we learn about their perspectives, and we hear the specific wording they use to describe their needs and brands' benefits. Ultimately, after conducting these interviews you should understand:

- The specific behaviors customers undertake as they "journey" through the category and select, try, and eventually commit to and use a brand.
- The information channels (social, online, and traditional) they use to gather or share feedback.

- The touchpoints they have with brands in the category.
- Their likes and dislikes along their journeys.
- The specific needs that arise throughout their journeys and their degrees of satisfaction with brands' abilities to meet those needs.

Figure 6.1 presents sample questions we have used in customer journey interviews.

Consider the answers you have given to the earlier Bs in the strategic process (the brand, the business category, and the bodies) in both developing interview questions and selecting the specific people you want to interview. The example in Figure 6.2 illustrates a customer journey map developed for the Peloton brand (mentioned throughout this book).

The customer journey map is built on the basis of interview data and includes common journey phases, current behaviors, and likes and dislikes. The last row in the interview summary contains customer needs – which, when the brand performs satisfactorily, we refer to as "benefits." These customer benefits are derived from analyzing the interview transcripts.

The strategic focus of the brand determines the target audience for these interviews. For Peloton, creating the at-home boutique fitness category, interviewees are from outside the category.

Customer journey interviews help us map the specific steps customers take in discovering categories and brands and eventually making purchase decisions. They are particularly useful in understanding the customer's perspective about categories and brands inductively, from the outside in.

Feature-Benefit-Value Laddering

In our consulting practice, we combine customer journey interviews with **feature-benefit-value laddering interviews** to develop a complete view of the customer perspective.

Feature-benefit-value laddering is a powerful research technique developed in the 1980s.[3] Like customer journey-mapping interviewing, laddering is designed to discover the less-obvious beliefs that drive brand preference. Unlike customer journey mapping, laddering starts with the brand and its features. In a laddering interview, we ask a target customer to select a specific brand feature they consider important, and we then we ask, "Why is that important?"

Awareness & Need Recognition	Search & Compare Alternatives	Trial & Purchase	Initial & Habitual Use	Reflect & Recommend
• What brands do you know, and what do you think about each of them?	• How do you compare alternatives?	• Do you trial products before you buy? How?	• How does the vendor organization handle your account?	• What happens at the end of contract / service completion?
• What information channels do you use?	• What information do you ask for?	• Who is involved in trials? How?	• Describe the install / initial use process.	• What do you say to others about the brands in the category (social media posts)?
• What is new, good, or bad about the category?	• How do you rank offers?	• How long does the purchasing process take?	• How do you request / receive service? Manage inventory?	• Does your preferred brand (and category as a whole) deliver good value to you?
	• Who is involved?	• What kind of contracts does your company look for?	• What goes well? What could be improved?	• What do you wish were different?
	• What works well / poorly about this process?	• What goes well / poorly during trial and purchase?		

FIGURE 6.1 Common customer journey interview questions to uncover beliefs.

	Awareness & Need Recognition	Search & Compare Alternatives	Trial & Purchase	Initial & Habitual Use	Reflect & Recommend
Current Behaviors (What, where, how?)	• I have worked out at my gym regularly for five years. • I talk to my friends at the gym about workouts and fitness.	• I've tried other workouts –cross fit, Orange Theory. . . • I always go back to my local gym.	I buy 10 class packages to make the finances work better – classes average $20 each or $160 per month.	• I have been working out at my spinning studio (~2x/ week) for three years. • I have made friends through my gym.	I recommend my local gym to people looking for energizing group classes.
Likes	• I enjoy my workouts.	• I like trying out new things. • I stick with what I know.	I like paying as I go.	• All I need to do is show up. • I like being on a first-name basis when I walk in. • It's nice to get out of the house.	• I am a better version of myself on days when I work out. • Overall, I am happy with my gym.

	Awareness & Need Recognition	Search & Compare Alternatives	Trial & Purchase	Initial & Habitual Use	Reflect & Recommend
Dislikes	Working out at my gym takes time out of my day. I interrupt my workouts when I get busy. Staying in shape is tough.	There may be no perfect workout, and I need to combine several to stay healthy.	I guess my gym is expensive.	Inconvenient schedules. I really like one trainer. . .her classes sell out.	I just wish I could use my gym more often.
Benefits/ Needs	• Convenience	• Ease of trial • Variety • Familiarity	• Accessibility (price) • Payment flexibility	• Convenience • Social connection, personalized attention • Personalized coaching • Time convenience	• Convenience / efficiency

FIGURE 6.2 Customer journey interview output example.

The goal of a laddering interview is to elicit benefits of the brand as well as how the brand appeals to someone's deeply held values. In conducting these interviews, we discover a range of functional, economic, and emotional benefits that target customers associate with the brand. Laddering interviews examine each of the major features of a brand systematically, starting from the brand and working toward the customer.

In laddering interviews, product by product, and feature by feature, the interviewer guides the target customer to discover associations, starting with specific features and linking each to abstract associations.

If questioning a customer of Peloton, the interviewer will focus on the hardware (the bicycle or the treadmill sold by Peloton), on the digital content and any other aspect of the customer experience. Imagine that, in discussing the bicycle, the target customer states that they like having a high-quality spinning bike at home. The interviewer might ask, "Why is it important to have the bike at home?" The interviewee might respond that by having the equipment at home they are able to access engaging spinning classes anytime, so there is no excuse to miss a workout. When asked why not having excuses is important, the respondent might say that not having excuses means that they work out more often, and as they do, they experience mental and physical benefits. Ultimately, having the bicycle at home appeals to their sense of accomplishing goals.

Take a look at Figure 6.3 for a laddering example for the Peloton brand. You should use laddering research to develop a deep understanding of brand benefits, not just the obvious functional advantages of using a product or service, but the emotional and values-based reasons customers choose brands.

Different customers will be more interested in different aspects of the brand, and even when examining the same features they might derive different benefits and connect them to different personal values. However, in conducting just a handful of these interviews we find recurring benefit words and dominant value associations.

In Chapter 3, I discussed how brands establish specific experience expectations. Laddering is a way of listening to the customers' version of the experiences they've had with the brand. As such, it is a critically important tool you will want to use to establish your brand's value proposition.

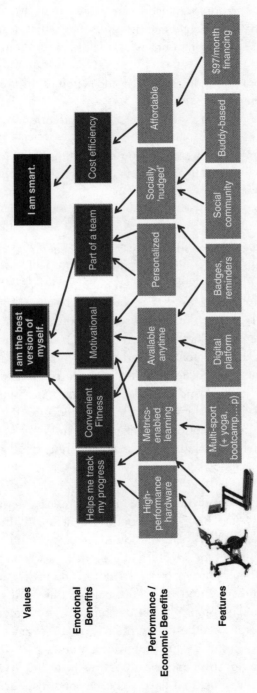

FIGURE 6.3 Feature-benefit-value (FBV) laddering – Peloton example.

By asking "why" about the features and benefits of the brand, the FBV interview elicits deeply held brand associations.

133

Customer journey mapping and laddering are two techniques every marketer needs to use to unearth customer insights. Insights are deep meanings about the true nature of customer behaviors. They are useful in two ways:

1. They direct your attention, resources, and activities toward what truly matters to customers.
2. They inspire content that will get customers' attention.

Both attention-grabbing messaging and compelling operational execution are required to sustainably change customer beliefs and behaviors.

Step Two: Evaluate Brand Benefits

Once you have collected customer needs, brand benefits, thoughts, and feelings evoked by the category and the brands within it, you should prioritize what you have heard in a systematic manner. For purposes of this discussion, I will refer to customer needs, thoughts, and feelings about brands, whether satisfactorily met by the brand or not, simply as *benefits*. The idea is that each of the items you have discovered through the journey mapping and laddering research is a potential brand benefit.

To initially sort customer benefits, put them in three groups by looking across the customer journey and the laddering output, in Figures 6.2 and Figure 6.3, respectively. These groups are value proposition opportunities, innovation insights (or perception) opportunities, and importance opportunities. I have created a matrix in Figure 6.4 containing these groups, and I discuss them here as follows:

- **Value proposition opportunities** are insights you have gathered about customer needs that have corresponding benefits. If the customer needs it and you have a great solution for it, you should be building and selling a product, or a feature of a product based on this. Comparing the customer journey map for Peloton and the feature-benefit-ladder (in Figures 6.2 and 6.3), you can see the word *convenience* appear in both. The brand's target customers wanted more convenience, and Peloton could credibly offer it; this is what the Peloton brand ultimately built its value proposition around.
- **Perception or innovation opportunities** are needs, uncovered by customer journey mapping, that have no corresponding benefits in your

<u>**Customer Need /Differentiation Matrix:**</u>

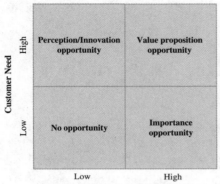

Customer Need /Differentiation Matrix:

- **Importance opportunity.** Lift importance through communications and RTBs
- **Value proposition opportunity.** Communicate importance and perception of benefit that meets need.
- **Perception / Innovation opportunity.** Lift perception of existing benefit or develop innovation (new benefit) to meet need.
- **No opportunity.** Low customer need and low fit with core competence.

FIGURE 6.4 Evaluating customer needs to brand benefits.

Evaluate the output of the customer journey map and feature-benefit- ladders by considering the relationship between customer needs and the brand's capacity to deliver on those needs now or in the future.

brand's feature-benefit-value ladders. This could be due to one of two reasons. First, your brand may offer the benefit, but customers do not recognize it. In this case, there is an opportunity to simply improve brand communication and increase perceptions. The second reason a need doesn't appear in your feature-benefit-value ladder is because your brand does not possess the benefit. In this case, your team should consider acting on the need, turning the need into a brand benefit and potentially changing the perception of the brand.

In customer journey mapping boutique gyms (Figure 6.2) you have uncovered that there is a need for customized trainer-based coaching / mentoring. There is no corresponding benefit (or feature) in the Peloton ladder (Figure 6.3). Peloton could eventually decide to offer a personalized one-on-one coaching service to its members, but it may also decide not to.

- **Importance opportunities** are brand benefits, discovered through laddering, that have no corresponding customer journey needs. These are benefits you can offer customers although they are not asking for them. To develop a value proposition around them, you will need to first make customers care about them, that is, increase their importance.

The next step in this process is to identify the single-minded benefit that you hope will become synonymous with your brand: the brand's *positioning benefit*.

Step Three: Choose the Positioning Benefit for Your Brand

Every brand needs a clear and compelling positioning to stand out from the cacophony that is the market. Positioning is the benefit word (or words) that customers strongly associate with a brand. The positioning of the Dyson brand is *air performance* and *good design*; Gillette's is *a close shave;* Toyota's is *reliability*; Nike's is *self-esteem*. Selecting a positioning benefit for your brand is possibly the most important decision you will make in the marketing strategy process. I introduced the *category plot* and the *competitive plot*, in Chapter 1. I expand on those tools and concepts now.

Once you have assembled a list of the benefits you wish to test, prepare a survey instrument to develop a quantitative assessment of brand-benefit importance and perceived performance. As before, focus your data collection on the group of customers you identified based on one of the four go-to-market strategies, using your 6Bs opportunity analysis.

We use that data to develop a *category plot*, which brings together benefit importance and brand perceived performance for all the brands in a category. If contemplating a category development strategy, plot your brand against other categories or substitutes whose customers you hope to attract – Peloton plots itself against two other categories. See Figure 6.5 for an illustrative category plots, one for the Peloton brand and another for a fictitious contact lens company, *ClearVu*.

You can use the category plot in combination with the *competitive plot* (see Figure 6.6), to select the *category benefit* and each brand's *differentiating* benefit.

By taking into account perception and importance ratings and the unit share or share of customers owned by each of the brands, you can use the *category plot* to identify the *category benefit*. The *category benefit* is the most important benefit in the category where the category leader is differentiated. The *category benefit* differentiates the category from other business categories and, in categories with clear leaders, the category leader from other brands within the category. The category benefit flows from the core competence of the category leader.

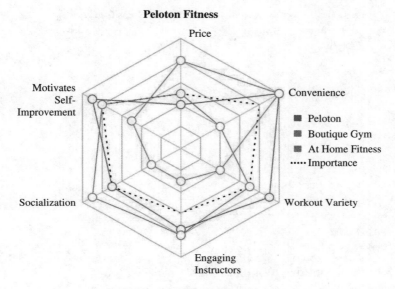

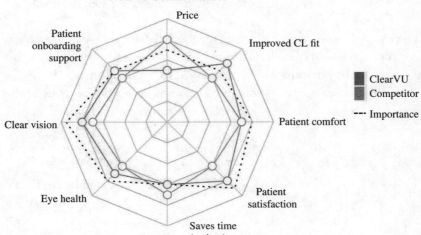

FIGURE 6.5 Category plot examples.

These illustrative category plots show importance and perception across categories (Peloton) and within a category (ClearVu), depending on the strategic focus of the brand under consideration.

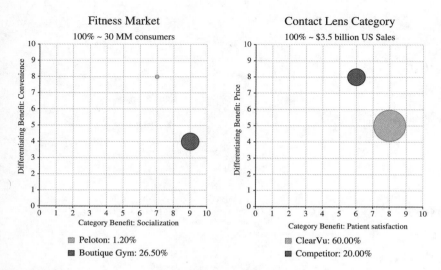

FIGURE 6.6 Competitive plot examples.

These plots illustrate the opportunity available to your brand if you position it on a specific benefit where you can outperform customers' best competitive alternatives.

For example, the category benefit for the fast-food category is convenience, and McDonald's, the creator and traditional leader of the category since the 1950s, dominates other brands on convenience. The brand achieves that differentiation through a core competence in food operations and store location, delivering a consistently convenient customer experience around the globe.

Another use for the category plot is as a proxy for brand value: the differentiation value of each of the brands within a category.

If the category plot contains all the key benefits evaluated by customers when faced with a brand choice, multiply each of the brands' perception scores on each benefit times its relative importance to create an overall brand score. That brand score should be correlated to the market shares of each of the brands in the category. And the brand that is perceived as the category leader should have the highest brand score because it outperforms others on the benefits that most matter to customers.

Each brand wishing to compete successfully in the category ought to perform within an acceptable range on the category benefit as well as on all the other benefits the category provides customers. In other words, brands in the category are considered "acceptable" to customers by performing at parity to competition on the benefits illustrated in the category plot.

And yet, to be preferred by a specific segment of customers within the category, each of the brands also needs to stand out on a single benefit, a *differentiating benefit*. The differentiating benefit is the basis for the brand's position in the category. Find your differentiating benefit by selecting a benefit where your brand can outperform other competitors.

The *competitive* plot helps you illustrate the customer opportunity available to your brand if you execute on a specific benefit that would motivate your target customers to change their behaviors. The *competitive plot* illustrates the positioning of two brands, generally the category leader and the brand seeking to compete against it. Accordingly, we generally plot the category benefit on the *x*-axis and the differentiating benefit on the *y*-axis.

For example, Peloton's competitive plot would examine the brand's perceived performance against boutique gyms whereas the ClearVu contact lens competitive plot would examine its performance relative to other contact lens brands. As illustrated in Figure 6.6, Peloton may execute a brand strategy centered around *convenience* against boutique gyms, known for their personalized workout approaches. The competitive plot illustrates the location of the two competitors in a perceptual space, and therefore the specific tradeoffs that customers make when choosing a brand.

The competitive plot illustrates how a brand could take share away from a competitor, generally the category leader, by performing close to the category leader on the *category benefit* and differentiating on an unrelated, *differentiating* benefit. Given the potential for competitive retaliation, the *differentiating* benefit should always arise from a core competence.

A winning positioning benefit meets multiple criteria: it can be made important to your target customers, it can differentiate your brand from competitive alternatives, and it possesses a long executional runway.

The brand team should feel excited at the prospect of building a rich executional plan around the positioning benefit. Execution includes content and messaging and, more importantly, the capability to achieve consistency across a variety of customer touchpoints in a revised customer journey we call the *brand customer experience*. The *brand customer experience* is designed to bring the brand's value proposition to life.

Being able to design a winning customer experience that articulates the value proposition requires a deep understanding of the brand benefit through the eyes of a customer. This is the function of the target audience persona.

Step Four: Write the Target Audience Persona

A target audience persona is a prototype of your target audience built in rich detail so as to enable your organization to locate them, engage them, and execute a compelling promise for them. In reviewing a target audience persona, ask:

- Is this a realistic customer?
- Would the salesforce be able to find members of our target segment, based on this?
- Does it articulate the benefit we have chosen for our brand in the words of a customer?
- Does this description bring the target audience to life for our internal teams who will be called on to execute a strategy centered on this target?
- Does the description include the likely objections our teams will need to overcome in accessing and motivating this person to work with our brand?

The primary goal of a target audience persona is to align the internal perspective of your organization with the external perspective of the customer around the positioning benefit.

The target audience persona is built using some of the qualitative insights your team has gathered through the customer journey and laddering interviews conducted earlier in the value proposition process. We also recommend that our clients conduct some additional interviews to complement their understanding of the brand positioning benefit they have chosen.

If your brand competes in a business category that requires large emotional and financial commitment, as most business-to-business categories do, it is also likely to involve multiple customer stakeholders. Although multiple stakeholders may meet to discuss your brand, your target audience persona should not be for a committee or a group, but rather for the individuals within that committee or group.

A useful target audience persona has four components:

1. **About.** A demographic and behavioral description of the customer in their habitat. This section of the target audience persona contains a name, income, career stage, general behaviors, and any other details that locate the target audience in their environment. It also contains other important contextual details that will aid execution. These include:
   - Where can they be found professionally?
   - Whom do they interact with?
   - What channels of communication do they generally use?
   - What general content are they most likely to be interested in?
   - What are their general attitudes about the category, their work environment, and life in general?
2. **Benefit description.** This is the core of the target audience persona. It is a description of the positioning benefit you have selected for your brand (category or differentiating benefit) from the perspective and in the words of a target customer.

   Knowing what a customer within your category is likely to understand when they hear the benefit promise of a brand – and therefore what they expect from the brand – is the key to successful execution. The meaning of benefit words like *reliable, easy to use, high-performing, operational control* is completely dependent on the context, so be sure you know what it means to the target audience.

   The benefit description should include the specific operational implications of the customer benefit. If you are positioning your service offering on being *easy to do business with*, you may include details like simple contracts, easy access to customer service, short time to get questions answered, and so on. In other words, what does your team need to deliver to meet customer expectations?
3. **Revealing behaviors.** Another critical component of a strategic target audience persona is the specific behaviors within the category and in

adjacent categories that reveal someone's latent need for our brand's positioning benefit.

It is difficult to locate the target audience because customers may not be able to recognize their own needs. For this reason, revealing behaviors are critical in a target audience persona. If you are targeting surgeons who need efficiency, do they call ahead on their way to work to check that the OR is running on time? Do they use equipment that may be more expensive but saves time during the procedure? Do they track intra-operative steps in ways others don't? If you are focused on surgeons who value aesthetic outcomes, do they stay in the operating room until the skin is closed to monitor how the resident sutures the outer layers? Are they constantly keeping abreast of minimally invasive operative techniques?

The target audience persona should contain rich descriptions of real people, including their goals and aspirations relative to the category. But goals and aspirations describe a person, rather than a product; accordingly, you may explore behaviors outside of the category that enrich the description of your target audience. The surgeon who values aesthetics may have a keen eye for design and may have decorated his office or keep a neat desk. You should feel free to include details in the target audience persona that help your salesforce locate the target, and your marketing communications colleagues develop messaging and contextual details (backgrounds, designs, ...) that are most likely to break through the cacophony that is the daily life of your target audience. Only then will you be able to get their attention and engage them in fruitful conversation.

4. **Objections and barriers.** Why won't this all work? The target audience is likely to have preoccupations, lack time, budget, or sufficient influence to compel the organization to select your brand. The objective of this section of the target audience description is to surface the most likely barriers you need to overcome to succeed in favorably changing beliefs and behaviors toward your brand.

Figure 6.7 contains target audience persona examples for a fictitious surgical robotics company.

Brand: Ada Pediatric Robotics
Benefit: Surgical Precision
Category: Robotics-enabled General Surgery
Strategic Focus: Category Development

	Surgeon	Hospital Administrator
Habitat/ Context	• Dr. Gagnon is a pediatric surgeon in Montreal at a large academic institution • Pressured to operate a lot • Treats complex cases (colon resections, complex tumors, …) • Wants to become a key opinion leader; feels pressure to publish	• Gloria Akalitus is the CFO at a large academic institution in Montreal • Oversees patient safety program • She manages a 500-bed hospital and is concerned about maintaining profitability while keeping the institution's research reputation
Customer perspective of the differentiating benefit (precision)	• Visibly reduces impact to adjacent tissue • Clinically proven outcomes related to precision (reduced bleeding, less invasive, fewer complications, …)	• Cares about patient care metrics (e.g., length of hospital stay, satisfaction) • Focuses on reducing complications
	• Requires experiential proof of precision • Needs outcome data to be able to sell internally	• Clinical outcome data is required for any capital investment • Requests in-facility trial period before signing any statements of work for new technology
Revealing behaviors	• Caring with patients (more follow ups than required) • Does clinical outcomes research • Interested in teaching opportunities	• Reviews patient care and safety metrics daily • Presenter on 'reducing complications' at hospital administration conferences • Follows clinical complications personally and closely
Barriers/Objections	• Too busy to attend at training program • Not very powerful in the hospital hierarchy	• Skeptical of return-on-investment data provided by vendors • Decision-making requires lengthy value-analysis-committee process

FIGURE 6.7 Target audience persona examples.

As there are two key decision makers who must support the brand choice, two target audience personas are needed.

Step Five: Develop the Value Proposition

A value proposition is the promise a brand makes to its target audience as to how they will specifically benefit from partnering with the brand. The Big Picture Strategy value proposition toolset is built with simplicity and strategic depth in mind.

Similar to having just 6Bs in our strategic decision framework, there are just six boxes, each tightly defined, in the 6Bs value proposition tool shown in Figure 6.8. The four boxes in each corner of the value proposition tool contain "I" statements: they are written in the first person because they represent the target customer perspective. The fifth box, the customer proposition, articulates what the brand wishes to communicate to customers. I describe them in the order in which they should be developed.

Current Do

This is the target customer behavior you want to change to achieve your brand's business goal. It reflects a customer behavior corresponding to the strategic focus of your brand. If contemplating a category development strategy, then the *current do* may read: "I don't use the category...," while for a category expansion strategy it would state: "I use *brand name* sometimes. . ." or, "I use a first-generation version of the product." For a

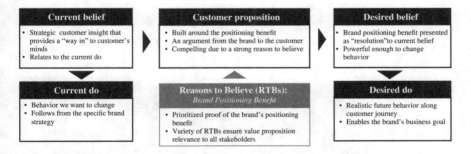

FIGURE 6.8 The value proposition 6-Box tool.

The value proposition tool links strategy and execution. It is built on a customer insight filtered and curated throughout the beliefs process described in this chapter. It contains a simple proposal to your customer that the entire organization supporting your brand can use to design the customer experience and that should be articulated through every brand customer touchpoint.

brand commitment strategy, it might read: "I use *two brands*...," while for a brand-switching strategy it might read: "I use *competitive brand*...."

Current Belief

This is the cornerstone of the value proposition. The current belief must connect to the *current do*; it should describe a belief that explains the current behavior we wish to change through the value proposition. It must also contain a customer insight (problem or opportunity) that the brand can solve better than anyone else; that resolution follows in the desired belief.

Marketers often think that the most important component of a value proposition is the customer proposition statement, the middle box in the value proposition tool. And yet, in my experience, the difference between a marketer's ability to develop a good versus great value proposition is the discovery of a strategic customer insight. That customer insight varies depending on the specific brand strategy you are utilizing. For Peloton, the customer insight was a lack of convenience associated with the boutique gym experience, as illustrated in Figure 6.9.

- Category development strategy insight: a frustration with a related category from which you will draw customers.
- Brand-switching strategy insight: a relative disadvantage of working with the category leader.

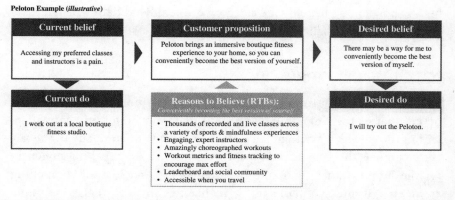

Peloton Example (*illustrative*)

Current belief	Customer proposition	Desired belief
Accessing my preferred classes and instructors is a pain.	Peloton brings an immersive boutique fitness experience to your home, so you can conveniently become the best version of yourself.	There may be a way for me to conveniently become the best version of myself.

Current do	Reasons to Believe (RTBs): *Conveniently becoming the best version of yourself*	Desired do
I work out at a local boutique fitness studio.	• Thousands of recorded and live classes across a variety of sports & mindfulness experiences • Engaging, expert instructors • Amazingly choreographed workouts • Workout metrics and fitness tracking to encourage max effort • Leaderboard and social community • Accessible when you travel	I will try out the Peloton.

FIGURE 6.9 The value proposition 6-Box tool, Peloton example.
The value proposition of a brand pursuing a category development strategy is built utilizing a customer insight from people outside the category. For Peloton, the insight is a frustration afflicting people who currently attend boutique gyms.

- Brand commitment strategy insight: how multibrand customers may be able to improve their relative experience vs. using another brand within their current brand set.
- Brand expansion strategy insight: what your customer is missing out on by only using your brand in a limited way.

Desired Do

This is the behavior you wish from a target customer stakeholder in the future, once your execution is successful. Conceptually, if you multiply the number of people in your target audience times the revenue impact of the change in behavior implied by this desired do, you should be able to approximate the sales goal associated with your strategy.

Keep in mind that the distance between the current do and the desired do must be realistic and represent how expensive and difficult it may be to implement the value proposition (and strategy). For longer distances, you can consider an intermediate behavior. You may wish a target customer to purchase a hybrid car model; the intermediate step may be for them to visit a dealer who is responsible for the personal selling of your brand.

Desired Belief

This is the belief that drives the desired do. It must relate to or contain the brand's positioning benefit (the category or the differentiating benefit). It's what the customer believes after we've executed our strategy.

The Customer Proposition

The essence of the customer proposition is the positioning benefit of your brand, that is, the single-minded benefit that your brand uniquely offers within the category. Written as a statement from your company to the target customer, the customer proposition presents a compelling *argument* for the brand, rather than simply a statement. And like all compelling arguments, it must contain some evidence to convince, that is, to transform the minds of your target audience so much so that they also change their behavior.

The Reasons to Believe (the Positioning Benefit)

This section of the value proposition tool contains a list of the most compelling proof you can develop. It should be an exploratory list of the key pieces of evidence your target customer stakeholders would find most convincing. I discuss reasons to believe in more detail immediately below.

Step Six: Develop Proof

What would make target customers believe our value proposition?

The delivery of a value proposition is your opportunity to educate prospective customers and, in doing so, create alignment within the client organizations. As you interact with your customers, this method should also ease the sales process by aligning their diverse functional members. An important goal of the Big Picture Strategy method is to align your team around common questions and single-minded goals. *Reasons to believe* are diverse proof types that align and convince.

Developing a winning value proposition requires combining seemingly contradictory goals of articulating a benefit with wide appeal to diverse stakeholders. This benefit is simultaneously single-minded and capable of differentiating the brand. It may be tempting to tell everyone what they want to hear about your brand, and yet using different value propositions to appeal to different customer segments or different stakeholder motivations is neither believable nor achievable.

A company's purchasing department may want the lowest cost, its C-suite may care about using the brand with the best reputation, and the direct user may care about functional features and benefits. A sales-driven organization might demand multiple value propositions to meet the diverging interests of these different customer stakeholders. Conversely, the marketing-led organization selects a single positioning based on its core competence and a differentiating customer insight. It then uses different types of evidence to *speak the language* of each of the customer stakeholders involved in selecting, using, and enjoying the final benefit of the brand.

The core of your value proposition, containing the positioning benefit, is ideally expressed in a few words that all client organization stakeholders know and value. The collaboration software brand Slack has a value proposition of *increasing teams' productivity*, Medtronic's Micra miniaturized pacemaker has a value proposition of *effectiveness with no physical sign of a pacemaker,* and the ride share company Uber offers the most *convenient way to get around.*

The reasons to believe in a value proposition can be classified by type of evidence, by content type, and by source (see Figure 6.10). Evidence can be hard or soft. Hard evidence is data and information. Hard evidence uses facts, logic, and numbers (economic proof, technical proof, market-based observational proof). Social – or soft – evidence is anecdotal (specific case studies, customer stories, expert opinions). Medtronic may state that its diabetes solutions are 99.9 percent effective in preventing hypo and hyper glycemia based on a randomized controlled study, or it may present patient case studies, which are essentially stories.

The source or channel you choose to deliver the information can add credibility. That source could be the brand (someone in your organization), the customer (peers, final consumers, or expert customers), or a third party (external experts, media, celebrities). The overall goal is to maintain focus on the *why* about your brand, while communicating it in a way that is memorable and persuasive by choosing the type of evidence, specific content, and delivery method that is most compelling to each of the recipients of your value proposition.

It is good practice to complete a structured evidence table, like the one in Figure 6.10, when starting to plan your value proposition containing different types of proof.

The best value propositions are not those that may appeal to everyone, as propositions with broad appeal are necessarily vague. Rather, a good value proposition is one that is highly specific about your brand but expresses how it will benefit client organizations in a variety of ways. Delivering the value proposition effectively requires not only that you consider what evidence to use, but also how to articulate it.

Value Proposition Considerations

As you prepare to finalize and articulate your value proposition, take into account how framing and messaging focus can increase attention and persuasiveness. Think through three factors as follows:

1. End-user focus
2. Gain versus loss framing
3. Importance versus perception focus

Content Type	Evidence Type		
	Hard Evidence • Experiments • Observations • Facts	**Social Evidence** • Anecdotes • Stories • Opinions / Reviews	**Soft Evidence** • Puffery • Drama • Humor • Product placements, Sponsorships
Brand	• 3M: One of the 2020 World's Most Ethical Companies by The Ethisphere Institute (B) • Alli: The only FDA approved OTC weight loss aid (B) • Purdue: "No antibiotics ever" (B)	• QuickBooks: "Join over 7 million customers globally" (B) • Neutrogena: #1 Dermatologist recommended skincare brand (B) • Sensodyne: "#1 Recommended brand for sensitive teeth" (B)	• Fiji Water: "Earth's Finest Water" (B) • Red Bull: "Gives you Wiings" (B) • Gillette: "The best a man can get" (B)
Product / service	• 3M Envision: GREENGUARD Gold Certification (B) • Samsung Air Purifier: "Protect your loved ones from up to 99% PM 2.5 & H1N1 Viruses" (B) • Mint: "#1 most downloaded personal finance app" (B)	• 3M™ Envision™ world's first non-PVC wrap films "... meet the world's most rigorous third-party testing standards for low emissions of volatile compounds into indoor environments" (B)	• Mini Cooper *The Italian Job* movie product placement (B)
Customer	• Peloton's: "96% customer retention rate" (B) • Allstate: "Drivers who switched saved $498" (B)	• Mint: "Join Mint. It's a phenomenal finance app." – Garion D. verified customer	• Peloton: Beyoncé, a customer, licenses her music to the brand (C)
Shared interest	• Mayo Clinic: "New Evidence supports ablation for heart failure patients with atrial fibrillation" (T)	• "Chewing gum after eating helps reduce cavities" A.D.A. statement on sugarless gum (T)	• Brand Sponsorships: e.g., Red Bull X Games (B)

(Source: Brand (B), Customer (C), Third Party (T))

FIGURE 6.10 Reasons to believe: Content, evidence, and sources.
Reasons to believe can be classified by the type of content topic, evidence type, and source.

End-User Focus

Although it may seem counterintuitive, if you are developing a value proposition for a business-to-business brand, focus your efforts on understanding and speaking about the ultimate end user. Your ability to differentiate your brand is predicated on your ability to demonstrate you can create maximum value for end users, as they ultimately drive demand for the final product. The larger your brand's contribution to end-user value, the more valuable it will also be to any other customer stakeholder in the chain.

If you work in health care, you will want to create a value proposition that aligns all partner organizations in creating value for patients. If you work within the music industry, keep listeners in mind. And if you code software, the users of the software and their ultimate project metrics should be top of mind. The more complex the industry, the more important it is to maintain your focus on the ultimate consumer of the entire value chain.

Walmart won in the retail value chain in the 1990s by capturing and analyzing consumer store shopping data, which could minimize cost in the entire value chain. Spotify became dominant in the music industry of the 2000s by offering the broadest highly curated music choices to listeners. Ride-share companies like Uber and Lyft emerged as winners in local transportation markets by offering convenience to end users.

Even if you never speak directly to end users, make yourself indispensable to your direct customers by creating end-user value. Now, how should you frame your value proposition? Should you adopt a gain or a loss frame? That is, should you state that your customer will be better off if they use your product or worse off if they don't?

Gain versus Loss Framing

Three decades ago, Kahneman and Tversky demonstrated that in motivating behavior, a loss frame is more effective than a gain frame. A simple example nicely illustrates this well-known human bias, called *prospect theory*.[4] Think of a program with a goal of decreasing the use of plastic bags in a grocery store. You can either pay your customers 10 cents each time they bring their own bag from home or you can charge them 10 cents if they do not bring their own. The program that charges customers is more effective.

People are much more likely to notice and react to programs that emphasize a potential loss than those that emphasize a potential gain. Many famous advertising campaigns have taken advantage of this principle and have used a loss frame. In the 1980s, as IBM was under attack from a lower-priced competitor, it developed the slogan: "No one ever got fired for buying IBM." And when you are driving on the highway, signs are more likely to remind you that if you don't wear your seatbelt you may die rather than telling you that seatbelts save lives.

Given this, should you adopt a loss frame? Loss framing can backfire by generating negative feelings about a brand. For this reason, loss frames are often used in public service announcements or healthcare campaigns (don't put off your cancer screening or else. . .) but may not always be advisable for brand messaging. When you use loss framing, you are essentially telling customers that what they are doing today is suboptimal or likely to lead to a loss. This can seem self-serving or arrogant coming from a number two brand in a category, especially if directed at noncustomers. And it may generate counter argument if the recipient of the message is loyal to another brand.

It is generally safer to *use loss framing when speaking to retained customers*, rather than when developing a value proposition to acquire customers. When IBM developed its famous "no one ever got fired" campaign, it was a category leader. The same is true for Michelin, "so much is riding on your tires," which encouraged car owners to not gamble with their children's lives by purchasing less expensive non-Michelin branded tires.

Despite the risk of generating negative associations toward the brand, a negative loss frame was successfully used by Apple in its "I'm a MAC" campaign seeking market share from corporate PC users. At the time, Apple was not the category leader in personal computers, and was investing in customer acquisition. Apple's success with this campaign, however, was likely due to most PC corporate users feeling "hostage" to PCs, rather than being fervently loyal. Of course, these images have shifted drastically with the success of Apple, now the dominant brand in that category. The focus of a brand's value proposition naturally changes as the brand strategy evolves.

Importance versus Perception Focus

As the next step in the value proposition process, consider the two dimensions to positioning beliefs – importance and perception – that I introduced back in Step 2. Importance is the relative value of a benefit to a potential customer; that is, the weight of a benefit among all the others considered in a purchase decision. Perception is the relative strength of the association between your brand and the benefit; that is, the perceived performance of your brand on the benefit.

Once you decide to position your brand on a particular customer benefit, you should lift both its importance and customers' perception of your brand. And yet, at times you will preferentially want to focus on importance or perception.

How to Change Importance

How is changing importance different from changing perception? I think about changing importance in terms of an economic-value formula, which states that economic value is the product of the frequency of an occurrence times its magnitude. To increase the importance of a benefit, highlight its frequency and the value allocated to each occurrence.

If you wanted to increase the importance of disinfection in a hospital, you might promote that hospital-born illnesses due to lack of disinfection occur much more often than people might have thought. To highlight the frequency of an event related to a benefit, you are likely to use hard data in your *reasons to believe*. You might also highlight the severity or cost of each individual infection.

Source credibility is critical to increase importance. Consider using a spokeperson who is one or two steps removed from your organization and who brings credibility to the issue at hand. To increase issue importance, medical device companies often use third-party researchers who may be clinical customers but are not directly associated with the company. Similarly, a company selling air purifiers may promote data from an independent air quality watchdog on the risks of breathing polluted indoor air as a way to increase the importance of air purification.

How to Change Perception

Changing perception requires that you convince potential customers of the performance advantage of your brand. You may use brand or product evidence, perhaps describing features or internal processes used to source and develop your product. For example, you could tell customers your process is more thorough, or your employees are better trained. You could leverage your brand equity by promoting the reputation of your brand or certifications or warranties that reassure would-be customers. You may disseminate specific performance data about your product, or you can use data collected from customers on how their performance has improved as a result of using your product or brand. And you can use experts or third-party sources to promote your brand.

Earlier in the book, I described how Hyundai improved its reputation over two decades through better manufacturing that resulted in more reliable products; offering the longest warranty in its category; and eventually spinning off its Genesis model as a premium offering that even well-heeled customers nowadays find an acceptable substitute for more traditional luxury car brands.

Importance Focus

A brand introducing an innovation, especially one that is novel enough as to merit a new business category, needs to focus on importance. This is because innovations bring to the world new benefits, positive customer outcomes that customers never demanded because they did not think they could have them. The Peloton brand introduced a benefit of convenience to customers of boutique gyms. Accordingly, it focused on increasing the importance of convenience.

At times, brands may also want to decrease importance. This is especially true for brands that are seeking to take share from a competitor. The challenger brand may want to decrease the importance of the category benefit to highlight a differentiating benefit. When Sprint sought to compete against Verizon in 2016, as mentioned in the four go-to-market strategies in Chapter 2, it advertised that its reliability was essentially the same, and that all other wireless brands also had similar reliability, as to diminish its importance while increasing the importance of price. In other settings, brands may deemphasize or eliminate discounts to increase the relative importance of performance.

Perception Focus

A brand seeking to expand frequency of use, through a brand expansion volume strategy, needs to focus on shifting perception. Arm & Hammer baking soda increased the amount of product that customers used by convincing them that baking soda was not just a baking ingredient but that it eliminates odors as well. McDonald's convinced customers to come into its stores more often by primarily telling them McDonald's had breakfast, and not just lunch and dinner.

Hybrid Focus: Importance/Perception and Perception/Importance

Brands may adopt a hybrid investment approach, trying to primarily change importance or perception while having a secondary emphasis on the other lever. On the whole, brands employing a brand-switching strategy will adopt an Importance / Perception approach. These brands are likely introducing an innovation that matches the category leader's performance on the category benefit but improves on a differentiating benefit.

As mentioned in Chapter 2, a share-focused brand can motivate customers to switch by first amplifying dissatisfaction. Amplifying dissatisfaction involves mining the competitive customers' experience with the category leader to uncover a latent or overt dislike, and making that benefit important, likely by discussing why it matters or the effects of its absence. The challenger brand then presents itself as a preferable alternative, working to also improve perception. When Subway successfully earned share away from McDonald's, it pointed out that some McDonald's customers were severely overweight and presented Subway as a healthier alternative.

Brands may also adopt a hybrid perception-importance focus. Especially for brands executing a brand commitment strategy, it is not uncommon to first demonstrate performance superiority on a benefit and later magnify its importance. Credit card issuers may promote their points-based reward systems as being better than other cards' and then showcase customers' stories about how allocating more spending to their cards has enabled them to achieve superior benefits.

The Beliefs Choice and the Four Go-to-Market Approaches

In selecting a positioning benefit for your brand, be mindful of how the role of your brand shifts with its commercial strategy, as illustrated in Figure 6.11. A brand that seeks to create a category or lead in an existing

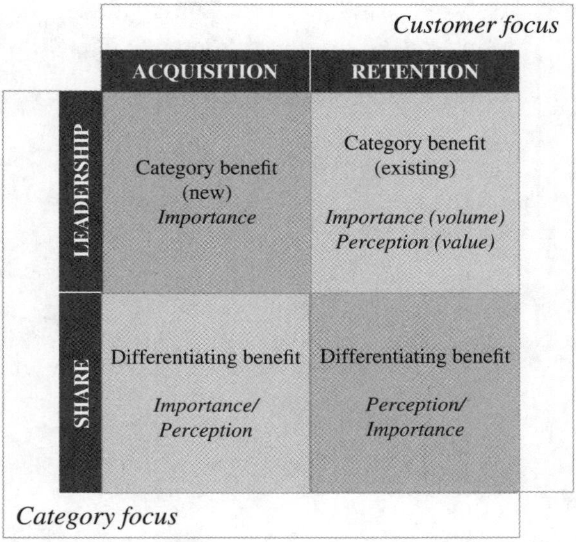

FIGURE 6.11 Belief emphasis by brand strategic focus.

The group of customers you are building a strategy around determines your choice of a positioning benefit for your brand as well as the relative focus on increasing benefit importance or perception.

category will want to establish its positioning benefit as the *category benefit*. In this way, to the extent that customers consider that benefit most important, the brand ensures its longevity and that of the category. A brand seeking to challenge a category leader through a share-focused strategy emphasizes a *differentiating* benefit that creates a wedge against the category leader. In addition, and depending on the strategy it has chosen, the brand team will carefully consider whether to invest to change importance or perception. This too depends on the brand strategy.

The value proposition is the overall promise a brand makes to its customers. Execution is the set of organizational behaviors required to make good on that promise. Accordingly, the brand value proposition becomes a guide as you execute your brand strategy. To align your strategy to your execution, you must first communicate a clear plan to cross-functional partners in charge of products, pricing, distribution, and communications. The marketing team designs a brand customer experience to create that alignment. The next chapter, Behaviors, discusses the implications of your strategy across all aspects of execution.

7 Behaviors: Designing Brand Customer Experiences

The brand's value proposition articulates a strategic hypothesis: if we change a belief widely held by our target customers, enough of them will change their behavior in a way that enables the brand's overall business goal. We now detail that hypothesis by designing a brand customer experience map, an exercise we use to visualize the future.

Developing the desired brand customer experience is the first step in the behaviors process. The brand customer experience bridges strategy and execution; it becomes the organization's North Star as your team starts working on your brand's execution.

To design the brand customer experience, start with the current customer journey and then transform it based on the value proposition for your brand.

For example, to design the brand customer experience for Peloton, start with the customer journey of the brand's target audience and ask how Peloton can deliver its value proposition of "conveniently becoming the best version of yourself." Working incrementally through each customer journey step, identify the opportunities to deliver on that promise.

Figure 7.1 corresponds to Peloton's category development strategy targeting boutique fitness enthusiasts (as discussed in Chapter 6 on beliefs). Peloton must first convince these customers that it offers at-home workouts comparable to those of a boutique fitness gym. Second, it must convince fitness enthusiasts that convenience is worth giving up

	Awareness & Need Recognition	Search & Compare Alternatives	Trial & Purchase	Initial & Habitual Use	Reflect & Recommend
Value Proposition: *Peloton brings the best boutique fitness experience to your home, so you can conveniently become the best version of yourself*					
Current Behaviors (What, where, how?)	I have belonged to my local spinning studio for over five years.	From time to time, I try new types of studio workouts: yoga, CrossFit (but it hurt my knees), Orange Theory.	I buy 10 class packages to make the finances work better – classes average $20 each or $160 per month.	I don't go to classes as much as I would like – the best classes sell out before I coordinate my schedule.	I recommend my spinning studio to acquaintances, if they are looking for energizing group classes.
Current Beliefs (Why?)	Boutique spinning with specialized classes and instructors provides a great workout.	Variety keeps exercise interesting	Single class rates and unlimited subscriptions are too expensive for me (on a per class basis).	Scheduling the best classes/instructors is a pain – requires too much organizing and planning.	Working out with other people is motivational.

158

Value Proposition: *Peloton brings the best boutique fitness experience to your home, so you can conveniently become the best version of yourself*

PELOTON	Awareness & Need Recognition	Search & Compare Alternatives	Trial & Purchase	Initial & Habitual Use	Reflect & Recommend
Desired Behaviors (What, where, how?)	I will learn more about at-home boutique exercising with Peloton.	I will go in-store to ride the bike.	I will trial/purchase a Peloton bike and subscription/accessories.	I have taken a variety of classes and instructors in the first two weeks.	I refer friends, take classes with them and engage others on leaderboard (high-five, follow).
Desired Beliefs (Why?)	There is now an at-home alternative to spinning at my local boutique studio.	The Peloton bike is high-quality and there's a variety of quality exercise content beyond just spinning.	The quality and variety of classes will make the bike/subscription economical on a per use basis.	I get all of the benefits of boutique fitness at my home, on my schedule.	Peloton is more than an exercise bike, it's a community.

FIGURE 7.1 Illustrative Peloton brand customer experience.

face-to-face interaction. And to do this, Peloton must first make a compelling case for why convenience is so important, and then deliver on an incredibly convenient experience.

With the above goals in mind, we can develop the Peloton brand customer experience by imagining the beliefs and behaviors of a boutique fitness customer who is now enjoying a super-convenient, highly motivating fitness experience through Peloton.

Create a brand customer experience that *articulates* and *delivers* the value proposition. Imagine how the customer journey could be transformed if the brand made good on the promise it has articulated.

All four brand strategies go through a similar brand customer experience design as in Figure 7.1. The differences among them relate to their starting point, the behavioral focus, and the value proposition.

Two of the four strategies – category development and brand switching– involve acquiring customers, and the other two – brand commitment and brand expansion – involve retaining customers. Accordingly, the focus of your marketing investment is either on the front end or the back end of the customer journey. Also, the leadership-focused strategies' brand customer experiences de-emphasize competition, whereas the share-focused strategies invite competitive comparison. Regardless of your brand strategy, the specific customer-journey transformation is dictated by your value proposition.

As you begin to create this desired journey, start by conducting an *unbound* brainstorm, and later add executional realities one by one, such as budget, timing, and overall scope. Simply imagine an ideal future where your team is able to flawlessly execute on a very specific promise and, in doing so, transform customer beliefs and behaviors. Peloton could build an always-available digital community and use behavioral science to deliver highly motivating workouts that keep people coming back and working toward self-improvement.

Note that the new customer-brand experience does not aim to "fix" every problem or satisfy every customer need discovered in the customer journey map. Customer needs that are unrelated to the value proposition are out of scope.

Once you have developed a brand customer experience map, you can turn to your executional tools: solutions (products and services), pricing, communications, and channels of distribution.

Products and Services as Brand Attributes

Products and services execute on the brand customer experience and reflect the core competence of the organization. The traditional divide between products and services is giving way to a continuum of tangible and intangible customer benefits. And as this happens, organizations shift their focus from product-and-service marketing to customer-experience marketing.

In customer-centric organizations that have adopted the Big Picture Strategy approach, marketing teams shift from being product marketers to becoming brand customer marketers. In this paradigm, the distinction between products, services, software, and any other attribute of the brand customer experience becomes purely tactical. When you prioritize the brand customer relationship, value propositions become central to the marketer's role because, more than any other single element in the marketing process, the value proposition links the brand with the customer.

Now, products and services are features of the brand prioritized according to their relative alignment to its value proposition. Let me explain this with a simple example. Imagine you are in charge of an organic grocery store brand with the value proposition *organic and locally sourced*. How would you execute on its brand experience design?

Naturally, you prioritize fresh produce, meats, and dairy over paper products and processed foods. They are the products that differentiate you against other stores, and you would therefore invest in their quality, feature them in your advertising, and price them higher than other stores.

The point is that product and service development arises from the brand meaning and the possibilities that your team's core competence and value proposition create for customers. Products, services, technology, and all other executional tools are tactical considerations that follow – rather than lead – the direction of the brand. As marketers, it is our job to organize and prioritize products and services, and their component features, according to the brand's strategic focus.

A Classification of Products, Services, and Their Attributes

Products and services are attributes of a brand; in turn, these are made up of attributes or components. Search-Experience-Credence, "SEC," is a well-known classification of product and service attributes. Searchable attributes are those that can be evaluated by a potential customer prior to purchase or use. A *search-dominant* product or service is one that has lots of *searchable* attributes; a Lenovo laptop can be considered a searchable product because many of its attributes – operating system, storage capacity, screen size, etc. – are also searchable.

In turn, *experience* attributes can only be evaluated after the product or service has been tried. And *experience-dominant* products and services are themselves made up primarily of *experiential* benefits. Services tend to be more experience-dominant than products. For example, a restaurant meal is made up of experiences: "location convenience," ease of reservations, table-side service, food presentation, taste, food menu, and wine selection.

Finally, *credence* attributes are hard to evaluate even after consumption or use. Products and services are considered to be *credence-dominant* if their most notable attributes rely on faith rather than proof. Despite the Fiji Water's claim that it is "the purest water on earth," there is no way to know for sure. And you can only hope that when seen in public carrying a hard-plastic and square bottle of this brand, people will think you are sophisticated. Credence attributes include *values* and *emotional benefits* such as feeling safe, powerful, beautiful, accomplished, or confident. They also include long-term outcomes of a product or service that become quality or reliability claims. Research may prove that drinking two liters of water daily improves liver health, but you can never really know whether your liver is healthier because you drink that volume.

The steps in the feature-benefit-value ladder tool (see Chapter 6) generally correspond to the SEC categorizations: features are *searchable*, functional and economic benefits are *experiential,* and emotional benefits and values are *credence* attributes. The SEC categorization is useful in connecting the product and service strategy to the overall brand strategy, as shown Figure 7.2.

Category Development Strategies: Solutions That Encourage Category Adoption

A brand creating a new category can describe a novel benefit, but it needs tangible proof that it can deliver on the category benefit. It should thus develop and promote attributes that meet three criteria:

1. **Attention-grabbing.** They are novel and *searchable* – making the brand tangible. The best products to drive category adoption are those that are easily understood by potential customers.

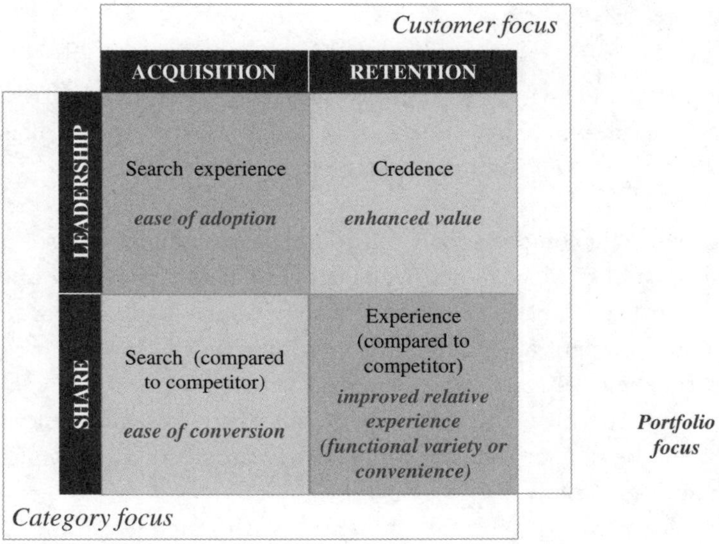

		Customer focus	
		ACQUISITION	**RETENTION**
LEADERSHIP		Search experience *ease of adoption*	Credence *enhanced value*
SHARE		Search (compared to competitor) *ease of conversion*	Experience (compared to competitor) *improved relative experience (functional variety or convenience)*

Portfolio focus

Category focus

FIGURE 7.2 Product and service attributes and the four go-to-market strategies.

Emphasize different solution attributes depending on your go-to-market strategy.

2. **Intuitive.** To successfully create new categories, innovations must appear to be breakthrough, while still being easy to use.
3. **Articulate the category benefit.** You may have a single opportunity to motivate cognitive and financial resource commitment to the new category and your brand. The first product or service interaction with a new customer is a proof of concept and must demonstrate the category benefit.

In 2011, Nest created the *smart home category* in launching a Wi-Fi enabled thermostat that could be remotely controlled from an iPhone and promised lower energy usage. The innovation was compatible with all major heating systems, was beautifully designed, easy to use – it could be programmed manually, through an attractive rotating wheel interface, or remotely. What's more, Nest sold for $200 but saved thousands in users' energy bills. The company targeted utility customers who were cost-conscious and liked the idea of modernizing their homes. By the time Google purchased the company for $3.2 billion in 2014, Nest had sold over one million thermostats in the United States.[1]

Brand-Switching Strategies: Solutions That Attract Competitive Customers

When executing a brand-switching strategy, use product and service attributes to create or amplify dissatisfaction – or at least indifference. Products and services in this case play an important role in:

- **Inviting favorable comparisons.** Your products and services must, in most ways, be like your competitive target's and better in at least one way. You must objectively benchmark your products and services to that of your competitor, on a feature-by-feature basis. Do they look similar? Do they deliver similar benefits? Be mindful, especially, of how well they perform on the *category benefit*, this is, the benefit espoused by the category leader as therefore a yardstick its customers will use to assess brands.

- **Demonstrating the differentiating benefit.** Although your brand needs to be similar to your competitor in many ways, it must be obvious to the target customer how you are better. Carefully curate the first product or service encounter the competitive target customer will have with your brand to ensure that it *articulates* the differentiating benefit.

- **Eliminating switching costs.** We are creatures of habit who loathe change. In some categories change is even more challenging if it requires relearning or reworking processes or replacing equipment. To motivate customers to switch brands you need to ease or eliminate the cost of switching. This might include financial incentives or trade-in options. In cases where customers are purchasing your competitor's entire portfolio, yours should not have any relative gaps so customers do not experience "a loss" in switching.

A successful example of a brand-switching strategy is that of Samsung against Apple. The successful launch of the iPhone in 2007 prompted Samsung to launch the Samsung Galaxy in 2009. Samsung set out to deliver an experience that in most ways was like that of the iPhone: similar design and functionality, app-capable, easy to use, delivered through the same distribution channels (wireless network firms as well as higher-end authorized electronics resellers). But one important aspect was better: the Samsung Galaxy aims to be ahead of the iPhone by having more advanced performance features.

Achieving parity with the iPhone required not just technical prowess. The device had to also deliver on the promise of "cool." To achieve this, Samsung organized its product development team to include not just R&D engineers, but also designers and marketers. Traditional Samsung appliances had been sold through discount electronics stores, but to compete against Apple the company refocused on premium electronics retailers. And to overcome switching costs, the company developed software to "make ditching your iPhone a snap." New Samsung users could download a free app aptly called Smart Switch that eased the transfer of pictures, contacts, and other apps into the new Galaxy.[2]

Brand Commitment Strategies: Solutions That Deliver Relative Experience

A brand seeking to increase customer commitment at the expense of others within a set must be able to compel customers who currently use it occasionally to see its products and services in a new light, motivating them to substitute use occasions of other brands.

Multibrand usage generally arises for one of two reasons. First, it may be due to a perception that your brand performs well in one aspect but not in others. Or second, absent a specialized preference, customers are somewhat indifferent to brands within a set and choose among them based on convenience. Most streaming video or audio service customers subscribe to multiple services, as they seek to have access to a greater variety of content that matches their preferences.

Regardless of why multibrand usage is occurring, the role of products and services in a brand commitment strategy is to offer an improved relative experience that motivates customers to substitute usage within a group of preferred brands. However, depending on whether the multibrand usage is driven by specific preferences or by convenience, product and service execution under this strategy diverges.

- **Performance enhancement.** If customers use your brand sometimes and a competitive brand at other times due to functional or performance differences, increase your performance to drive increased commitment. In the streaming wars waged amongst Disney+, Netflix, and Amazon Prime in 2020, Disney's investment in content through the exclusive release of blockbuster movies like the *Star Wars* series and *Wonder Woman* were key to that network's growth. Although Netflix still leads the category with 195 million subscribers, Disney is expected to assume leadership by 2024 with over 250 million customers.[3]

- **Convenience enhancement.** If your customers use your brand as part of a set within which they are relatively indifferent, enhancing your top-of-mind status, of mental or physical availability, may be the most efficient way to increase their commitment to your brand. Multibrand usage is common in the hotel, airlines, streaming, online shopping, credit cards, and many other categories. The average American has four credit cards, and to capture a larger share of their customers' wallets, credit card companies routinely launch convenience features, for example, by pre-filling credit card information on frequently used websites, making it easier for card holders to automatically charge frequently purchased items.[4]

When working with multibrand customers, emphasize the relative experience of your brand by also improving its performance on your differentiating benefit. Improving convenience alone, without a change in the emotional value of the relationship may not translate into true loyalty.

Brand Expansion Strategies: Solutions as Tools to Drive Increased Volume or Value

If growing your brand with customers who are already loyal, rely on the benefits they already like and amplify their experience to move from a rational or habitual relationship to a more emotional one, one that moves from *experience to credence*. I think of the ideal customer experience here as one of *suspended disbelief*, where product and service benefits artfully combine so customers focus less on how products and services work and can establish an emotional connection to the brand. When the brand is able to connect with customers at an emotional level, through credence elements, customers can enter a loyalty phase characterized by trust in the brand that transcends the operational aspects of service and product delivery.

Expanding your customers' connection to your brand by lifting their value or their volume requires slightly different executions as follows:

- **Expand value.** Increasing the value customers obtain from the brand – and pay – requires you to improve their experience by creating meaningful progressive changes to products and services. To this end, companies commonly improve products over time. Dyson launches new generations of its vacuum cleaners, with updated design and functional benefits. Companies also execute on brand expansion strategies by wrapping new services, software, or digital insights around existing products or services that augment their value to customers. Medical device companies are launching "smart" versions of their devices that use artificial intelligence algorithms to provide clinicians with more timely information that enables greater surgical precision.

- **Expand volume.** Increasing your customers' volumes or use frequency requires that you provide more uses for your products and services. Arm & Hammer baking soda successfully increased use of its product by teaching customers the "countless" ways in which they may use baking soda in their homes to clean, deodorize, bake, and even maintain their swimming pools.[5] Allergan, the company that sells Botox Cosmetic, similarly increased its customer's use frequency by obtaining FDA approval for many applications of the product, from treating frown wrinkles, to treating forehead, lip, chin, crow's feet around the eyes. In noncosmetic applications, Botox also increased customer volumes by expanding its therapeutic uses, now treating afflictions as diverse as migraines and incontinence.

Search, experience, and credence attributes can be overlaid on the customer journey (see Figure 7.3) as they naturally correspond to the product and service portfolio's role in creating attention on behalf of the brand, drawing customers in, motivating them to try it, delivering a specific experience, and building loyalty.

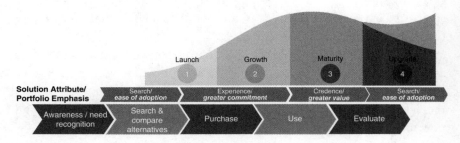

FIGURE 7.3 Solution attributes, the product life cycle and the brand customer experience.

Emphasize different product attributes along the customer journey and product life cycle.

Search-dominant attributes are critical to getting your target customers' attention. Whether you are hoping for a competitive conversion or wish to drive adoption of a new category, you should be able to answer this question: What are my target customers' most likely first tangible interactions with the brand? Experience attributes are critical in garnering commitment, and these require trial or use. A potential customer's first experience with a brand can make the difference between wanting to increase the commitment or deciding not to pursue the relationship further.

Finally, if you wish to extend your brand's reach from rational tit-for-tat calculated commitment to higher-level ego-involved emotional loyalty, appeal to customers' inner motivations, and their values. For customers who have already committed to the brand and are loyal, the brand can earn long-term commitment by communicating at the *credence* level. In doing this, the intent of the marketer should not be to manipulate or deceive, but rather to find like-minded individuals whose values match those espoused by the brand. The fitness clothing brand Lululemon was successful not only because it was able to create a new category of fitness clothing stylish enough to be worn outside the gym, but also because its fashion actually encouraged fitness: there is evidence that Lululemon customers actually feel "fitter" and are likely to have a healthier lifestyle when wearing the clothes.[6]

Pricing as a Communication Tool

Prices might seem objective because they are expressed numerically; however, how price is perceived is quite relative. The Big Picture provides a structured approach to consider all the factors that affect the perception of price. We use the 6Bs for this purpose.

Starting with the first B, **brand**, its identity, the type and strength of its associations, and the degree of differentiation it holds will impact price perceptions. The **bodies**, people's prior experiences with other brands in the category, whether they have purchased similar products before, and how much they have paid for them, affects whether they think the brand is well-priced or expensive. Also, potential customers' budgets and purchasing dynamics affect price perceptions: if the cost is shared among a group or if it is a small percentage of someone's overall budget or income, customers tend to be less price sensitive. Effectively planning to change customer behavior through pricing requires that you consider the specifics of your target customer context.

And this brings us to thinking about the **business** category; a category with lots of competition and readily available price benchmarks is one where customers are likely to be price sensitive. A category that is purchased out of impulse or due to a sudden need, like Valentine's Day gifts or medical emergency care, is likely to arouse less price sensitivity than one that involves planned purchasing.

Then there are customer **beliefs**, the centrality of the value proposition to your target customers, that drive their perception of your price. If you are selling a high-performance product to people who believe performance is very important, they will be less sensitive to the price than people who don't value performance.

Customer beliefs drive their **behaviors**. Out of all our executional levers, pricing is the easiest to change quickly, the one that is easiest to communicate, and the one that most directly affects customer behavior. Sampling programs or random discounts can generate a sense of urgency in customers, increasing their likelihood of making a purchase. Persuasion principles – *reciprocity*, the innate drive to give back to those who give us something; *scarcity*, our drive to hold in higher esteem things that are rare; *authority*, our innate drive to listen to experts and to want to emulate them; and *commitment*, our tendency to follow through with initial promises – function as additional factors that also affect how pricing is perceived and that can be manipulated by marketers to increase the likelihood that target customers will react to pricing tactics.

The **benchmarks** that get prioritized in a business also affect how pricing is handled. A surprisingly high number of companies focus on market-share metrics even when they are category leaders. A blind focus on market share can result in frequent discounting, which is proven to make customers more sensitive to price.

How to Set Price: Pricing Strategy

The basic method to set value-based pricing is common to all four go-to-market strategies. First, select a price reference, which is the price of the most likely substitute your target customers associate with your brand, sometimes referred to as the "next best competitive alternative." Then, estimate the differentiation value: this is the difference in value to the customer between the reference and the solution your brand offers. The differentiation value stems from your value proposition, as the positioning belief about your brand is generally the most valuable aspect of your solution versus the customer's best alternative.

The strategic focus selected for your brand affects the price because the four go-to-market strategies target different customers – and therefore have different references (see Figure 7.4).

If executing a category leadership strategy (category development or brand expansion), you can influence the price references used by customers in the category by establishing a specific narrative. When Spiked Seltzer launched the hard seltzer category, the brand was priced slightly higher than nationally distributed light beer and at a discount to premium craft beer. The brand sought to attract a young audience, people between 21 and 29 years old, who liked beer but were health conscious and open to a low-calorie alternative.[7]

However, if you are seeking instead to take share in a category, and therefore implementing either a brand-switching or commitment strategy, the brand you are comparing yourself to will set the reference. You will set your price slightly higher or lower than the reference set by the category leader,

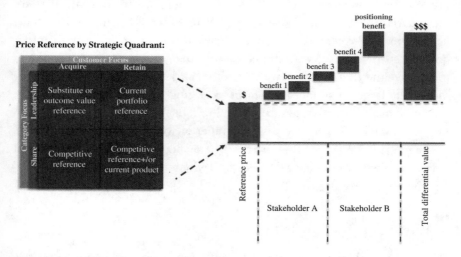

FIGURE 7.4 The price waterfall and the four go-to-market strategies.

While there is a common methodology to setting prices based on customer value, the choice of a go-to-market strategy affects the reference price, that is, the benchmark for your differential value.

depending on the relative value of your differentiating benefit. When the Boston Beer Company introduced Truly in 2016, they priced their drink just below the then hard-seltzer category leader, White Claw.

Once you determine the price by following the strategic-value-based method suggested above, consider enacting short-term programs to motivate customers to either try a brand or to increase their commitment to a brand they already purchase.

Pricing as a Behavioral Tool: Pricing Tactics

Pricing tactics are aptly divided into *trial* and *continuity*.

Trial pricing programs aim to remove price as an objection to trying a brand, and they include samples, temporary discounts, and coupons or rebates for new customers. Discounts and cash-back offers lower customers' willingness to pay the regular price, and as a result can be damaging to the brand longer term. Samples or a free trial period are preferable to temporary discounts because no price is communicated, and as a result, they have a smaller negative impact on willingness to pay.

Well-executed trial pricing programs educate the brand's prospective customers enabling the best possible initial purchase and use experience with the brand. Trial pricing programs work well when the customers' willingness to pay as a result of the trial, goes up more than the discounted price lowers it. Second, although many trial programs emphasize the amount of the discount, to create willingness to pay it is critical to emphasize the regular price rather than the discount.

Also, the purpose of a trial program is to experience the brand, and as a result, trial pricing programs should be structured around the number of uses rather than simply a period of time. This number of uses should be set based on an estimate of the number of interactions the customer needs to realize the intended experience with the brand. If developing a sampling program for an iPhone app, the trial period could be based on number of logins rather than simply time.

Trial pricing programs should be assessed on a cost–benefit basis. On the benefit side, they increase purchases by new customers, although at a lower contribution margin; while on the cost side, they lower customers' willingness to pay the regular, nondiscounted price. To assess the profitability of a trial pricing program, look at its costs and benefits over the retained customers' lifetime.

Continuity pricing programs are designed to retain customers by building their loyalty to the brand. Loyalty is made up of both a behavioral and a belief component; accordingly, these programs are successful only if they increase both purchase behaviors and the relationship with the brand.

The most common types of continuity pricing programs include discounts for large volumes and price rebates. Rebates are generally preferable to upfront volume discounts, because when volumes are not realized, clawing back the discount can be challenging and disruptive. Since the 1990s, companies have developed a variety of continuity pricing programs under the general banner of loyalty programs. These commonly include accrual of points, number of units purchased, dollars spent, or some other volume metric. In exchange the customer receives a discount, additional service, or a product reward. One drawback with many loyalty programs is that extrinsic rewards can decrease loyalty, so paying to retain customers keeps them coming back but can actually erode their relationship with your brand. The most effective loyalty programs reward customers with service gifts, rather than cash, and do so in a way that is unexpected by the customer. In these cases, the more business a customer does with the brand, the more intimate the relationship becomes.

An example of a "random" nonprice loyalty program is the Delta Airlines 360, reserved for the highest-revenue generating customers of this US-based airline. The airline does not publish criteria for membership. These customers are rewarded with special perks like a dedicated service phone line, priority upgrades, and random acts of kindness from agents, like getting priority processing through customs and immigration lines or sometimes being rushed to a connecting gate in a Porsche. Whether you use a creative non-price-based loyalty program or use price to motivate behavioral change, the key to these programs working long term for your brand is to tightly integrate them to your strategy.

Without a clear strategic approach that integrates all 6Bs, you become mired in the complexities of managing pricing and lose sight of the bigger picture: price is just one element brands use to change customer beliefs and behaviors. The 6Bs help you price congruently by tying the price to your overall brand strategy, as shown in Figure 7.5.

Category Development Strategies: Pricing the Category

Imagine you wish to create a new category, which you call the seamless writing category. You have just developed keyboard technology that enables writing at 10 times the speed of conventional keyboards. What should the price be? No, it should not be 10 times the price of a conventional keyboard.

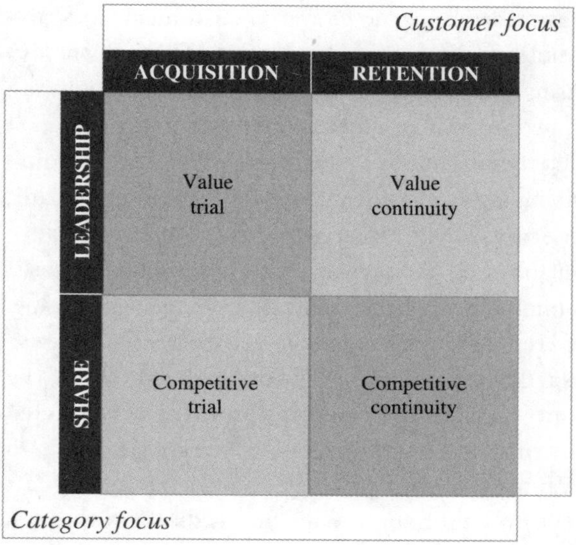

FIGURE 7.5 Pricing and the four go-to-market strategies.

Take a different approach to price setting and to pricing tactics, depending on the strategic quadrant.

To determine an optimal price, first select a target audience for the product among current nonusers. Should you target millions of students who are under a time-crunch to turn in term papers? Or perhaps thousands of professional writers, who are already adept at using conventional keyboards but who value their time at much higher rates and who may be able to expense the seamless keyboard?

To set a price when developing a new category, answer questions like the following: Who is the target customer? How important can the category benefit become to them? What other factors affect their willingness to pay?

Noncustomers are naturally diverse; this is because people have a variety of reasons to not do something. And yet, people must still share a common need to adopt a new category and brand. Your ideal customers are people who have both the motivation and means to pioneer a new way of doing things.

For Tesla, these were people who could afford a luxury car but felt a latent guilt about its environmental impact. For Peloton, it was people who were spending a great deal to stay fit and felt frustrated at their seeming inability to reach their goals due to what it took to get a workout in.

Choose a reference that is premium to the price and tell a great story. You may be launching an incredible innovation, but customers need to relate it to something they know to make sense of the value (and the price). Peloton referenced gyms charging $20 per group class and a monthly membership fee. It showed target customers that they could save money by purchasing a Peloton membership, even after also buying a sophisticated spinning bicycle. Similarly, at almost $80,000 for the base model in 2015, the Tesla S was expensive relative to other all-electric cars available then, but similarly priced to luxury sedans.

Also, it's always preferable to show, rather than simply "tell," the value. Quantifying value for breakthrough innovations is really difficult, because people cannot imagine exactly how it will work for them. Monetize the value by listing all the ways in which the innovation helps the selected target customers. Conduct in-depth interviews with a few customers to collect good data on the value. Test your pricing estimates by having target customers use a prototype or simulation while you walk them through your value narrative. Tell them exactly how they are going to benefit from the product. Listen for the one or two ways that the value seems greatest, and which benefits seem less important. And let them tell you how you are wrong and adjust and iterate until you feel confident about the price.

And finally, implement trial pricing programs that educate customers on how the innovation is valuable and how to successfully enjoy that value. If the innovation has a strong experiential benefit, getting target customers to try it is critically important. The goal of a trial pricing program is to maximize the value of the brand experience for customers, so that they will be willing to pay the regular price.

Pricing to Get Customers to Switch Brands or Increase Brand Commitment

As stated previously, all elements of your brand execution should help articulate the value proposition of the brand. Accordingly, the role of pricing when executing a share-focused strategy (brand switching or brand commitment) is to encourage comparisons and demonstrate superior cost-benefit to the competitive brand.

Share-focused brand strategies utilize *competitive pricing* strategies. This means pricing similarly to the targeted brand in general and at least initially; brands that are priced similarly are assumed to offer similar features. Price slightly lower or higher than the targeted brand, depending on the relationship between the category benefit and your differentiating value proposition.

If you are Subway and are trying to earn share from McDonald's by emphasizing that your product is healthier, you would benchmark and probably price a little higher than McDonald's because health is a premium benefit relative to convenience. That also means that if McDonald's changes its price either up or down, you have to change your prices as well to keep a consistent difference between the two brands.

Pricing Tactics to Encourage Brand Switching

Use short-term pricing programs, *trial-pricing tactics*, to encourage switching. Programs that effectively motivate customers to switch brands are tailored to overcome the specific switching costs faced by competitive customers considering your brand. Will they have to learn a new operating system, as PC users did when switching to Apple computers? Will they need to give up capital equipment that still works and purchase yours instead? Will they have to incur contract breakage fees? Successful brand- switching programs, like those implemented by Apple in 2007 to displace PCs, Komatsu versus Caterpillar, and Verizon versus AT&T in the first decade of the 2000s were effective, in part, because they addressed the specific one-time learning, capital, and legal switching costs that would-be customers faced in converting their businesses.

Pricing Tactics to Drive Brand Commitment

When pricing to encourage increased customer commitment, use continuity pricing tactics that are tailored specifically to motivate customers to substitute within a brand set. Continuity pricing tactics, in general, work best when they are perceived by customers as being random and when they offer a benefit to the customer that goes beyond simply lowering the price.

In brand commitment strategies, you are working with multibrand customers and are seeking to tilt the scales of their wallet toward your brand. Credit card companies do this by emailing specific offers that promote rebates or more convenient payment to customers based on recent purchases, as a way to get them to use their card instead of another credit card.

Brand Expansion: Pricing to Motivate Loyalty

When pricing to encourage current loyal customers of your brand to upgrade their use or increase the volume they purchase, use value-based pricing relative to your own portfolio. When Apple introduces a new iPhone version each year, it makes it marginally more expensive than the previous latest model, and the price differential between the two models is based on the magnitude of the value the upgrade brings to the customer.

Use continuity pricing programs to reward or delight customers for their loyalty, encouraging them to increase the volume (or dollar amount) of their purchases. *Random and nonprice rewards* are preferable to price discounts, or a program where the customer gets more value in direct relationship to their spend with the brand. The rewards are varied to avoid creating an expectation from the customers who are getting them. In industries where compliance rules prevent giving rewards with any significant monetary value, you can use innovation or customer council membership, podium presentations, visits by senior managers, and other "rewards" that meet compliance rules and still delight customers.

Pricing: Putting It All Together

Your brand's pricing strategy should be based on broader strategic decisions. If you are positioning your brand as a category leader, emphasize its uniqueness by setting price references and by making price comparisons difficult; if focusing on taking share from a competitor, instead enable price comparisons to the competitive target (see Figure 7.5).

When executing a customer acquisition strategy, consider using trial pricing programs with a focus on educating noncustomers to ensure a great first experience with the brand.

Brand-switching strategies also utilize trial pricing specifically targeting competitive customers and emphasizing the relative advantage of your brand and lowering or eliminating switching costs. Well-executed trial pricing programs teach customers about the brand and take away the price as an objection to trial.

If you are executing a customer retention strategy, encourage customer intimacy through continuity pricing programs that go beyond discounting and aim to convince customers that the more they rely on the brand, the more value they will obtain.

Communications: Telling the Brand Story

Executing a flawless communications plan is difficult, particularly for business-to-business brands, because the company tends to speak with many voices including a diverse salesforce, its professional education content, peer-to-peer reviews, and the cacophony customers create on social media. Together, these may drown out the brand's strategic messaging. Therefore, when developing the communications effort, keep in mind the many challenges that can cause your team to lose focus. You need simple yet profound messaging that is both easy to understand and powerful enough to align all the stakeholders who use their voice on behalf of your brand.

As with the other executional elements, your communications plan needs to wrap around the desired behaviors and beliefs spelled out by your brand customer experience. Communications plans have four key elements: communications objectives, communications content, channels, and metrics. I address metrics in Chapter 8, Benchmarks. Here I address the other three elements and how your choice of a go-to-market strategy affects communications.

Why We Communicate: Communications Objectives

There are five communication objectives: *basic awareness, top-of-mind awareness, information, behavior,* and *image.* These five objectives generally follow the customer journey.

Basic awareness, also called *aided awareness,* aims at getting customers to simply recognize our brand.

Top-of-mind awareness is built through many positive associations between the brand and the category benefit. The goal of top-of-mind awareness communications is to develop positive symbiosis between the business category and the brand. Top-of-mind awareness brands, like Apple and Samsung in smartphones, have built an equivalence between the category and the brand. Regardless of actual market shares, these brands have mindshare leadership.

More than 85 percent of communications contain **information**, and most of it is about the product or service being advertised.[8] The overall goal of information communications is to get the target audience to acquire specific knowledge about the brand. Strategic information communications is focused on the overall "why" of the brand and its differentiating benefit, not just any features and benefits.

Behavioral communications aim to motivate people to take a particular action, such as to go to a website, post on social media, call a toll-free number, or make a purchase. The language-learning brand Rosetta Stone uses bright yellow in its advertisements and displays messages like "Call

Now" or "Buy Now" to create a sense of urgency around learning a foreign language. Its longer television and web-based commercials depict vignettes of people landing in a foreign country and immediately falling in love with a local, hence the urgency to speak the language.

Finally, an **image** objective is that of a brand that seeks to get its current customers to become advocates, which happens when they identify with the brand. Achieving image is a complex process. It requires personalizing the brand, developing vocal advocates who are influencers or celebrities or otherwise admired by the target audience. Image objectives focus on developing intimacy with real customers. Image objectives can be achieved by both direct-to-consumer and professional brands. Caterpillar, the earth-moving equipment company, has achieved this objective with some of their customers, a few of whom tattoo their machines on their bodies. The surgeon customers of Gore Medical Products feel supported and align with the values and mission of the organization. A vascular surgeon recently told me she was a "Gore girl," she felt so intimately connected to that brand. The Dove Beauty image campaign, launched in 2006, featured female customers in underwear under the banner "Real Beauty." The goal was to normalize real female anatomy as a way to lift women and girl's self-esteem, while presenting Dove as an ally in this mission.

Communications objectives naturally develop along the customer journey. Your particular strategy, however, will focus your investment in one or two of these objectives at a time (see Figure 7.6).

Once you have determined your communications objective and located your target audience, develop content and orchestrate how to reach your target audience through the right channels.

What to Say: Communications Content

Your content strategy refers to the specific communications assets, the "what" of your communications. With the advent of social media, customers expect authenticity when interacting with a brand's content. Unfortunately, a surprisingly large number of companies outsource content creation to a third party, and as a result may appear less than honest in their communications.[9]

Communications content stems from the execution of your "reasons to believe" plan developed in the Beliefs stage discussed in Chapter 6, and includes evidence about your brand, a specific product or service and its

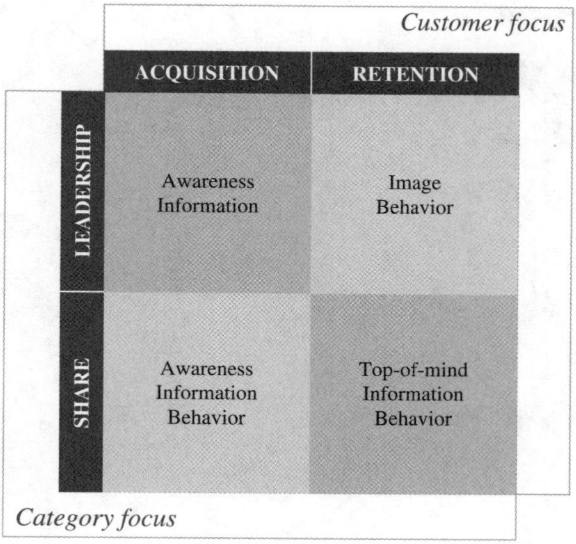

	Customer focus	
	ACQUISITION	**RETENTION**
LEADERSHIP	Awareness Information	Image Behavior
SHARE	Awareness Information Behavior	Top-of-mind Information Behavior

Category focus

FIGURE 7.6 Communications and the four go-to-market strategies.
The four go-to-market strategies correspond to specific communications objectives.

components, your customers, and shared interest data that showcases your team's expertise within your business category. Figure 7.7 presents examples of content types that may be used.

Content can be repurposed across multiple customer journey steps. Carefully consider how to best align content types to specific communications objectives and customer stakeholder targets.

How to Reach Your Target Audience: Communications Channels

Communications channels are the conduits that deliver content to your target customer. To effectively use communications channels, first you must know where target customers habitually interact with brands in the category. Gather this information as part of your target audience persona interviews, or through your customer journey mapping research. Although customers receive communications through a variety of channels daily, focus on channels that are most capable of succeeding relative to your communications objective and message (see Figure 7.8 for examples).

Customer Journey	Awareness & Need Recognition	Search / Compare	Trial & Purchase	Initial & Habitual Use	Reflect & Recommend
Communications objective	• Awareness	• Information	• Top-of-mind awareness • Behavior	• Information • Behavior	• Image • Behavior • Top-of-mind awareness
Content types:	• Brand equity • Customer context • Shared Interest	• Product / solution • Customer context • Shared Interest	• Customer context • Product/ solution	• Product/ solution • Customer context	• Brand equity • Customer context
Content purpose:	• Ignite a need and drive interest • Frame consideration set	• Deliver benefit (USP) • Convince • Differentiate brand • Drive choice	• Gain stake-holder approval • Motivate action • Show economic value of the solution	• Engage, inform, support the customer in initial usage • Ensure a positive experience	• Remind customers about the positives • Encourage advocacy

Customer Journey	Awareness & Need Recognition	Search / Compare	Trial & Purchase	Initial & Habitual Use	Reflect & Recommend
Format Examples: Content listed to the right can be delivered and re-purposed across multiple stages of the communications plan.	☐ Videos ☐ Print/digital advertisements ☐ SEO & paid search ☐ Social content: tweets, stories ☐ Blogs ☐ Webinars ☐ Infographics ☐ Interviews/podcasts ☐ Press/news ☐ Newsletters ☐ Presentations ☐ Product placement	☐ Brochures, Infographics, ebooks, guides ☐ Demo videos ☐ White papers ☐ Clinical studies ☐ Articles ☐ Evaluation tools ☐ Data sheets ☐ Case studies ☐ Testimonials ☐ Ratings & reviews ☐ User-generated content	☐ ROI tools/calculators ☐ Case studies ☐ Evaluation tools ☐ Tailored presentations ☐ Solution demos ☐ Stakeholder education/training	☐ Training videos ☐ Tip sheets ☐ In-service (personal and non-personal) ☐ Call center messaging ☐ Sales/technical support messaging ☐ Customer satisfaction surveys	☐ Targeted communications (e.g., email, text) ☐ Peer-to-peer advocacy/testimonials

FIGURE 7.7 Content types along the customer journey.

181

Communications Channels	Awareness & Need Recognition	Search / Compare	Trial & Purchase	Initial & Habitual Use	Reflect & Recommend
Objective	• Awareness	• Information	• Top-of-mind awareness • Behavior	• Information • Behavior	• Image • Behavior • Top-of-mind awareness
Priority:	• Deliver content to wide audience. • Place brand in relevant context.	• Achieve ubiquity without over-exposing the brand. • Use channels that are "positional" to the brand.	• Use appropriate conduit to reach specific stakeholders.	• Use multiple channels to enable customer support and feedback.	• Amplify brand message. • Enable advocacy.
Examples:	☐ Digital (earned/paid): Websites, blogs, newsletters ☐ Social (earned/paid): FB/Instagram, Twitter, LinkedIn, WeChat, online communities ☐ Print: magazines, journals ☐ Online and In-person events: conferences, symposia, webinars, livestreams ☐ Sponsorships ☐ Email ☐ TV and radio	☐ Online search ☐ Brand website ☐ Digital (earned/paid) ☐ Social (owned pages): YouTube, FB/Instagram, LinkedIn, Slide share ☐ Influencers ☐ Podcasts	☐ Sales and technical representatives ☐ Brand website ☐ Targeted meetings/events ☐ Distribution outlets	☐ Sales and technical representatives ☐ Brand website ☐ Call center ☐ Podcasts ☐ Newsletters	☐ Word of mouth: peers, influencers ☐ Digital/social ☐ Targeted emails

FIGURE 7.8 Channel types along the customer journey.

Channels need to be carefully aligned to the communications objective and content delivered at each stage of the customer journey.

Public channels are useful at the outset of the customer journey, when your focus is customer acquisition. Banner ads, journal print advertising, sponsorships and trade shows, and web and TV advertising are capable of reaching a broad audience and creating exposure for your brand. Some of them are also capable of efficiently broadcasting short brand messages to create awareness.

To convey more complex messaging and encourage customers to move into the *search and compare* phase of their journeys, transition to **participatory channels.** Social media channels like Twitter or LinkedIn, as well as organic and paid search, can facilitate engagement and two-way information exchange. Of course, carefully plan your web presence to maximize your customers' search success. Although most large companies invest in paid search, it is critical to the trust in your brand to manage content carefully to maximize organic search results.

Finally, **private channels** such as text, email, and web, and direct sales are designed for two-way synchronous communication and are appropriate once the customer is engaged with the brand through a clear indication of serious consideration. And certainly, private channels are appropriate once customers have solicited a trial, have further committed through a purchase, or have engaged more deeply in a contractual relationship. In these stages of the customer relationship, private communications channels afford customers the opportunity for greater intimacy.

No content strategy is complete without a solid interdependent channel strategy.

Carefully align channel types to specific communications objectives, content, and customer stakeholder targets.

Category Development Strategies: Creating the Category Narrative

If you are launching a brand to create a new category, focus on *awareness* and *information* objectives. Communicate first to create awareness of the category and to gain attention. In the initial stages of your brand's communication plan, create excitement about the innovation, and almost immediately establish credibility by showing your brand's ability to deliver on the promise the category establishes. Tesla did this by leveraging its well-heeled investors and its celebrity CEO, who took to mass communication channels to announce the launch of the first luxury all-electric car. It then also established credibility by holding VIP-only events to showcase its technology and invite celebrities to purchase its vehicles.

Brand-Switching Strategies: Motivating Customers to Consider Alternatives

The communications plan for a brand-switching strategy must focus on capturing the attention and interest of customers currently engaged with the competitive brand you are targeting. This strategy will still primarily focus on *awareness and information* objectives while placing your brand as a plausible alternative to the competitive brand. To do this, you need to be in the same communications channels as the targeted brand and provide content that first amplifies latent dissatisfaction and later presents your brand as a better alternative. You must establish a performance or cost advantage.

Apple first gathered attention for its Macintosh computer through its famous 1984 commercial, where PCs were impersonated by a Big Brother voiceover. This was effective in creating awareness.

Once awareness is established, you should pivot to an *information* objective, communicating searchable differences between your brand and the competitive product or service. Apple did this while continuing to amplify dissatisfaction in the 1990s by articulating that PCs were unintuitive and prone to viruses. It used television and print, and later billboards, to successively create attention, amplify dissatisfaction, and offer a solution in its computers. Once information has been delivered to target customers to get them engaged in a search process, the strategy moves to a *behavioral* objective, asking target customers to switch brands.

Brand Commitment Strategies: Creating Top-of-Mind Awareness

When executing a brand commitment strategy, focus on *behavior, top-of-mind awareness,* and *information* as communication objectives. You are communicating to current customers of your brand who are also purchasing or using other brands. *Awareness* has already been established; now deliver *information* to increase relative preference for your brand. 5-Hour Energy ran a share-focused campaign relative to coffee showing that 5-Hour energy is preferable to coffee some mornings, when there just is no time to make coffee.

When multibrand usage is due to relative availability or convenience, also create *top-of-mind awareness.* As mentioned earlier in the chapter, an aim of a brand commitment strategy is to increase your share of customers' spend and commitment, by increasing your brand's mindshare. *Top-of-mind awareness* is important in categories where the brand that comes to a customer's mind first is the one that gets pulled off the shelf, in categories like beer and soda, and other impulse items. In business-to-business environments, *top-of-mind awareness* might also be critical if the brand that comes to mind gets the first call when request-for-proposal terms are being developed or if competitive products are also in distribution and being pulled off a shelf, as in a hospital environment.

Brand Expansion Strategies: Getting Customers to Identify with the Brand

For these strategies, move from delivering information to delivering either *image* or *behavior*. This is because information keeps people in a cognitive state. To inspire customer loyalty, move people away from evaluating your brand rationally on features and benefits because that is where your brand is most vulnerable to the competition. Volvo succeeded in lifting its customers into emotional loyalty by executing image-focused communications. Since the 1980s, it has focused on appealing to its customers' identities as safe drivers, people who take care of their families, rather than simply providing features and functional benefits.[10]

Distribution Channels: Managing Delivery of the Brand Experience

Channels are systems of interdependent organizations, and they establish how you go to market; they are *how* the brand experience gets delivered. When thinking about the ways to reach target customers, first design all touchpoints between the brand and the customer based on your overall brand customer experience. Controlling the delivery of the brand experience affords the opportunity to forge deeper and more knowing relationships with customers.

Sadly, in most of our client companies, channel management is not a marketing function. Managing sales and distribution generally rests with sales leadership, and, unfortunately, channel structure decisions are heavily weighted by short-term efficiency considerations. While efficiency is a necessary component of effective channel management, to design an optimal channel, first consider the ideal customer experience you wish to create, and then construct a structure that optimally balances cost and benefit.

Last, there is the issue of conflict. Distribution channels are mired in conflict because they involve organizations with different motivations and incentives. An important goal of the Big Picture Strategy approach is to integrate distribution channels into the brand strategy, designing channels by first considering the desired brand customer experience.

Using the Brand Customer Experience Map to Design Touchpoints

As with the other elements in execution, the starting point in channel design is the brand customer experience map (Figure 7.1). Start the work of channel design by carefully mapping all the interactions needed between the brand and the customer. Your go-to-market strategic choice is helpful, as the number and location of your customer touchpoints depend on whether you are establishing a new category, leading in an established category, or competing against another brand.

If executing a category leadership strategy, ideate customer touchpoints from a white-canvas perspective, that is, re-imagining how to interact with customers. However, if focused on earning share from a competitor, consider the expectations that brand has already established as to how customers interact in the category. In this case, it may be more efficient to follow the path predetermined by your competitor, unless your differentiating benefit is directly related to distribution. This was the case with Dell in the 1990s. The company executed a share-focused strategy against more traditional computer manufacturers like HP and IBM by going directly to consumers and offering the opportunity to purchase computers with customized components.

In building a map for customer touchpoints, describe the substance of the interaction in terms of three channel flows: product, money/risk, and information. Although efficient management of money and tangible products flows is critical to the health of a brand, it is the information flow that has the most long-term strategic value. Emerging as a channel leader requires the ability to innovate based on end-consumer needs and to directly measure and communicate the value you contribute to that end user. Intel processors, Gore-Tex fabrics, and Vibram shoe soles are examples of ingredient brands that increase consumers' willingness to pay for products because consumers recognize their value. All three companies invest considerable resources in conducting end-user research and in communicating directly to the end consumer. Once your ideal customer touchpoints are designed, think through an ideal channel structure.

Channel Structure

Channel structure answers questions regarding who will be involved in interacting with customers and how they will be organized. There are three dimensions to channel structure: length, breadth, and depth.

Length refers to the number of channel members involved in reaching the end consumer. At the extremes, your brand may go direct or indirect: in a direct sales channel your employees are the only people selling and handling customer interactions, while in an indirect channel, distributors are handling those tasks. Companies use intermediaries for a combination of cost and specialized skills. When first going to market, either because you are creating a new category or entering a new geography, hiring salespeople and establishing logistics flows, like transportation and warehousing, can be daunting and expensive. In some categories, there are logistics partners who possess specialized skills to perform those tasks and who may be able to execute them more efficiently as well.

In a customer-acquisition strategy, indirect channels can help the brand by increasing its capacity to penetrate a market or customer segment. In a customer-retention strategy, conversely, going direct to customers affords the brand greater control: direct access to customers can be key to improving products and services and helpful in establishing brand loyalty. You not only need to worry about who will be involved in your channel, but also how available your brand will be – its breadth.

Breadth refers to the availability of your brand to customers. Will you be ubiquitous (intensive), or harder to find (selective)? A brand that is distributed intensely is much more visible than one that is distributed selectively. Of course, being widely distributed is key in some categories, such as perishables or those requiring frequent in-person service. Beyond category considerations, whether to make your brand widely available also depends on whether you are seeking to build heart loyalty by making your brand seem exclusive. Of course, brands perceived as being sophisticated are not immediately available everywhere.

In the early 2000s, Starbucks had pioneered the premium coffee category and developed an ardent following. Over the last decade, the brand went from being *selectively* distributed to being *intensively* distributed, adding more than 20,000 outlets. The company's increased revenue base is undoubtedly key to its share price growth: Starbucks' share prices grew fivefold in the decade between 2010 and 2020.[11]

Depth is the degree of control over channel partners. You may want to own all intermediary agents (such as distribution networks or financing partners), you may control their actions as much as possible through long-term iron-clad contracts, or you may have more casual relationships.

Here again, ownership is costly and less flexible. However, consider exerting control over touchpoints that help establish differentiation for your brand while outsourcing those that are less central to your positioning. Starbucks aims to deliver a premium coffeeshop experience. As such, it either owns its stores or licenses them to certified and tightly-monitored retail partners who promise to abide by its brand standards and agree to the company's controls. This level of supervision is not necessary for its packaged products, which represent a brand extension. In fact, Starbucks sold its packaged coffee business to Nestlé in 2018.[12]

Channel Benefits

The purpose of a distribution channel is to augment the commercial competences of your organization by helping you deliver the parts of the customer experience that your organization cannot do as well as a specialized or more efficient alternative.

Distribution channels offer product and service value, time convenience and place convenience/availability as follows:

1. **Product and Service Value:**
   - **Package sizing and amount.** Channel members break down large quantities and enable customers to purchase exactly the amounts they desire.
   - **Variety or assortment.** Dealers and distributors (for B2B customers) and retailers (for B2C) may offer a one-stop-shop experience (variety) or a selected group of brands that fit the needs of specific customer segments (assortment).
   - **Customer service.** Value-added services to the customer include assistance in purchasing, restocking, record-keeping, or using the product or service.

- **Information and education.** Pre-purchase or post-purchase education features enable the customer to maximize the value they derive from the brand.
- **Lower financial risk.** Channel members can lower financial risk to end consumers and also help them better manage their cash flow (for example, through leasing or subscription programs).

2. Time convenience: Channel members can shorten waiting and delivery times, to purchase or receive a product or service.

3. Place convenience / availability: This refers to the distance between the customer and the channel outlet to obtain, use, or service the product or service.

The above are general categories; as you work through your customer touchpoint maps, you can be more specific about the exact benefit exchange in each. Now that we have established some ways to organize channel structure decisions and channel benefits, we can think about how each of the four go-to-market strategies interact with them (see Figure 7.9).

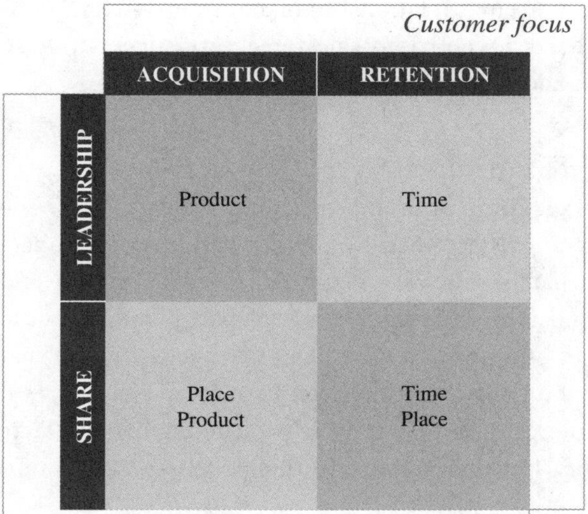

FIGURE 7.9 Benefits of distribution channels and the four go-to-market strategies.

Structure distribution channels to emphasize different benefits depending on your go-to-market strategy.

Category Development: Establishing Go-to-Market Infrastructure

When executing a category development strategy, build your channel with two ideas in mind: maximizing category penetration while establishing your brand as the leader in the new category. To achieve these dual aims, set up a channel capable of *availability* and *information / education delivery*. If being a first mover is important because customers become sticky to the first brand they use within a category, build a channel utilizing *indirect distribution* and maximizing *breadth* to ensure your target customers can find your brand, try it, and purchase it easily. If your product or service is at all complex, arm the channel member with *information dissemination* and *educational* resources to ease the adoption of your category and brand. Sometimes these two goals are somewhat incongruent; despite the need to build scale quickly to get ahead of other premium car brands and also to become financially viable, Tesla decided to avoid car dealerships and instead created stores. They believed customer intimacy was necessary for adoption, and they did not want to outsource the initial service encounter to a third party.

Using a virtual salesforce can help with both *availability and education*. The leader in cloud-based customer relationship management (CRM) software, salesforce.com, utilized a web-based salesforce very successfully to sign up and educate small and medium-sized businesses.

Brand Switching Strategies: Relative Availability

As mentioned earlier, if executing an brand switching strategy, study the customer touchpoints already established by the brand whose customers you seek. Ask yourself what benefits are being delivered by whom and where. Then categorize those benefits into points of parity and potential points of differentiation. In other words, establish a channel structure that matches that of your competitor in some ways, yet in other ways diverges if that divergence enables you to better deliver your positioning benefit. Here again, prioritize *availability*, but now relative to the brand whose customers you seek.

When seeking competitive conversions, being available is sometimes opportune: your brand may be purchased when the competitive brand is out of stock or experiences a failure. A key to the growth of the Vizio brand in televisions in the early 2000s was due in part to its distribution focus. The brand placed its TVs, which looked almost exactly like Sonys and

Samsungs, in the same stores (Costco and Sam's Club) and literally next to its competitors. Customers looking for an LCD TV could afford a 47-inch Vizio for the price of a 32-inch Sony.[13]

Brand Commitment Strategies: Relative Ubiquity

When working to increase the commitment multibrand customers make to your brand, add variety or convenience to improve their relative experience of using it versus a competitor's. Your distribution channel focus will depend on which path you pursue. If you are enhancing customers' experiences by adding functional variety, train the sales and distribution channel to deliver that experience. Their focus then may be on *product variety* or *assortment*. Streaming services like Netflix direct specific message customers about content that is similar to other content they have viewed as a way to increase their share of viewership versus competitive streaming services.

If you elect to lift commitment by making your brand more visible or convenient at the point of purchase or use, the distribution channel should focus on delivering *availability and timeliness* relative to the competitive brand you are seeking to displace. Amazon uses its customers' browsing history to display ads that specifically target them and redirect them to Amazon.com to make a purchase. Many customers visit a brand's website to conduct product research but, having seen Amazon's offer, will go to Amazon to finalize the transaction and take advantage of its convenient payment and shipping features.

Brand Expansion Strategies: Serving Up the Brand

Loyal customers generally know how to find your brand and how to call for service and supplies. Given that loyalty has already been established, consider becoming more selective, that is, having fewer points of distribution. Also, as part of your brand expansion strategy, it is natural to sell more value-added services or to try to engage customers through a subscription rather than an outright sale. Customers who know and trust the brand are more likely to be willing to engage on a longer-term committed relationship through a subscription. When executing a brand expansion strategy, the brand's channel focus is to deliver *timely customer service* to facilitate upgrades and longer-term contractual relationships with the customer. The Michelin tire brand offers its small fleet and truck owner–operator customers the option of joining its Advantage Program. Michelin Advantage, in turn, offers 24/7 roadside assistance, lowest price guarantees across the Michelin dealer network, and order tracking and productivity tools to improve the longevity of trucking tires.

Regardless of the go-to-market strategy you choose, anytime you use channel partners you are subject to conflict, due to divergent motivations and goals. Channel leaders emerge from managing that conflict and organizing the channel to maximize profitability and value to the end consumer.

Managing Channel Conflict

Proactively manage channel conflict by assembling a complete list of all channel members, and then conducing an analysis of their capabilities, cost added to the final product versus the benefit to the end consumer, and the motivations of each. Then think through how to best align each of the channel members through training, incentives (payments and contracts), and sharing of information (end-customer satisfaction and other total channel cost and financial metrics). This type of analysis, for a car-buying customer experience, is shown in Figure 7.10.

Aligning channel members requires understanding their role – and benefit to the end consumer – as well as their motivations.

Channel Member	Role and Skills	Benefit to End Consumer	Motivation (Goals/ Needs)	Alignment Actions
Manu-facturer salesforce	Manage product development, availability and dealer relationships	• Product	Maximize commission	• Back-end incentives to encourage support of profitable dealers
Dealers	Manage customer relationship (acquisition and retention)	• Product • Time • Place	Relationship/ customer lifetime value	• Profit incentives • Second-car purchase incentives • Referral incentives

Channel Member	Role and Skills	Benefit to End Consumer	Motivation (Goals/ Needs)	Alignment Actions
Dealer used car departments	• Used car valuation, negotiations, used car wholesale sales • Facilitate purchase by offering competitive trade-in	• Product • Time	Short-term profit	• Sales reporting in exchange for limited promo $ • Training support
Internet info sites	• Enable customer research • Car evaluation / review • Car valuation • Market data acquisition and analysis	• Information	Unique visitors / distribution	• Training and new product introduction "peak preview" • Co-promotional dollars
Mini financial services	• Underwriting and documentation	• Financing fees • Time - product		• Collaborate on a model-by-model basis through co-financing offers

FIGURE 7.10 Aligning your channel partners.

	Awareness & Need Recognition	Search & Compare Alternatives	Trial & Purchase	Initial & Habitual Use	Reflect & Recommend
Desired Behaviors (What, where, how?)	I will learn more about at-home boutique exercising with Peloton.	I will trial the digital app and go in-store to ride the bike.	I will purchase a Peloton bike and subscription/accessories.	I have taken a variety of classes and instructors in the first two weeks.	I refer friends, take classes with them, and engage others on leaderboard (high-five, follow).
Desired Beliefs (Why?)	There is now an at-home alternative to spinning at my local boutique studio.	The Peloton bike is high-quality and there's a variety of quality exercise content beyond just spinning.	The quality and variety of classes will make the bike/subscription economical on a per use basis.	I get all of the benefits of boutique fitness at my home, on my schedule.	Peloton is more than an exercise bike, it's a community.
Executional Emphasis:					
Solutions	New retail stores Develop Peloton Apparel	Digital content app Hotel gym trials	Installation service Set up video tutorials	10,000+ classes Customized content High-five feature Video chat feature #Tags, Challenges	Referral program Homecoming event (NYC) Celebratory rides: Holidays, Pride, Ethnic Heritage,....) High-five feature Merchandise
Price			Value-based vs. premium gym memberships		
		30-day free app trial, Monthly pricing option for equipment Digital app introductory price, "$100 refer a friend" Bundled accessories trial offers		Flat household pricing Referral program	
Communications: Content	Product videos Product placement: (Olympics) Product reviews	Product demos/info In-store trial Peloton app content	Financing tools Accessory details Trial follow-up	Peloton quick start guide Peloton tips Monthly workout summary	Milestone shoutouts Spotify Peloton playlists
Communications: Channels	Social (paid), Word of mouth, TV, Fitness magazines, Events	Brand website Retail stores Social media sites (owned)	Retail stores Brand website Customer service	Delivery rep Email, App Brand website	Email Brand website (owned) Socials (owned), WOM

FIGURE 7.11 Brand experience and execution for Peloton.

Use the brand customer experience map to ensure execution is aligned to the belief and behavior change stipulated by your marketing strategy.

Summary: Aligning the Brand and the Customer Journeys

Perhaps the most important word to an organization seeking to deliver a consistent and differentiated customer experience is *alignment*. Your organization needs to internalize its go-to-market strategy to be able to execute it well. The brand customer journey, built around the belief and behavioral changes you wish to motivate as expressed in the brand's value proposition, is a powerful tool to bring about that alignment.

In this chapter, I used two powerful tools to align strategy and execution: the customer journey map and the four go-to-market strategies. The work of execution starts by designing a brand customer experience that articulates the value proposition to target customers at each step of their journeys with the brand. With the brand customer experience on hand, you need to work with your cross-functional team to layer in executional tools that can close the gap between the current customer journey and that desired experience.

Accordingly, the brand customer experience serves as a wireframe to organize the sequence of your major executional priorities (Figure 7.11). Ultimately, great strategy without execution is a useless exercise, and great execution without a strategy is a missed learning opportunity. Both strategy and execution must be integrated to maximize your chances of learning and sustained growth for your organization.

8 Benchmarks: Learning from Our Work

Whether creating a new category, igniting investment in an existing one, or working to grow your brand at the expense of a competitor, sustaining brand performance requires a tight alignment of strategy and execution. **Strategy** is your long-term plan – based on a series of logical hypotheses – about the best way to take your brand to market to achieve a goal. **Execution** is all the organizational behaviors performed in service of achieving that goal.

Great strategy without execution equates to unrealized potential. Great execution without a strategy can deliver short-term performance but, as market conditions change, is unlikely to sustainably continue to deliver. The reason is simple: lacking a feedback loop between actual organizational behaviors – as experienced externally by the market – and the plan that drives them, the company will just run in place not getting anywhere.

The image the comes to mind when I think of an organization that doesn't integrate strategy and execution is that of a hiker in a deep forest running in circuitous loops. To avoid this, you need **metrics**: tools that quantify actions or trends. Organizations are complex systems that operate in broader and even more complex markets. Metrics establish learning processes that guide the organization in its path toward its particular goals.

Within the Big Picture Strategy method, marketing metrics are the tools used to confirm or disprove the hypotheses that underpin your strategy (building intelligence about market trends, competition, customers), operationalize those strategies, and evaluate their results. We call these metrics strategy-integrated metrics, or SIMs.

Using Marketing Metrics to Evaluate Strategy

Developing a go-to-market strategy is always uncertain, despite the fact that market data is proliferating. That's because more information does not necessarily correlate to more knowledge. Transforming information into knowledge requires asking the right questions, rather than making assumptions.

The Big Picture framework, through the 6Bs system of integrated choices, provides a structured approach to such go-to-market inquiries. Once the 6Bs questions are framed, use metrics to assess opportunity, reducing uncertainty. Figure 8.1 shows the fundamental metrics you can use to evaluate and select a strategy, among the four archetypes presented in Chapter 2.

This dashboard shows some of the most common metrics used to assess the worthiness of a go-to-market strategy relative to alternatives as well as to assess progress in the execution of a particular strategy, as it is operationalized.

Although specific benchmarks may be specific to each strategy, here are some of the fundamental metrics you need to know.

Brand

- **Brand awareness and top-of-mind awareness.** This is the percentage of the target population that is aware of or mentions your brand. It is simple recognition, while top-of-mind awareness requires unaided brand recall. Measuring brand awareness used to require performing surveys; however, today you can also use analytical tools to listen for your brand name in social media and web channels.
- **Brand preference.** The percentage of your target population that *prefers* your brand. You can use surveys combined with social listening to develop measures that go beyond mere mentions to emotional associations. What is the chatter on Twitter, LinkedIn, or Facebook? Are the conversations and mentions in blog posts and websites positive? Are the online reviews of your brand positive?
- **Brand associations.** What are the specific associations that your target customers have with your brand? Use social listening tools and search data to understand the words most often associated with your brand, and their emotional tenor.

Strategy	Brand	Bodies	Business Category	Beliefs	Behaviors	Financial Benchmarks
Brand Development	• Brand awareness • Brand preference among non-users • Brand associations	• # non-customer qualified leads • # non-customers at each step in the customer journey: awareness and searching; trialing / educated; using (multibrand vs. loyal); retained (repurchasing); advocating	• Total available market (TAM) • Category size (#, $); also called total addressable or served market • % category penetration (categorize size/total available market)	• Awareness, attitudes, and usage (AAU) • Category benefit importance and perception ratings • Customer satisfaction score (CSAT)	• # inquiries • # customers trained • # trials; trial rate (trials / qualified leads) • # new customers from outside category • $ revenue from new customers • Acquisition rate	• Dollar or unit sales • Acquired customer $ margin

FIGURE 8.1 Key 6Bs metrics by go-to-market strategy.

Strategy	Brand	Bodies	Business Category	Beliefs	Behaviors	Financial Benchmarks
Brand Switching	• Brand awareness • Brand preference among competitive customers • Brand development index (BDI)	• # competitive customer qualified leads • # competitive customers at each step in the customer journey	• Brand served market (brand size / category size) • Unit or revenue market share; relative market share • Brand penetration (# brand procedures/ # available in account)	• Differentiating benefit importance and perception ratings	• # inquiries or trials from competitive customers • # customers acquired; competitive acquisition rate (%)	• Unit or revenue market share • Competitive prospect CLV
Brand Commitment	• Brand top-of-mind awareness • Brand preference among multibrand customers • Brand development index (BDI)	• # multibrand customers (or as % of total customers) • % head loyal; % hand loyal (or #)	• Brand served market (brand size / category size) • Category development index	• Differentiating benefit importance and perception ratings	• $ purchases by multibrand customers • # incremental product purchases by multibrand customers • % heavy usage index	• Unit or revenue share of wallet • Retained customer margin ($ or %) • Multibrand customer CLV

Brand Expansion					
• Brand value • Brand top-of-mind awareness	• # retained customers (or retention rate %) • Attrition rate	• Category size (total addressable or served market)	• Category benefit importance and perception ratings • % top-of-mind awareness • % heart loyal • Customer satisfaction score (CSAT) or net promoter score (NPS)	• # or $ purchases per customer/ total # or $ brand sales • % upgraded • % heavy usage index • % multiple product or relationship customers • Contract utilization rate ($ or # units / $ or # contracted) • Retention rate • Willingness to search	• # or $ per retained customer • $ CLV • $ profit • $ retention cost/ customer • Retained customer $ margin

FIGURE 8.1 (Continued)

- **Brand development index (BDI).**[1] BDI is an index of how well your brand performs within a specific customer group or subcategory—or within a specific targeted segment—as compared to how it performs in the broader customer group or category (or market). This is a useful metric if creating a new category by drawing from a broader one, as Tesla did from luxury cars or Peloton did from boutique fitness gyms.

$$BDI = \dfrac{\left(\dfrac{\text{Subcategory brand sales (\$)}}{\text{Subcategory customers}} \right)}{\left(\dfrac{\text{Total category brand sales (\$)}}{\text{Total customers}} \right)}$$

- **Brand value or equity.** Conceptually, the value of your brand should translate into higher prices for your products (if positioned on a performance, service, or other premium benefit) or higher sales than your competitors (if positioned on an operational excellence or cost-related benefit). Unfortunately, brand equity is difficult to measure. The BAV Group uses a tool it calls the Brand Asset Valuator, a survey that combines customers' perceptions on four dimensions: differentiation (specific associations with the brand that are different from those with competitors), relevance (connection of the brand to its target customers), esteem (consumers' attraction to the brand), and knowledge (awareness and understanding of its positioning).

  Develop your own brand value index by multiplying customer importance and perception scores on the category benefits across you and your competitors. This is the information used in Chapter 6 to develop a category plot. Although this method may not be scientifically sound in terms of estimating the actual value of your brand, tracking this brand value proxy over time and asking why it may be trending up or down can be enlightening. It is akin to measuring your weight on a scale that doesn't weigh accurately but keeps the proportions constant—the absolute number may not be valid, but the measurements are reliable and therefore changes are informative.

Business Category

Although traditional approaches to marketing may simply accept existing category definitions, the Big Picture Strategy method places category definition at the core of strategic choice. In developing brand strategy, you can act like a category leader or take share from another brand, and this decision is dependent on the definition of the category. It is likely you will choose a category leadership strategy if your market share or mindshare in the category is dominant and you have a large number of loyal customers (brand expansion strategy). You may also choose a leadership strategy if you redefine category boundaries because you have a significant innovation that brings new benefits to customers, (*category development strategy*).

Alternatively, select a strategy that allows another brand to lead the category and focus on growing your brand at the expense of a competitor (in a brand-switching or brand commitment strategy).

Either way, assess the size of your business category relative to your brand and agree on how to measure category leadership. Set metrics that will trigger a reconsideration of your strategic focus (leadership or share) as your relative position in the category changes.

Here are some of the key metrics to use relative to the business category:

- **Total available market (TAM).** Defining the available and addressable market is akin to delineating who in the world has a need for the benefits your category delivers. Within that group, identify who you would compel to join the category so as to obtain those benefits. The difficulty in measuring TAM varies depending on the category. People may be unaware that they have a particular need—in health care, people may be unaware that they are suffering from a disease or may not report it if they do due to a variety of reasons. Either way, TAM is generally measured in either number of people or potential unit sales.
- **Category size** (or addressable or served market). This is the portion of the total available market, the category, within which your brand competes. As discussed in Chapter 3, narrow categories are defined around the product or service you sell. Broader categories are generally defined around the benefit the product or service brings to customers. It is generally easier to measure narrow categories using dollars or units, whereas broader categories may require that you estimate the number of potential customers.

    Peloton could estimate the dollars or number of subscriptions sold in the *at-home boutique fitness category*, as the brand competes against similar brands, including Northface, FlyWheel, Hydrow, and Echelon. To estimate the category in terms of boutique fitness enthusiasts, Peloton could also investigate the sales of franchise fitness studios and then also look up independent studios in major metropolitan areas.

- **Category penetration.** This is the number of customers in a product category as a percentage of customers in the total available market. If selling cochlear implants for moderate to severe deafness, measure the number of people wearing cochlear implants as a percentage of the population who suffer from moderate or severe deafness of the inner ear, and who are indicated to wear cochlear implants.
- **Category development index.** This index measures category sales within a specific subcategory or customer segment relative to sales of the brand in the broader category (or addressable market). This index can give a sense of whether your segmentation strategy is yielding the effectiveness hoped for. If you were targeting surgeons who perform complex procedures within a disease state, were you successful in penetrating that specific segment? Calculate the category development index using the following formula (note that you can substitute sales units for sales dollars).

$$\text{Category development index} = \frac{\left(\dfrac{\text{Category sales to a group}(\$)}{\text{Customers in the group}(\#)}\right)}{\left(\dfrac{\text{Total category sales}(\$)}{\text{Total customers in category}(\#)}\right)}$$

- **Category share (market share).** Share metrics are generally referred to as *market share*; however, given the brand strategy focus of the 6Bs approach, the external context unit of analysis is the category rather than the broader market. As a result, I use the terms *revenue category* and *unit category share.*
  - **Revenue category share.** Sales revenue as a percentage of category sales revenue. Revenue share is also called value share.

$$\text{Revenue category share} = \frac{\text{Brand dollar sales }(\$)}{\text{Total category dollar sales }(\$)}$$

- **Unit category share.** Unit sales as a percentage of unit sales. Unit share is also called volume share.

$$\text{Unit category share} = \frac{\text{Brand unit sales }(\#)}{\text{Total category unit sales }(\#)}$$

- **Relative category share.** Brand share of the category divided by largest competitor share of the category. Relative category share gives a sense of your brand's relative competitive strength. It is preferable to a simple market-share metric if you are trying to decide whether to select a category leadership or share-focused strategy. Remember that share-focused strategies require not only that your brand be small relative to the category opportunity, but that there be a larger brand that customers consider an exemplar for the category.

$$\text{Relative category share} = \frac{\text{Brand's category share (\%)}}{\text{Largest brand category share (\%)}}$$

- **Brand penetration.** Understand the relative acceptance of your brand among a target customer group (the entire category or a segment). Brand penetration is calculated by dividing the number of customers buying your brand by the total number of target customers.

Bodies

To measure the effectiveness of your marketing strategy, you need to measure how well you do in identifying qualified prospects and in moving them through each of the steps of the customer journey. Importantly, to select a strategic focus, categorize potential customers into prospects, competitive targets, retained customers, and multibrand customers, and assess how attractive each of these groups is to your commercial organization.

Construct a specific customer conversion funnel for your brand, following the categories that illustrate your brand's customer journey, including qualified leads; potential customers aware of your brand; potential customers actively searching for your brand or requesting proposals; customers engaged in final product selection; customers under contract; customers who have been trained, or are installing or using; satisfied customers willing to recommend your brand; or full-fledged advocates for your brand. Ideally, track customers as they filter through the funnel, assessing how many are in each stage of the journey, and what internal and external factors impact their progress toward loyalty and advocacy. Figure 8.2 illustrates such a funnel.

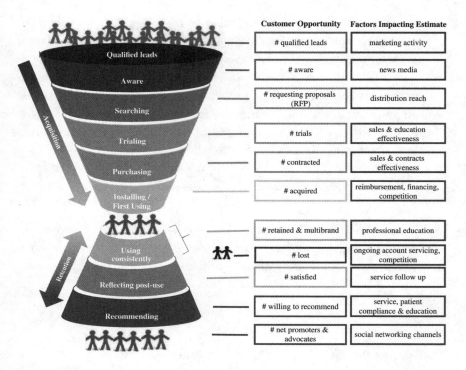

FIGURE 8.2 The customer opportunity funnel: tracking customer journey progress.

Develop a customer opportunity funnel to share with your entire organization to track (and celebrate) your team's successes in helping customers progress through their journeys.

A customer is not simply someone who purchases or uses your brand. You should think about developing brand-specific definitions for the following:

- **Loyal customers** must both *behave* (buy, use, receive, or recommend) in a way that results in profitability (frequently enough or with sufficient spend) and *believe* in the brand (prefer it to competitive alternatives).
- **Multibrand customers** rely on the brand but do so at a lower level than loyal customers. Establish what that level is for your brand as well as other brands they use. Communicate the degree of brand

loyalty by counting the number of loyal and multibrand customers or express those metrics as a percentage of your customer base. A loyal customer may or may not be buying your brand exclusively. Conversely, depending on how you sell your brand, exclusive use may also not equate to loyalty. If in your category, customers purchase sole-source contracts, you may be locking out competitors but not gaining the customer's preference for your brand.

- **B2B customer stakeholders.** In a business-to-business setting, it is tempting to state that customers are accounts rather than individuals. At first and for convenience, you may decide to equate customers with purchase orders. Over time, and despite the difficulties, consider developing a more nuanced understanding of your customers and track customer stakeholders (purchasers, users, influencers, indirect users). CRM software makes this task achievable.
- **Noncustomers** are prospects or *qualified leads*. Define them using both demographic (income, profession, career stage, work affiliation) and behavioral data (category membership and brand usage). Locate noncustomers of the category by asking: what category do they belong to currently? Peloton primarily targeted boutique fitness customers. Tesla primarily targeted luxury car owners. And, in defining *competitive targets*, specify which competitor those customers use primarily. Samsung targeted Apple users, the way that years earlier Apple targeted PC customers.
- **Retained customers, retention rate, and attrition rate** metrics are very important. A retained customer is someone who renews a contract at the end of life or repurchases the brand (rather than switching to another brand or leaving the category). The retention rate is the number of customers retained divided by the number at risk. If you are selling magazine subscriptions, the retention rate is a percentage corresponding to the number renewed divided by the number expiring. The attrition rate is the inverse: 1 − retention rate.
- **Head, heart, and hand loyalty** are different types of customers. Measure the number of loyal customers in your customer base by type (see Chapter 5), especially if executing a brand expansion strategy. Use a survey instrument to do this.[2]

Beliefs

Beliefs are central to our work as marketers. Big Picture Strategy is a brand strategy method, and a brand is a collection of customer beliefs. Accordingly, measure beliefs to assess your progress as you implement the approach. Here are some of the key metrics to track:

- **Customer perception ratings.** Measure overall perceptions of your brand and perceptions of your brand's performance on specific benefits. Measure perceptions by using ratings scales (1 to 5, 1 to 7, or 1 to 10) or ask respondents how strongly they associate your brand with specific benefits or overall perceptions. Rating scale questions may be less discriminating but are widely used. Common perception questions include the following:
  - **Perceived value for money.** Generally asked as a rating question; customers or noncustomers rate their level of agreement with a sentence such as "This brand represents good value for the money."
  - **Perceived performance** (on the category or differentiating benefit). Generally asked as a rating question, "How would you rate the performance of this brand on (benefit)?"
- **Benefit importance ratings.** This is the relative weight of different benefits in the brand selection decision. Measure *stated* benefit importance by asking target customers how important a benefit is on a rating scale (0 to 10 or 1 to 10 depending on whether you offer a neutral middle rating). I recommend not using stated importance questions because the ratings tend to not be very discriminating, as you are likely asking about benefits that are all important and the questions can be subject to biases. Instead, use a *max-diff method,* also called *best–worst scaling method,* where you present respondents a set of benefits and ask them which is their most and their least preferred.
- **Customer satisfaction score (CSAT).** This is the percentage of total customers who report a high or very high level of satisfaction with their brand experience. To compute a CSAT score, measure stated satisfaction on a 1- to 5-point scale and count 4s and 5s as a percent of total respondents. CSAT scores are highly correlated with customer retention rates.[3]
- **Net promoter score.** The percentage of customers who report they would recommend the brand to a friend or colleague minus those

who would not. NPS ratings are generally collected on a scale of 1 to 10. The NPS score is calculated by adding respondents who provided a 9 or 10 rating (promoters) minus those who rated the brand as 6 or below (detractors) as a percent of total respondents. Frederich Reichheld found evidence that NPS scores are positively correlated to revenue growth although other researchers have questioned the predictive power of this metric.[4]

- **Awareness, attitude, and usage (AAU) studies.** These aim to correlate customer attitudes and behaviors to test go-to-market hypotheses such as "Increasing the brand's perceived performance on a differentiating benefit amongst competitive customers will motivate them to switch brands." Measuring AAU requires surveying customers and noncustomers about their awareness of, attitudes toward, and usage of your brand. If you can, triangulate actual usage by measuring sales from the people responding to your survey.

Behaviors

The best way to measure customer behaviors is to collect actual behavioral data (search data, call-center data, web-behavior data, and trial-and-usage data). Depending on your business category and strategy, measure *frequency* or perhaps the value of the purchases made by your target customers (both are useful in brand expansion strategies) or the recency of their interactions with the brand. Of course, to assess communications or salesforce performance, measure more specific behaviors.

There are some other common metrics to be familiar with. Here are just a few:

- **Trial rate.** The percentage of target customers who purchase your product or service (or brand) for the first time in a given period. If last year your salesforce targeted 1,000 qualified leads and 100 of them tried your brand for the first time in that period, your trial rate would be 10 percent.
- **Willingness to search.** Measures the percentage of your customers who are willing to delay or reduce purchases rather than switch brands. Willingness to search is a measure of high-commitment loyalty – either head or heart. Hand loyal customers are likely to switch brands if your brand is not available or back ordered. If measuring

willingness to search, keep in mind that there are significant category effects. In some categories (medical and pharmaceutical, necessity consumables, financing, and others) purchases are not elective.

- **Intentions / purchase intention.** Measure target customers' stated intent with a question like: "Would you be willing to switch brands if your favorite were not available?" If you are unable to triangulate customer awareness and perception survey responses to actual behaviors, ask about purchase intentions as a proxy to future behavior through a question like: "How likely are you to purchase this brand?" However, keep in mind that intentions are generally not great predictors and tend to overestimate future behaviors.

- **Usage.** Measure customers' self-reported behavior if you cannot triangulate actual sales data to other survey responses (about awareness, importance, or perception). Question examples include: "What brands of moisturizing cream did you last purchase?"; "How many times in the past year have you purchased moisturizing cream?"; "How many brands of moisturizing cream do you currently have in your home?"; and "Do you have any Neutrogena moisturizing cream in your home at the current time?"

- **Heavy-usage index.** The heavy-usage index is also called the weight index. It compares how heavily your customers use the category relative to the average customer in the category. The heavy-usage index may be helpful for either of the customer-retention strategies. When executing a brand expansion strategy, expect the index to trend up as your customers use your brand more frequently, or upgrade. Also, when executing a brand commitment strategy, you want the heavy-usage index to trend up, as customers substitute other brands in the brand with yours.

Heavy usage index(I)

= Avg. total category purchases by brand customers (# or $)

/Avg. total category purchases by all category customers (# or $)

- **Contract-utilization rate.** This is simply a customer's sales divided by their contracted volume calculated based on number of products sold, price, or margin ($ or %). It may be helpful in a brand commitment strategy or brand expansion strategy to assess whether your customers are fully utilizing the capacity reserved for them. If rewarding higher volumes with discounts, calculate the actual versus forecasted margins to make sure you are not misallocating discounts to customers who are not purchasing as much as they promised.

(Financial) Benchmarks

As marketers, we earn credibility in our organizations by demonstrating our impact on business goals. One way we do this is by establishing linkages between leading brand performance indicators (brand awareness, brand preferences, benefit importance and perception, customer satisfaction, and loyalty) and lagging business outcome indicators (customer behaviors and financial outcomes). I discussed some financial metrics in the section above regarding the business category (market share, category penetration). Other key financial indicators include the following:

- **Net present value of a marketing investment.** Net present value is the discounted value of cash flows over time. The basic net present value technique consists in understanding the cost of an investment (any marketing project, business acquisition, or customer acquisition) and projecting the cash flows it will generate over time, then applying a discount factor to consider their total value today compared to their current cost. The discount factor (or discount rate) is normally established by the company, or it can be the average cost of borrowing (interest rate). Calculating net present value is critical to calculating customer lifetime value and the value of any other marketing activities expected to benefit your company over time.
- **Customer lifetime value.** Customer lifetime value is the present value of the cash flows attributable to a customer over their life with the company. To calculate, know the customer margin ($M), the retention rate (r), the discount rate (d), and the net cost of acquisition ($A). The customer margin is the profit of serving a customer (over a period of time, typically a year), taking into account the profitability of the products and services they purchase or use and their frequency. The retention rate, defined earlier in this chapter, is the percentage likelihood that a customer will continue as a customer from one year to the next. The discount rate is the same used to calculate net present value. To calculate the acquisition cost, perform some activity-based costing (ABC) analysis[5] and estimate the

total sales and marketing expense required to acquire the customer. The customer lifetime value formula with constant retention rates and margins is:

$$CLV(\$) = Margin~(\$) * \frac{Retention~rate~(\%)}{1 + Discount~rate~(\%) - Retention~rate~(\%)}$$
$$- Acquisition~cost~(\$)$$

- **Prospect CLV.** The projected net present value of a customer, taking into account the likelihood of acquiring them (measured by the acquisition rate), the cost of acquiring them, the purchase they will make immediately after being acquired, and their long-term customer lifetime value.

$$PLV = Acquisition~rate(\%) * \$~Initial~customer~margin + CLV(\$)$$
$$- Acquisition~cost~(\$)$$

- **Marketing return on investment (MROI or ROMI).** This measures the financial value created by the dollars allocated to specific marketing initiatives. Estimate the incremental *contribution margin* generated by a specific marketing activity net of its cost. The MROI must be greater than zero!

$$\begin{aligned} &Marketing~return \\ &on~investment~(MROI~\%) = \frac{\substack{Incremental~financial \\ value~created(\$) - Cost~of~marketing(\$)}}{Cost~of~marketing(\$)} \end{aligned}$$

- **Share of wallet (% of # or % of $).** This is a key metric in brand commitment strategies as it measures the relative commitment of multibrand customers to your brand relative to their total spend within the brand set. Calculating share of wallet does require that you specifically designate your brand's direct competitors—the other brands your multibrand customers use in addition to yours. For Netflix to estimate share of wallet, it must specifically select the other streaming services their customers also watch, estimate the total number of hours they view streaming content, and compare it to the number of hours they watch Netflix. Share of wallet may be estimated as a percent of units (as in the Netflix example) or as a percent of revenue in dollars.

$$\text{Share of wallet } (\%) = \frac{\text{Brand purchases } (\# \text{ or } \$)}{\text{Total purchases from brand set } (\# \text{ or } \$)}$$

The 6Bs metrics presented in this chapter and detailed in Figure 8.1 are foundational marketing metrics used to assess the attractiveness of a particular strategy relative to another one. Once one of the four strategies is selected, use these metrics to track progress overall in execution and to establish when to pivot.

Of course, it makes sense that you will go into a new market with a customer-acquisition strategy, either developing a new category or executing a brand-switching strategy. Afterward, you may pivot to a brand expansion strategy or execute a brand commitment strategy, depending on the number of loyal customers created (relative to multibrand customers). Long term, you will find great efficiency in a brand expansion strategy, still putting some money into customer acquisition, but directing the majority of investment toward growing with current customers, people, and organizations whose capabilities make them a great match for your firm.

Using the Brand Experience Map to Operationalize the Strategy and Assess Execution

Working through the brand, business category, and bodies phases of your marketing strategy requires self-awareness, other-awareness, and purpose. First choose a brand to represent your organization in the market, with awareness of your team's core skills and strategic assets. Select a business category where your brand will compete. And then define an ideal customer for that brand and assess customer-based opportunity. The idea of the 6Bs is to bring specificity and focus to your go-to-market execution, both to conserve resources and to learn from execution. Figure 8.3 shows some of the key metrics used to assess execution.

The executional metrics dashboard should reflect your go-to-market strategy as well as the value proposition of your brand.

	Awareness & Need Recognition	Search & Compare Alternatives	Trial & Purchase	Use	Reflect & Recommend
Products & Services	• # products & services that target new customers • # ease of adoption / switching features • # search features	• # inquiries from non-users • Target customer perceptions of search features • # qualified leads attending product-focused webinars	• # trials • # salesforce or web demos • # new customers trained • % intent to purchase • % intent to upgrade	• # products upgraded / # products in portfolio • % new product revenue	• # customer product reviews • # positive vs. negative social media posts • % customers reordering or retained
Pricing	• $ trial program revenue and $ margin	• Price vs. key competitor's average • Perceived value ratings	• Trial rate % • # cross-selling trial pricing tactics available • Avg selling price vs. list price	• $ volume / margin from continuity pricing tactics available • Avg selling price vs. list price	• Perceived value ratings • Product satisfaction ratings
Channels	• Brand availability (% of eligible outlets, # salespeople / qualified leads)	• # sales visits / qualified competitive leads • #RFP responses / total RFPs in category	• # salespeople / qualified leads • # sales meetings / # new customers • # demos or trials • % contract win rate	• # sales visits / retained customers • % first-time issue resolution	• # relationships/account

	Awareness & Need Recognition	Search & Compare Alternatives	Trial & Purchase	Use	Reflect & Recommend
Communications	• Impressions (# times a piece of content is served to visitors)* • CPM (cost per thousand impressions) • Organic search ranking • Awareness development and media spend / total	• Pageviews (# times a page has been shown to a user) • # downloads • Clickthrough rate % (clickthroughs (#) / impressions #) • Bounce rate (# single page visits / # total visits) • Cost per click • Organic search ranking • Total website traffic	• Total website traffic • Behavior (purchase) development and media spend / total • Cost per order • Conversion rate (purchasers/visitors) • Email open rate (%), email clickthrough rate (%), email unsubscribe rate (%)	• Total website traffic • Website bounce rate • Usage development and media spend • Avg media display time (#) (= total media display time (#) / total media impressions) • Email open rate (%), email clickthrough rate (%), email unsubscribe rate (%)	• # likes, # followers, # supporters • Advocacy (#, %)

*Impressions > pageviews if a page has multiple pieces of content.

FIGURE 8.3 Key executional metrics.

Product Metrics

Use product and service input metrics to track whether your product and service execution is aligned to your brand strategy. In Chapter 7, I presented products and services as tools to deliver the brand value proposition and to change behaviors, motivate, drive adoption, commit, switch, or expand use of your brand.

Set product and service metrics to help track your organization's executional alignment. If you are executing a category development strategy, are your products and services significantly innovative, and are they easy to adopt? Are you providing appropriate customer education to ease adoption? Set evaluation metrics to help track the effectiveness of your product and service portfolio. Are customers actually adopting, switching brands, increasing commitment, upgrading, and recommending? Some of these behavioral metrics may be set at the brand level, as I discussed earlier in this chapter. Your product and service teams may need to also set more specific product metrics.

Pricing Metrics

The development and measurement of pricing policy and programs belongs to marketing. I don't mean the marketing department should shoulder all the responsibility of setting and managing price; rather, anyone performing that task should have an understanding of the multidimensional role price plays in the brand strategy process.

The price set communicates the brand value proposition. It is critical to how noncustomers, whether competitive or from outside the category, first interact with the brand. Trial pricing metrics should be constructed with an adoption or brand-switching objective, and therefore should include extrinsic and intrinsic motivation for the customer to try the brand. Continuity programs should not just be conceived as back-end rewards for high-volume customers. The best loyalty programs enhance the brand experience for mid-tier customers and effectively build their loyalty. In assessing whether trial and continuity programs are working, consider both their impact on brand perceptions as well as their impact on longer-term financial outcomes.

Distribution Metrics

Distribution channel metrics are also multidimensional because distribution channel partners have structural and customer experience roles. Channel partners enable multiple flows to end-customers (product/service, money/ risk, and information) and also deliver a variety of benefits associated with those flows. The three categories of performance include customer reach (volume and coverage), operating efficiency (cost to serve), and service quality (effectiveness and customer retention). Given this, distribution metrics should help assess whether to interact with end-customers in a way that optimizes efficiency (should you perform a task or have someone else who is better at it take it on instead?) and effectiveness (do you have control over the right elements of your target customers' experience?). For this reason, use a combination of metrics to manage your channel execution, from metrics that assess sales coverage efficiency (e.g., salespeople/customer, frequency of sales interaction with customers, customers' time and distance to sales representative, sales cost/account size) as well as the effectiveness of that effort (perceptions of service availability, timelines, expertise, selection, and assortment).

Communications Metrics

Communications metrics help you understand whether you are reaching your target audience efficiently and with the right intensity, and they should help you optimize the use of communications channels. Specifically, web and social metrics enable direct-response measurement; they reveal what content is effective in attracting attention and engagement. Beyond that, they can help you monitor what is working in motivating customer behaviors.

Communications metrics will continue to evolve as social and web channels develop further, and as artificial intelligence (AI) automates measurement. Additionally, although companies are adopting an omnichannel strategy, it is important to organize and integrate your activity by thinking very specifically about your brand and target audience. Use the strategic goals and value proposition to guide what content to broadcast, through what channels, and to what end in terms of target audiences' beliefs and behaviors.

A Final Note about Metrics

In designing a metrics dashboard (such as the ones in Figures 8.1 and 8.3), adopt an overall design philosophy that prioritizes learning over simply declaring success. The metrics others use may not be the best ones for your brand, as their strategy is likely different.

Also, what is easiest to measure (for example, market share or top-line sales) may not provide the right insights or the right incentives. Ultimately, great brands, just like great relationships, are not built overnight. Both require compatible partnering, and both develop through a learning process fed by careful observation, analysis, and experimentation. Metrics enable you to build on your relative successes and iterate on your relative failures.

Notes

Chapter 1

1. Sergei Kelbnikov, "Streaming Wars Continue: Here's How Much Netflix, Amazon, Disney+ and Their Rivals Are Spending on New Content," *Forbes,* May 22, 2020, https://www.forbes.com/sites/sergeiklebnikov/2020/05/22/streaming-wars-continue-heres-how-much-netflix-amazon-disney-and-their-rivals-are-spending-on-new-content/#62d35eec623b

Chapter 2

1. Tom Lauricella, "How Barclays Became a Force in ETFs," *Wall Street Journal,* November 1, 2004, Barclays shares: https://www.wsj.com/articles/SB109927249793760816
2. "GE Launches Mini-Ultrasound for Use in the Intevetional Setting," *Imaging Technology News,* September 23, 2009, https://www.itnonline.com/content/ge-launches-mini-ultrasound-use-interventional-setting
3. Camila Domonoske, "Half a Million 'Hoverboards' Recalled over Risk of Fire, Explosions," NPR, July 6, 2016, https://www.npr.org/sections/thetwo-way/2016/07/06/484988211/half-a-million-hoverboards-recalled-over-risk-of-fire-explosions
4. David Hochman, "Instant Pot Inventor Explains Why the World's Gone Mad for Slow Cooking," *Forbes,* January 24, 2018, https://www.forbes.com/sites/davidhochman/2018/01/24/instant-pot-inventor-explains-why-the-worlds-gone-mad-for-slow-cooking/?sh=60fc22d47c35 https://www.digitalcommerce360.com/2017/06/05/startup-instant-pot-became-amazon-prime-day-star/
5. The brand ceased to be independent when it was purchased by Ford in 1999, and approximately a decade later sold to the Chinese company, Zheijang Geely Holding Group.
6. David Frederick, "Volvo's XC90 Launch Campaign Revved Sales," *PR Week,* February 10, 2017, https://www.prweek.com/article/1423879/volvos-xc90-launch-campaign-revved-sales

7. https://www.instantbrands.com/catalog/storage

8. "A Brief History of Baking Soda," *Angi,* October 8, 2019, https://www.angieslist. com/articles/brief-history-baking-soda.htm

9. Tugba Sabanoglu, "Share of Amazon Customers Who Are Amazon Prime Members as of December 2019," Statista, November 30, 2020, https://www. statista.com/statistics/234253/share-of-amazon-prime-subscribers-in-the-united-states/#:~:text=As%20of%20December%202019%2C%2065,members%20in%20the%20United%20States

10. Peter Csathy, "Amazon Prime Video: The Stealthy, Ominous Streaming Force," *Forbes,* January 31, 2020, https://www.forbes.com/sites/petercsathy/2020/01/31/ amazon-prime-video-the-quiet-ominous-streaming-force/?sh=22ef4dc71f1a

11. Bereskin & Parr LLC, "Round Two of the 'Bunny Brand' Battle – Energizer Brands, LLC v The Gillette Company, 2020 FCA 49, Lexology, March 2, 2020, https://www.lexology.com/library/detail.aspx?g=8e35661e-00fa-4153-94b7-2cfef1449d90

12. Statista Research Department, "Market Share of the Leading Battery Brands in the United States in 2016," Statista, December 1, 2016, https://www.statista. com/statistics/380309/market-share-of-the-leading-alkaline-battery-brands-in-the-us/; Jack Neff and Jack Neff, "Duracell vs. Energizer – One Charges Up, One Sputters," *AdAge,* November 6, 2013,https://adage.com/article/news/ duracell-energizer-charges-sputters/245108

13. Toni Fitzgerald, "How Many Streaming Video Services Does the Average Person Subscribe To?" *Forbes,* March 29, 2019, https://www.forbes.com/sites/ tonifitzgerald/2019/03/29/how-many-streaming-video-services-does-the-average-person-subscribe-to/?sh=555fb6bc6301

14. https://www.duracell-me.com/technology/the-longevity-of-a-duracell-battery/

15. Timothy Cain, "Hyundai Sales Figures – US Market," Good Car Bad Car, n.d., https://www.goodcarbadcar.net/hyundai-us-sales-figures/

16. Jonah Engel Bromwich, "With Sprint, Former Verizon Actor Says, You Can Hear Him Just Fine" *New York Time,* October 14, 2016, https://www.nytimes. com/2016/10/15/business/sprint-verizon-hear-me-now-paul-marcarelli.html; Tomi Kilgore, "This Guy Helped Sprint's Stock to Its Biggest One-Day Gain" *MarketWatch,* July 26, 2016, https://www.marketwatch.com/story/this-guy-helped-sprints-stock-to-its-biggest-one-day-gain-2016-07-25; https://www. statista.com/statistics/199359/market-share-of-wireless-carriers-in-the-us-by-subscriptions/

17. Danny Sullivan, "Is Microsoft's Scroogled Campaign Working? Not if Gaining Consumers Is the Goal," *Marketing Land,* October 16, 2013, https://marketing-land.com/microsoft-scroogled-campaign-61887

Chapter 3

1. David Aaker describes three components of brand equity: awareness, differentiation, and loyalty. *Managing Brand Equity* (New York: Free Press, 1991), ISBN-10: 0029001013

2. "GDP by Industry," https://www.bea.gov/data/gdp/gdp-industry, US Bureau of Economic Analysis, March 29, 2021.

3. Raynor de Best, "Share of All New U.S. Vehicles That Are Leased 2017–2020," Statista, February 12, 2021, https://www.statista.com/statistics/453122/share-of-new-vehicles-on-lease-usa/; Aaron M. Kessler, "Auto Leasing Gains Popularity Among American Consumers," *the New York Times*, January 8, 2015, https://www.nytimes.com/2015/01/09/business/auto-leasing-gains-popularity-among-american-consumers.html

4. Chris Stokel-Walker, "Inside the Collapse of Dyson's Electric Care Dream," *Wired,* October 14, 2019, https://www.wired.co.uk/article/dyson-electric-car-cancelled-inside-story

5. "Porsche Speeds Ahead as World's Most Valuable Luxury and Premium Brand," *Brand Finance,* October 23, 2019, https://brandfinance.com/news/porsche-speeds-ahead-as-worlds-most-valuable-luxury-and-premium-brand/.

6. "Porsche, Part of the Volkswagen Group, Develops Technologies that Advance Vehicle Performance, Improve Safety, and Spur Environmental Innovations within the Automotive Industry," Interbrand, 2021, https://interbrand.com/best-global-brands/porsche/

7. "How Hyundai Sells More When Everyone Else Is Selling Less," Knowledge@Wharton, June 20, 2009, https://knowledge.wharton.upenn.edu/article/how-hyundai-sells-more-when-everyone-else-is-selling-less/

8. C. K. Prahalad and Gary Hamel. "The Core Competence of the Corporation." Harvard Business School Reprint, 1990. *Harvard Business Review* 68 (3), (May–June, 1990).

9. Michael Treacy and Fred Wiersema, *The Discipline of Market Leaders* (Reading, MA: Addison-Wesley, 1995).

10. "The World's Most Valuable Brands," https://www.forbes.com/powerful-brands/list/; and "The World's Most Admired Companies," https://fortune.com/worlds-most-admired-companies/2019/

Chapter 4

1. "Joint Pain and Arthritis," https://www.cdc.gov/arthritis/pain/index.htm

2. https://www.botoxcosmetic.com/what-is-botox-cosmetic/frequently-asked-questions

3. Elaine Watson, "US Retail Sales of Stevia Sweeteners Rose 11.9% in the Past Year as Sales of Artificial Sweeteners Continue to Slide," Food Navigator, October 1, 2018, www.foodnavigator-usa.com/Article/2018/10/01/US-retail-sales-of-stevia-sweeteners-rose-11.9-in-the-past-year-as-sales-of-artificial-sweeteners-continue-to-slide#

4. "Dell: Notice of Annual Meeting and Proxy Statement, 2003," http://edgar.sec-database.com/1992/95013403007092/filing-main.htm#012

5. Nathaniel Meyersohn, "Tide Pods: P&G Big Innovation Gone Wrong," CNN Money, January 29, 2018, https://money.cnn.com/2018/01/19/news/tide-pods/index.html; "Laundry Detergent Pods Market Size to Reach USD 3,567.7 Million by 2023 at 5.04% AGR, Predicts Market Research Future," Global Newswire, March 29, 2019, https://www.globenewswire.com/news-release/2019/05/29/1856251/0/en/Laundry-Detergent-Pods-Market-Size-to-Reach-USD-3-567-7-Million-by-2023-at-5-04-CAGR-Predicts-Market-Research-Future.html

6. "Global Trust in Advertising," Nielsen, September 2015, https://www.nielsen.com/wp-content/uploads/sites/3/2019/04/global-trust-in-advertising-report-sept-2015-1.pdf.

7. John Legere, "T-Mobile's CEO on Winning Market Share by Trash-Talking Rivals," Harvard Business Review, January–February 2017, https://hbr.org/2017/01/t--mobiles-ceo-on-winning-market-share-by-trash-talking-rivals#comment-section; Tiffany Hsu, "Sprint and T—Mobile Loved to Attack Each Other. Then They Decide to Merge." The New York Times, July 26, 2019, https://www.nytimes.com/2019/07/26/business/t-mobile-sprint-merger-ads.html; Aaron Pressman, "John Legere Will Go Down in Corporate History as One of the Greatest Turnaround Stories of All Time," Fortune, February 12, 2020, https://fortune.com/2020/02/12/john-legere-will-go-down-in-corporate-history-as-one-of-the-greatest-turnaround-stories-of-all-time/; Jacob Kastrenakes, "T-Mobile Just Spent Nearly $8 Billion to Finally Put Its Network on Par with Verizon and AT&T, The Verge, April 13, 2017, https://www.theverge.com/2017/4/13/15291496/tmobile-fcc-incentive-auction-results-8-billion-airwaves-lte

8. Erica Ogg, "The Secret of Vizio's Success," CNet, August 20, 2007, https://www.cnet.com/news/the-secret-of-vizios-success/#:~:text=Vizio's%20strategy%20essentially%20revolves%20around,better%20and%20more%20personal%20service; Paul Gagnon, "TCL Surges to the Top of the North American TV Market Amid US-CHINA Trade Turbulence," OMDIA, June 3, 2019, https://technology.informa.com/614549/tcl-surges-to-the-top-of-the-north-american-tv-market-amid-us-china-trade-turbulence accessed August 21, 2020.

9. Geoffrey Cain, "Samsung vs. Apple: Inside The Brutal War for Smartphone Dominance," Forbes, March 13, 2020, https://www.forbes.com/sites/forbes-digitalcovers/2020/03/13/samsung-vs-apple-inside-the-brutal-war-for-smartphone-dominance/#2d9fc3a44142

10. Robert D. Buzzell, Bradley T. Gale, and Ralph G. M. Sultan, "Market Share – A Key to Profitability," *Harvard Business Review*, January 1975, https://hbr.org/1975/01/market-share-a-key-to-profitability

11. SGB Executive, "iFits President Discusses the Home Fitness Boom," SGB Media, July 29, 2020, ihttps://sgbonline.com/ifits-president-discusses-the-home-fitness-boom/

12. James Vincent, "Apple Lawsuit Says 90 Percent of 'Official' Chargers Sold on Amazon Are Fake," *The Verge*, October 20, 2016, https://www.theverge.com/2016/10/20/13343682/fake-apple-chargers-amazon-lawsuit

13. Christopher Rosen, "What Does Tenet's Rough Run Mean for Theatrical Blockbusters?" *Vanity Fair*, September 14, 2020, https://www.vanityfair.com/hollywood/2020/09/tenet-box-office-what-now

Chapter 5

1. "Amazon Shares Give Up 2011 Gains on Profit Concern," FoxBusiness, March 4, 2016, https://www.foxbusiness.com/features/amazon-shares-give-up-2011-gains-on-profit-concern

2. https://techcrunch.com/2010/05/10/apple-att-iphone-agreement/

3. Jenna Wortham, "AT&T and Verizon Trade Aunts Over iPhone," *New York Times,* January 10, 2011, https://www.nytimes.com/2011/01/11/technology/11phone.html

4. Sarah Cavill, "Toilet Paper Is Having a Moment, But Which Brand Will Win the War?" *Insights,* March 23, 2020, https://insights.digitalmediasolutions.com/news/toilet-paper-wars

5. Marta Dapena-Baron, Thomas W. Gruen, and Lin Guo, "Heart, Head, and Hand: A Tripartite Conceptualization, Operationalization, and Examination of Brand Loyalty," *Journal of Brand Management* 27 (2020): 355–375, https://doi.org/10.1057/s41262-019-00185-3

6. James G. Maxham III and Richard G. Netemeyer, "Modeling Customer Perceptions of Complaint Handling over Time: The Effects of Perceived Justice on Satisfaction and Intent," *Journal of Retailing* 78 (4) (2002): 239–252.

7. Pamela N. Danziger, "How to Make a Great Loyalty Program Even Better? Sephora Has the Answer," *Forbes,* January 23, 2020, https://www.forbes.com/sites/pamdanziger/2020/01/23/how-to-make-a-great-retail-loyalty-program-even-better-sephora-has-the-answer/#6f5837d6287a

8. Jack Houston and Irene Anna Kim, "Prime Day Deals Aren't the Only Way Amazon Gets You to Spend More. Here Are 13 of the Company's Sneaky Tricks," *Insider,* October 13, 2020, https://www.businessinsider.com/amazon-prime-members-spend-more-money-sneaky-ways-2019-9

Chapter 6

1. https://news.delta.com/investor-day-recap-2018-success-showcases-deltas-durable-business-model
2. D.D. Gremler, The Critical Incident Technique in Service Research," *Journal of Service Research* 7 (1) (2004): 65–89. doi:10.1177/1094670504266138.
3. T. J. Reynolds and J. Gutman, "Laddering Theory, Method, Analysis, and Interpretation," *Journal of Advertising Research* 28 (1) (1988): 11–31.
4. Daniel Kahneman and Amos Tversky, "Prospect Theory: An Analysis of Decision under Risk," *Econometrica* 47 (2) (1979): 263–291. *JSTOR*, www.jstor.org/stable/1914185. Accessed 5 Jan. 2021.

Chapter 7

1. Marcus Wohlsen, "What Google Really Gets Out of Buying Nest for $3.2 Billion," *Wired,* January 14, 2014, https://www.wired.com/2014/01/googles-3-billion-nest-buy-finally-make-internet-things-real-us/
2. "How Samsung's Marketing Strategy Transformed Them into a Global Brand," Proecho Solutions, June 6, 2020, https://proechosolutions.com/asheville-marketing/how-samsungs-marketing-strategy-turned-them-into-a-technological-powerhouse
3. "Disney and Warner Make Big Bets on the Small Screeen," *The Economist,* December 16, 2020, https://www.economist.com/business/2020/12/16/disney-and-warner-make-big-bets-on-the-small-screen
4. Alexandria White, "Americans Have an Average of 4 Credit Cards – Is That Too Many?" CNBC, December 1, 2020, https://www.cnbc.com/select/how-many-credit-cards-does-the-average-american-have/#:~:text=The%20average%20American%20have%204,2019%20Experian%20Consumer%20Credit%20Review
5. https://www.armandhammer.com/baking-soda
6. Jamie Wiebe, "Psychology of Lululemon: How Fashion Affects Fitness," *The Atlantic,* December 12, 2013, https://www.theatlantic.com/health/archive/2013/12/psychology-of-lululemon-how-fashion-affects-fitness/281959/
7. https://nogood.io/2020/11/10/whiteclaw-seltzer-growth-marketing-strategy/; https://firstkey.com/the-implications-of-hard-seltzer-pricing/; Tom Huddleston Jr., "How White Claw and the Hard Seltzer Craze Are Taking on Beer – and Taking over America," CNBC, December 5, 2019, https://www.cnbc.com/2019/12/05/how-white-claw-and-the-hard-seltzer-craze-are-taking-on-beer.html

8. J. Scott Armstrong, *Persuasive Advertising* (New York: Macmillan, 2010): 38.

9. "Essential Content Marketing Statistics for 2020," *Smart Insights,* February 20, 2020, https://www.smartinsights.com/content-management/content-marketing-strategy/essential-content-marketing-statistics/

10. Stuart Schwartzapfel, "Real 'Mad Men' Pitched Safety to Sell Volvos," *New York Times*, March 23, 2012, https://www.nytimes.com/2012/03/25/automobiles/real-mad-men-pitched-safety-to-sell-volvos.html

11. "Starbucks Corp." CNN Business, https://money.cnn.com/quote/chart/chart.html?symb=SBUX

12. "Nestlé and Starbucks Close Deal for Global License of Starbucks CPG and Foodservice Products," Starbucks, August 7, 2018, https://stories.starbucks.com/press/2018/nestle-and-starbucks-close-deal/

13. Erica Ogg, "The Secret of Vizio's Success," CNet, August 20, 2007, https://www.cnet.com/news/the-secret-of-vizios-success/#:~:text=Vizio%20also%20emerged%20with%20an,Mart%2C%20Sears%20and%20Circuit%20City

Chapter 8

1. P. W. Farris, *Marketing Metrics: 50+ Metrics Every Executive Should Master* (Upper Saddle River, NJ: Wharton School Pub., 2020).

2. Marta Dapena-Baron, Thomas W. Gruen, and Lin Guo. "Heart, Head, and Hand: A Tripartite Conceptualization, Operationalization, and Examination of Brand Loyalty," *Journal of Brand Management* 27 (2020): 355–375, https://doi.org/10.1057/s41262-019-00185-3.

3. Roland T. Rust and Anthony J. Zahorik. "Customer Satisfaction, Customer Retention, and Market Share," *Journal of Retailing* 69 (2) (1993): 193–215.

4. https://www.netpromotersystem.com/about/; T. L. Keiningham, B. Cooil, T. W. Andreassen, and L. Aksoy, "A Longitudinal Examination of Net Promoter and Firm Revenue Growth," *Journal of Marketing* 71 (3) (2007): 39–51.

5. Robert S. Kaplan and Steven R. Anderson, "Time-Driven Activity-Based Costing," *Harvard Business Review,* November 2004, https://www.intercom.com/blog/what-is-customer-acquisition-cost/; https://hbr.org/2004/11/time-driven-activity-based-costing.

Acknowledgments

The methodology presented in this book evolved over many years of teaching, coaching, and consulting. I am indebted to my clients, who in learning this strategy-through-execution method, provided new insights and challenges that helped me refine and improve it.

I have learned from visionary leaders at organizations like Stryker, Medtronic, bioMérieux, Johnson & Johnson, Terumo, ABN AMRO, GE, and Futura Industries. The leaders I admire are as diverse as the brands they represent. And yet upon reflection, great leaders like Kevin Lobo, Tim Scannell, Don Payerle, Cindy Schawe, Kristen Fletcher, Diane Gomez-Thinnes, Simon Fraser, Sue Johnson, Laura Angelini, Sergio Rial, Maarten Potjer, Christophe Beck, and many others, inspire their teams by communicating simple impactful visions. I hope that others who read this book may be able to use it to ascend to that type of profound and motivating messaging for their teams.

The decision-based strategy method I present in this book is the natural evolution of the Big Picture methodology presented in the book I co-authored, *Marketing Management: The Big Picture* (Wiley, 2014). My colleagues and I have used the Big Picture method with many global clients and taught thousands of executives and MBA students. The basic philosophy of the method is that integrative strategies that create continuous improvement in organizations require alignment between beliefs and behaviors, internally within the organization first, and then with its customers.

It is my great pleasure to acknowledge my colleagues at The Big Picture Partners, Drew Boyd, Shelly Cropper, and especially Tom Gruen. Tom contributed greatly to this project through many hours of sage counsel and many edits. Thank you also to Visa Pawittranon, who helped organize the madness of figures and tables all over the text. Thank you as well to Alice LaPlante for giving my writing a well-deserved *haircut*.

About the Author

Marta Dapena Barón, EdD, is the co-founder and president of The Big Picture Partners, a marketing strategy training and coaching firm, and is the co-author of *Marketing Management: The Big Picture*.

Marta helps her clients close the gap between their strategic and executional efforts by teaching the marketing strategy methodology presented in this book. She helps clients in a wide range of industries such as health care, manufacturing, financial services, retail, and airlines. Marta's clients span the globe and include Johnson & Johnson, GE, Sealed Air, W.L. Gore, Medtronic, Stryker, and Olympus. In addition to her teaching and writing, Marta develops training simulations that elucidate key strategy and marketing concepts and their application in the real world.

Prior to founding The Big Picture Partners, Marta was the vice president of Marketing for GE Capital's US Equipment Dealer Leasing Business and worked as a strategy consultant for McKinsey & Co. She also spent eight years at ABN AMRO Bank in a variety of roles including being the director of Strategy reporting to the North American chairman; heading up the product development function for the Global Trade business; and advising and financing privatization projects in Latin America.

Marta holds a Chief Learning Office Doctorate (EdD) and a MS in Education from the University of Pennsylvania, an MBA in finance and international business from the University of Chicago, and a BA in Economics summa cum laude from Kenyon College.

Index